beginner's
ITALIAN
grammar

Vittoria Bowles

TEACH YOURSELF BOOKS 458.242
Bow

The author of *Teach Yourself Beginner's Italian* and *Teach Yourself Italian Vocabulary*, Vittoria Bowles Protej has taught Italian for 24 years and is currently lecturing at the University of Brighton.

For UK orders: please contact Bookpoint Ltd, 39 Milton Park, Abingdon, Oxon OX14 4TD. Telephone: (44) 01235 400414, Fax: (44) 01235 400454. Lines are open from 9.00–6.00, Monday to Saturday, with a 24-hour message answering service. Email address: orders@bookpoint.co.uk

For U.S.A. & Canada orders: please contact NTC/Contemporary Publishing, 4255 West Touhy Avenue, Lincolnwood, Illinois 60646–1975, U.S.A. Telephone: (847) 679 5500, Fax: (847) 679 2494.

Long renowned as the authoritative source for self-guided learning – with more than 30 million copies sold worldwide – the *Teach Yourself* series includes over 200 titles in the fields of languages, crafts, hobbies, and other leisure activities.

British Library Cataloguing in Publication Data
A catalogue entry for this title is available from The British Library.

Library of Congress Catalog Card Number: On file.

First published in UK 1999 by Hodder Headline Plc, 338 Euston Road, London, NW1 3BH.

First published in US 1999 by NTC/Contemporary Publishing, 4255 West Touhy Avenue, Lincolnwood (Chicago), Illinois 60646–1975, U.S.A.

The 'Teach Yourself' name and logo are registered trade marks of Hodder & Stoughton Ltd.

Typeset by Transet Limited, Coventry, England.
Printed in Great Britain for Hodder & Stoughton Educational, a division of Hodder Headline Plc, 338 Euston Road, London NW1 3BH by Cox & Wyman Ltd, Reading, Berkshire.

Impression number   10 9 8 7 6 5 4 3 2 1
Year   2004 2003 2002 2001 2000 1999

CONTENTS

iii

PREPOSITIONS

INTRODUCTION

Why learn a foreign language?

Acquiring the tool of communicating in another language (in itself a useful practical achievement) can enhance personal development and self-assertion, improve one's attitude to and understanding of other people and can expand one's outlook on life in general. The way in which the grammar of a particular language functions can provide a fair insight into the personality and background of the native speakers.

About learning techniques

The process of learning a language is not always easy or straightforward, and mastering the grammar of a second language can be quite a challenge. One of the main reasons that this grammar book has been developed is to give the student the opportunity of learning a few rules at a time, in a logical sequence, and to then immediately be able to practise them.

Those who speak another language have probably already developed their own personal learning strategies. The newcomer will need to discover the way which best suits him/her. One thing is certain for most of us – practice makes perfect. Reading and re-reading, writing and re-writing, saying and saying again. Once a basic structure has been acquired, the student can try modifying the sentences in the book, by changing a noun, a verb or a gender, etc. to suit their own purposes. Verbs can be memorised by dividing them into groups with similar patterns. Some people record them and then listen to them wherever they can – in the car, in the bath, in bed!

How to use this book

This book is designed to be consulted either in sequence, at random or as a reference book, according to the needs of the learner. In general, the units are grouped progressively in grammar topics. The main rules of a topic, e.g. the gender of nouns, are immediately followed by more in-depth units. The book can be used in strict numerical sequence, although a beginner may wish to study only the first one or two units of each grammar topic initially and then return to the more complex units as proficiency grows. The exercises, placed immediately opposite the rules, make it easy to refer back as needed to reinforce the points being learned. Consult the index as necessary to find the information you require, and the glossary whenever you encounter an English term which you do not understand.

Buon divertimento e buon lavoro!

1 UNIT | What goes into a sentence?

Sentences are made up of different elements: the most important of these are the subject and the verb.

A At least two elements are required for a sentence to make sense: a subject and a verb. For example, **Carla** is a noun and **mangia** is a verb. **Carla mangia** (*Carla is eating*) is a whole expression with sufficient meaning to stand by itself.

Usually, though, more words go into a sentence: **Carla mangia una pesca** (*Carla is eating* (what?) *a peach*). **Una pesca** is called the complement (or object) because it illustrates the object of the action expressed by the verb (**mangiare**).

B Of course you could say or write something more complex like:

> **Carla mangia una pesca perché ha**   *Carla is eating a peach because she*
> **una gran fame e non ha nient'altro**   *is very hungry and she doesn't have*
> **di commestibile in casa.**   *anything else edible in the house.*

This sentence is formed by several clauses: **Carla mangia una pesca** is the main clause since it can stand by itself; **perché ha una gran fame** and **e (perché) non ha nient'altro di commestibile in casa** are two dependent clauses since they can't stand by themselves.

C Traditionally speech contains nine parts:

1 Article: **il, lo, la, l', i, gli** (*the*) **un, uno, una, un'** (*a, an*)
2 Noun or names of things, animals and people: **strada** (*road*), **gatto** (*cat*), **Maria** (*Mary*), **bellezza** (*beauty*).
3 Adjective: **buono** (*good*), **chiaro** (*clear*), **intelligente** (*intelligent*).
4 Pronoun: **io** (*I*), **mi** (*me*), **lo** (*it/him*), **gli** (*to him*), **il mio** (*my*), **questo** (*this*).
5 Verb: **parlare** (*to speak*), **vedere** (*to see*), **partire** (*to leave/depart*).
6 Adverb: **lentamente** (*slowly*), **bene** (*well*), **presto** (*soon/early*).
7 Preposition: **di** (*of*), **a** (*to/at*), **per** (*for*), **dopo** (*after*), **vicino** (*a near*).
8 Conjunction: **e** (*and*), **anche** (*also*), **oppure** (*or*), **perché** (*because/why*).
9 Interjection: **ahimè!** (*alas!*), **ahi!** (*ouch!*), **coraggio!** (*take heart!*).

Of these nine, the following five have variable endings which agree in gender and number with the subject: article, noun, adjective, pronoun and verb. The other four (adverb, preposition, conjunction and interjection/ exclamation) are invariable, that is they do not undergo any change.

➤ See Glossary for more explanations.

1 Using the words in the box complete the sentences to give a title to each of the four pictures.

a La mamma _____
b I libri che ho ordinato _____
c Il treno _____
d Mariella _____

Il treno delle 6.45	arriverà	una lettera
The 6.45 train	*(it)will arrive*	*a letter*

La mamma
Mum   la settimana prossima   arriveranno
            next week   *(they) will arrive*   in ritardo
scrive   *late*
is writing   il pasto   Mariella
            the meal   *Mariella*
prepara   per il bambino
is preparing   I libri che ho ordinato   *for the child*
            the books I ordered

2 Break down the sentences in the above exercise and write each word under the appropriate heading below.

Articoli (*Articles*)	Sostantivi (*Nouns*)	Aggettivi (*Adjectives*)	Verbi (*Verbs*)	Preposizioni (*Prepositions*)	Congiunzioni (*Conjunctions*)

3

2 UNIT The order of words

A In Italian, the grammatical form of words, including their appropriate endings, is very important, whereas the actual order of words is less so. The subject, for example, can be placed almost anywhere in the sentence.

Tomorrow Renza is going to Sori can be translated as: **Domani Renza va a Sori**; **Renza va a Sori domani**; **Va a Sori domani Renza**; **A Sori va domani Renza**.

The difference in meaning is in the change of emphasis.

B Subject pronouns **io** (*I*), **tu** (*you*), etc. are omitted except when needed for emphasis: **Esco** (*I am going out*), **Io esco** (*I am going out*). When placed after the verb, the emphasis is even greater: **Esco io** (*I (not you) am going out*).

C To make a question in Italian, you don't need to alter the order of the words: a question mark at the end of the sentence suffices:

Costa caro. *It is expensive.*   Costa caro? *Is it expensive?*

D The negative form requires only a **non** before the verb.

Non costa molto.   *It doesn't cost much.*

⚠ *Do*, *did*, *does*, etc. in questions or the negative are NEVER translated.

E Adjectives generally follow the noun but not necessarily (see Unit 18). You can say:

Angelo vive in una casa grande.
Angelo vive in una grande casa.   *Angelo lives in a large house.*

In the former example, the emphasis falls on the adjective **grande**.

F The position of adverbs is usually before the adjective, if there is one …

Paolo è un bambino molto vivace.   *Paul is a very lively boy.*

… and after the verb:

Carlo vive lontano.   *Charles lives far away.*

Il martedì vado sempre a Brighton. *On Tuesdays I always go to Brighton.*

With compound tenses, adverbs of time (e.g. **sempre** (*always*) are placed between the auxiliary verb and the past participle, as in English:

Sono sempre stata magra.   *I have always been slim.*

Non sono mai stata a Roma.   *I have never been to Rome.*

➤ See subject pronouns in Unit 34, compound tenses in Units 49, 50, 51 and 57, negatives in Units 88 and 89, adverbs in Units 82–84.

4

2 UNIT The order of words – Exercises

1 Following the example on the left-hand page (*Domani Renza va a Sori*, etc.), write the sentence below in as many different ways as possible.

Dopodomani   Gino   arriva   da Roma.
The day after tomorrow   Gino   will arrive   from Rome.

2 Add the subject pronouns to add emphasis.

E.g. leggo (*I read/I am reading*) → io leggo, leggo io!
a parlo (*I speak/I am speaking*)
b pago (*I pay/I am paying*)
c vengo (*I come/I am coming*)

3 Put the sentences below into the interrogative and negative forms.

E.g. Devo finire. (*I must finish.*) → Devo finire? Non devo finire. Non devo finire?
a Posso andare. (*I can/may go.*)
b Posso parlare. (*I can/may speak.*)
c Devo pagare il conto. (*I must pay the bill.*)
d Devo scrivere la lettera. (*I must write the letter.*)
e Devo leggere questo libro. (*I must read this book.*)

4 Form four sentences taking the words from the box below, using this example as a pattern.

E.g. Angelo vive in una casa grande.

adjectives	nouns	verbs
interessante *interesting*	**Francesco/un cantante** *singer*	**ha** *has*
blu *blue*	**Elisa/un libro** *book*	**legge** *is reading*
enorme *enormous*	**Filippo/un'automobile** *car*	**è** *is*
famoso *famous*	**Mario/un vestito** *suit*	**indossa** *wears*

5 Re-write the sentences below adding *molto, sempre* or *mai*.
a Non vado al cinema.   *I (never) go to the cinema.*
b Gino va a teatro.   *Gino goes to the theatre (a lot).*
c Ho pagato i conti.   *I have (always) paid my bills.*

3 UNIT | Alphabet, accent, apostrophe

The other five letters (j, k, w, x, y) are used to write words of classical or foreign origin, e.g. **xilofono** (*xylophone*), **box** (*lock-up garage*).

A In Italian, some words carry an accent on the last letter. It may be either grave (è) or acute (é): **qualità** (*quality*), **più** (*more/plus*), **è** (*s/he/it is*) **perché** (*why*). The grave accent is used at the end of those words which are pronounced with an open -**e** (as in 'red') such as: **caffè** (*coffee*), **tè** (*tea*), **cioè** (*that is (to say)*). Acute accents go on words pronounced with a closed -**e** (as in 'they') at the end: **perché** (*why/because*), **sé** (*oneself*), **né** (*neither*), **benché** (*although*), **poiché** (*since*).

B When two vowels come together, at the end of one word and the beginning of the next, the final vowel of the first word is replaced with an apostrophe ('). This is compulsory with the articles **lo**, **la** and **una** and with combined prepositions and articles.

l'amico *the friend*   l'ala *the wing*   un'arancia *an orange*
nell(o)'orto *in the vegetable garden* dell(o)'ortolano *of the greengrocer*
sull(a)'altalena *on the swing*   dall(o)'arco *from the arch*

Often **di** is also treated this way: **d'inverno** (*in winter*), **d'argento** (*in silver*).

⚠ When you say these pairs of words, they run together.

C Other expressions which take an apostrophe are:

d'ora in poi	*from now on*
senz'altro	*without any doubt*
nient'altro	*nothing else*
tutt'altro	*on the contrary*

In most other cases it is either strictly forbidden or only optional and thus avoidable.

► See Unit 30 for the apostrophe on quello, bello, grande, santo.
See Units 74, 75, 76, 77, 80 for combined prepositions.

3 UNIT Alphabet, accent, apostrophe – *Exercises*

1 Write the appropriate accents on the last vowels of this list of words:

a ne
b e
c benche
d se
e cioe
f perche
g poiche
h te

2 Use an apostrophe with the pairs of words below if appropriate.

E.g. la elica (*propeller*) → l'elica.

a lo zero (*zero*)
b di estate (*in summer*)
c dallo autobus (*from the bus*)
d di oro (*in gold*)
e un problema (*problem*)
f una arancia (*orange*)
g una amica (*friend*)
h un aereo (*plane*)
i una ala (*wing*)

3 Join each word in the first column to the appropriate word in the second column.

a una   1 altro
b un'   2 dubbio (*doubt*)
c senza   3 automobile
d senz'   4 macchina
e di   5 metallo
f d'   6 autunno

4 UNIT | Shortening words

Sometimes in Italian a vowel or even a whole syllable is lost at the end of a word.

A The loss of a vowel – or sometimes a whole syllable – can occur at the end of a word without the use of an apostrophe. With words ending in **-re**, **-ne**, **-le** and **-ra**, **-na**, **-la**, it is optional and used only to produce a better sound:

mal(e) di gola *sore throat*   cuor(e) di leone *lion heart*

B The apostrophe occurs only before a vowel, whereas a shortened word can also occur before a consonant (except **-z**, **gn**, **-ps**, **-x** or **-s** followed by another consonant).

C **Signore** (*Sir/Mr*), **professore** (*teacher/professor*), **dottore** (*doctor*), **ingegnere** (*civil/naval engineer*) always lose their final vowel when followed by a surname.

il signor Cervi *Mr Cervi*   il professor Neri *Professor Neri*

D Infinitives can also be shortened, particularly before another infinitive.

poter andare *to be able to go*   lavorar sodo *to work hard*

E **Quello** (*that*), **bello** (*beautiful*), **grande** (*large/great*), **santo** (*saint*) are shortened before a word beginning with a consonant.

quel libro è mio *that is my book*   un bel bambino *a beautiful child*
They take an apostrophe before a vowel.

quell'uomo   *that man*
Also **quale** often drops the final **-e**:

Qual è …?   *Which is …?*

Similarly, **buono** (*good*), **uno** (*one/a/an*), **alcuno** (*any*) and **nessuno** (*nobody*), drop their final vowel.

un buon amico *a good friend*   nessun uomo *no man*

F Generally words are not shortened in the plural.

buoni amici   *good friends*

G There are a few cases where a word which has lost its last vowel or syllable does use an apostrophe, irrespective of the following word: **po'** = **poco** (*little*), **mo'** = **modo** (*way/manner*), plus the imperatives **da'** = **dai** (*give!*), **sta'** = **stai** (*stay!*), **di'** = **dici** (*say!*), **va'** = **vai** (*go!*), **fa'** = **fai** (*do (it)!*), **to'** = **tieni** (*take!*).

➤ *See Unit 58 for imperatives; for more on quello, etc, see Unit 30.*

1 Correct the expressions below by dropping the final vowel or syllable when possible.

a il male di denti
b la prova scritta
c il male di testa
d il male di cuore
e il Mare Adriatico
f un cuore d'oro
g quale è?
h stai attento
i un poco di vino
j il professore Rossi
k la professoressa Rossi
l l'ingegnere Bianchi

Quel bel ragazzo ha un cuor d'oro!

2 In the list for exercise 1, write an asterisk before the nouns requiring the loss of the last vowel and two asterisks in front of those requiring an apostrophe.

E.g. * il mal. ** un po'

3 Translate the following into Italian.

E.g. a beautiful child → un bel bambino

a a friend
b a good friend
c that man
d Which is …?
e good friends
f to be able to go
g no friends
h to work hard
i that book
j take!
k Mr Cervi
l Doctor Green

5 UNIT The gender of nouns (1)

A Italian nouns are either masculine or feminine and, except for a few Latin words or words of foreign origin such as **bar**, **film** and **album**, which are mostly masculine, they end in either **-o**, **-a** or **-e**.

Most nouns ending in **-o** are masculine: **uomo** (*man*); **cavallo** (*horse*); **bambino** (*little boy*); **ragazzo** (*boy*); **aeroplano** (*airplane*); **treno** (*train*); **orario** (*timetable*); **oro** (*gold*).

Most nouns ending in **-a** are feminine: **donna** (*woman*); **bambina** (*little girl*); **ragazza** (*girl*); **casa** (*house/home*); **banca** (*bank*); **commedia** (*play/comedy*).

Nouns ending in **-e** can be either masculine or feminine. The dictionary will give you the gender; next to the noun you will find s.m. (= sostantivo maschile) for the masculine form and s.f. (= sostantivo femminile) for the feminine one: **carne** (s.f.) *meat*; **cane** (s.m.) *dog*; **colore** (s.m.) *colour*

B Some nouns do not follow the above rule.
Masculine
clima; pigiama; programma; telegramma; tema; diploma; problema; profeta; sistema; poeta; pianeta; duca; dramma; papa; vaglia; cinema(tografo)
Feminine
mano; radio; dinamo; crisi; auto(mobile); moto(cicletta); foto(grafia); eco

C Most often masculine nouns referring to people change their **-o** ending into an **-a** to form the feminine: **zio/zia** (*uncle-aunt*); **cittadino/cittadina** (*citizen*). The dictionary gives the masculine form of such nouns, followed by **-a** (or other suffix), to indicate its feminine equivalent.

D Nouns ending in **-tore** form the feminine with **-trice**: **attore/attrice** (*actor/actress*), **pittore/pittrice** (*painter*), BUT **dottore/dottoressa** (*doctor*).

E Nouns ending in **-e** form the feminine in two ways: some change the **-e** into **-a**: **infermiere/infermiera** (*nurse*); **cameriere/cameriera** (*waiter/tress*); others, usually those indicating profession or title, change the **-e** into **-essa**: **professore/professoressa** (*lecturer*); **dottore/dottoressa** (*doctor*). In spite of this rule, academic, office, rank and many professional titles are more often used in the masculine form: **l'ambasciatore Signora** ... (*the (female) ambassador*), **il sindaco Signora** ... (*the mayoress*).

 ➤ For more on the gender of nouns, see Units 6, 12, 13 and 14.

1 Write the name and gender (m. or f.) under each picture.

a)

d)

b)

e)

c)

f)

2 In each line there are five words (translated in the box below) divided into syllables and mixed up. Can you find them? Write them down and indicate their genders.

a pro co rio ble o to re ma lo ra re ne ca dot

b fo bam com bi ban na ca me o dia to ro

gold	bank	doctor	dog	colour	little girl/child
	photo	problem	timetable	play	

3 Some of the words on the opposite page have not been translated. Without the help of the dictionary, match the words below to their Italian equivalent.

a programme　　　　　　　　**h** theme
b radio　　　　　　　　　　　**i** motorbike
c problem　　　　　　　　　　**j** pyjamas
d photo　　　　　　　　　　　**k** hand
e climate　　　　　　　　　　**l** cinema
f aunt　　　　　　　　　　　　**m** drama
g poet　　　　　　　　　　　　**n** crisis

6 UNIT | The plural of nouns

A Masculine nouns (ending in **-o** or **-a**) form their plural with **-i**.

bambino → bambini (*children*); problema → problemi (*problems*)

BUT

uomo → uomini (*men*)

B Feminine nouns ending in **-a** form their plural with **-e**:

mamma → mamme (*mums*); scatola → scatole (*boxes*); gonna → gonne (*skirts*)

C Nouns ending in **-e** (masculine and feminine) form their plural with **-i**.

luce → luci (*lights*); fiore → fiori (*flowers*)

D Nouns ending in **-co**, **-go**, **-ca** and **-ga** do not always behave in the same way but usually acquire an **-h** between the **-c/-g** and the ending (**-i** or **-e**).

buco → buchi (*holes*); fungo → funghi (*mushrooms*);

banca → banche; (*banks*); diga → dighe (*dams/dykes*)

⚠ Nouns ending in **-ico** (NOT **-ica**) follow the normal masculine rule.

medico → medici (*doctors*); sindaco → sindaci (*mayors*); amico → amici (*friends*); nemico → nemici (*enemies*); greco-greci (*Greeks*); porco → porci (*pigs*); farmaco → farmaci (*medicines*); stomaco → stomaci (*stomachs*); monaco → monaci (*monks*)

E Nouns ending in accented vowels do not change in the plural.

città (*city, cities/town, towns*); qualità (*quality, qualities*); virtù (*virtue(s)*); caffè (*coffee(s)*)

F Nouns ending in **-io**, where the stress falls on the **-i** (there are not many), have a regular plural by changing the **-o** into an **-i**: **zio** → **zii** (*uncles*). All the others lose the **-o**:

viaggio → viaggi (*trips*), figlio → figli (*sons*)

G Words ending in **-cia** and **-gia** tend to form their plural in one of two ways. If **-c** and **-g** are preceded by a vowel, they keep the **-i** and add an **-e**:

camicia → camicie (*shirts*), valigia → valigie (*suitcases*)

If preceded by a consonant, they lose the **-i** and add an **-e**:

spiaggia → spiagge (*beaches*).

► For more on plural of nouns, see Units 14 and 15.

1 Write the singular form of the nouns below.

E.g. dighe → diga

a fiori
b bambini
c problemi
d uomini
e mamme
f gonne
g banche
h luci
i strade
j borse
k funghi
l scatole

2 Below is a list of nouns: some take an *-h* between *-c* or *-g*, others do not. Can you sort them out?

farmaco	buco	porco	banca	amico
	greco	stomaco	medico	

3 Write the plural form of the nouns below.

E.g. una città (*one city*) → due città (*two cities*)

a una virtù (*one virtue*) → due _____ (*two virtues*)
b un caffè (*one coffee*) → _____ (*two coffees*)
c un tè (*one tea*) → _____ (*two teas*)
d una qualità (*one quality*) → _____ (*two qualities*)
e una quantità (*one quantity*) → _____ (*two quantities*)
f un giovedì (*one Thursday*) → _____ (*two Thursdays*)

4 Give the plural of the following nouns.

a viaggio (*trip/voyage*)
b figlio (*son/child*)
c zio (*uncle*)
d leggio (*book rest/music stand*)
e specchio (*mirror*)
f brusio (*buzz/hum*)

7 UNIT | *The*: the definite article

Several words translate the *in Italian*. These vary according to the gender, number and the first letter of the following noun.

	masculine	feminine
singular	**il ragazzo lo zero l'aereo**	**la ragazza l'arancia**
plural	**i ragazzi gli zeri gli aerei**	**le ragazze le arance**

A The article **il** precedes the majority of singular masculine nouns:

il libro (*the book*); il problema (*the problem*); il fiore (*the flower*)

Its plural form is **i**:

i libri (*the books*); i problemi (*the problems*); i fiori (*the flowers*)

B However, **lo** precedes masculine nouns starting with:

- **s** followed by consonant: lo specchio (*mirror*); lo sci (*ski*)
- **z**: lo zucchero (*sugar*), lo zero (*zero*), lo zio (*uncle*)
- **x**: lo xilofono (*xylophone*), lo xenofobo (*xenophobe*)
- **pn, ps**: lo pneumatico (*pneumatic/tyre*)*; lo psicologo (*psychologist*)
- **gn, sc**: lo gnocco (*dumpling*); lo sciopero (*strike*); lo sceicco (*sheik*)
- **i** followed by another vowel: lo ione (*ion*), lo iettatore (*jinx*)

*You will, however, often hear **il pneumatico → i pneumatici**

C The form **lo** becomes **l'** before masculine nouns starting with a vowel:

l'aereo (*plane*); l'elicottero (*helicopter*)

⚠ Lo is used instead of **il** in adverbial expressions like **per lo più** (*mostly*) and **per lo meno** (*at least*).

D The plural form of **lo** and **l'** is **gli**. **Gli** can become **gl'** before a noun starting with **i-** but the whole form is better.

gli studenti (*students*); gli zeri (*zeros*); gli xenofobi (*xenophobes*); gli pseudonimi (*pseudonyms*); gli scioperi (*strikes*); gli aerei (*planes*); gli elicotteri (*helicopters*); gli Italiani (*Italians*)

Gli is also used instead of **i** before **dei** (*gods*): gli dei.

E The feminine article is **la**: la giacca (*jacket*); la borsa (*bag*); la zia (*aunt*)

La before a noun starting with a vowel becomes **l'**.

l'isola (*island*); l'arancia (*orange*); l'auto (*car*)

The plural form of **la** or **l'** and **le**: le signore (*ladies*); le cravatte (*ties*).

Le NEVER becomes **l'**: le ore (*hours*); le unghie (*finger nails*)

7 UNIT *The*: the definite article – *Exercises*

1 **Write the definite article before the following nouns.**

E.g. elicottero → l'elicottero

a _____ gnocco
b _____ casa
c _____ aereo
d _____ sciopero
e _____ psicologo
f _____ xenofobo
g _____ auto
h _____ sci
i _____ arancia
j _____ specchio
k _____ problema
l _____ ora
m _____ zia
n _____ fiore

2 **Change all the nouns and their articles from exercise 1 into the plural.**

E.g. l'elicottero → gli elicotteri

3 **Correct the wrong definite articles.**

E.g. ~~lo~~ il libro

a le scioperi
b i dei
c la auto (pl.)
d i elicotteri
e i gnocchi
f le unghie
g lo pseudonimi
h la borse
i l'ore
j le studenti
k la isole
l i aerei

4 **Write at least three nouns from the left-hand page for each of the articles below.**

E.g. il fiore

il   lo   l'   la   i   gli   le

8 UNIT The use of the definite article (1)

The definite article (*the*), is used in the following cases:

A Geographical names such as continents, countries, regions, counties, large islands, lakes, mountains.

l'Italia (*Italy*); il Kent (*Kent*); il Monte Bianco (*Mont Blanc*); la Toscana (*Tuscany*); la Corsica (*Corsica*); la Cornovaglia (*Cornwall*).

⚠ After the preposition *in*, the article is omitted providing it is not qualified by an adjective or an adjectival phrase.

Abito in Inghilterra. *I live in England.* Vado in Spagna. *I am going to Spain.*

BUT

| nell' (in+l') Inghilterra di Cromwell | *in Cromwell's England* |
| nell'Italia Meridionale | *in Southern Italy* |

B Titles. il signor Rossi (*Mr Rossi*); il duca d'Aosta (*the duke of Aosta*)

C Women's surnames. La Loren è molto ammirata. *Loren is much admired.*

D Expressions of time and dates. Sono le tre. *It's three o'clock.*

Lavoro dalle nove alle cinque. *I work from 9 to 5.*
  (da + le) (a + le)

BUT È mezzogiorno/mezzanotte. *It is midday/midnight.*

Il 1993 è stato un anno molto bello. *1993 was a lovely year.*

Mario è nato nel 1966. *Mario was born in 1966.*

E Names of languages except with the verb **parlare**.

Francesca studia il cinese. *Francesca studies Chinese.*

Parla inglese? *Do you speak English?*

F Parts of the body, clothes and objects we own, such as cars. In these cases Italian uses the definite article rather than the possessive adjective.

Mi lavo le mani. *I am washing my hands.*

Vado a prendere la macchina. *I am going to get my car.*

G Nouns used in a 'general' sense.

Amo la musica. *I love music.*

I gatti sono indipendenti. *Cats are independent.*

H Expressions such as **tutti e due**, **ambedue**, **entrambi** (*both*).

tutti e due/ambedue/entrambi i bambini *both children*

➤ See possessive adjectives and pronouns in Unit 21; reflexive verbs in Unit 47; combined prepositions in Units 74, 75, 76, 77, 80.

1 Below is a list of geographical names. Write the definite article, when required, before them.

E.g. Inghilterra → l'Inghilterra

a _____ Cina
b _____ Francia
c _____ Spagna
d _____ Cornovaglia
e _____ Londra
f _____ Madagascar (m)

g _____ Milano
h _____ Roma
i _____ Cassino
j _____ Toscana
k _____ Calabria

2 Write each of the geographical names above (omitting the towns) using *abito in ...* and *vado in.*

E.g. Abito in Inghilterra. → Vado in Inghilterra.

3 Translate the following into Italian.

a Loren is a much admired actress (**attrice**).
b It is five o'clock.
c I work from 10 to 6.
d It is midday.
e 1995 was (**è stato**) a lovely year.
f I am going to get my umbrella (**ombrello**).
g I wash my face.
h I love sport.
i It is midnight.
j Fish is expensive.
k Both cats are black (**neri**).
l Dogs are faithful (**fedeli**).

4 Make questions by joining each verb in the box to each of the adjectives of nationality listed below.

E.g. Parla tedesco? Studia il tedesco?

	Parla	Studia

a francese	French	**f** portoghese	Portuguese	**k** polacco	Polish
b inglese	English	**g** turco	Turkish	**l** danese	Danish
c tedesco	German	**h** arabo	Arabic	**m** svedese	Swedish
d spagnolo	Spanish	**i** russo	Russian	**n** norvegese	Norwegian
e greco	Greek	**j** olandese	Dutch	**o** finlandese	Finnish

9 UNIT The use of the definite article (2)

Here are some more cases in which the definite article is used in Italian but not in English.

Italian uses the definite article in the following situations:

A With prices, weights, measures and other figures such as percentages.

Questo vino costa tremila lire al (a + il) litro.	*This wine costs 3000 lire per litre.*
il 30% della popolazione	*30% of the population*
Una lezione costa 25 sterline all' (a + l')ora.	*A lesson costs £25 per hour.*
Il prezzo è aumentato del (di + il) dieci per cento.	*The price has increased by 10%.*

B With names of towns when accompanied by an adjective or adjectival phrase.

la Firenze del (di + il) Cinquecento *Florence of the 16th century*

C With certain expressions.

Mi piace vedere/guardare la televisione.	*I like watching television.*
Che cosa c'è alla televisione stasera?	*What is on television tonight?*
A che ora è la colazione/il pranzo/la cena?	*What time is breakfast/lunch/ dinner?*

D *The* is not translated with expressions like *to/in the mountains, to/in the office, to/in the country, in the car.*

Vado in montagna ogni anno.	*I go to the mountains every year.*
Abito in campagna.	*I live in the country.*
Vado/Sono in ufficio alle otto.	*I go to/am in the office at eight.*

➤ *For preposition + article, see Units 73, 74, 75, 76, 77, 80.*

1 **Use the left-hand page to help you find the answers to these questions:**

a Quanto costa al litro questo vino?

b Quanto costa una lezione all'ora?

c Di quanto è aumentato il prezzo?

d Quando vai in montagna?

e Che cosa ti piace fare?

f Dove abiti?

g A che ora vai in ufficio?

2 **Translate the following expressions into Italian and then read them aloud (see vocabulary at the bottom of page).**

a Soave wine costs 3,000 lire per litre.

b I like watching football on television.

c Ninety per cent of the population has a car.

d A lesson costs £25 lire per hour.

e Imperial Rome

f Dinner is ready (**pronto**).

g What time is breakfast?

3 **Translate the expressions shown in English into Italian.**

a Vado *to the mountain* ogni estate.

b Tullio va *to the country* domenica prossima.

c A che ora vai t*o the office*?

d Alle tre ero *in the office*.

e Abito *in the country*.

f Gisella ha una casa *in the mountains*.

g Gabriella va *to the swimming pool*.

h Marco è *at the swimming pool*.

i Il mio amico mi aspetta *in the car*.

il calcio	*football*	**estate**	*summer*
la piscina	*swimming pool*	**aspetta**	*waits/is waiting*
domenica	*Sunday*	**pronto**	*ready*
la cena	*dinner*	**prossima**	*next*

10 UNIT A, *an*: the indefinite article

The indefinite article is used for non-specified nouns, that is, a friend as opposed to the friend. In Italian it has four forms; un, uno, un' and una.

A **Un** precedes masculine nouns.

un amico (*a friend*); un attore (*an actor*).

It becomes **uno** before **s** followed by a consonant, before **z**, **x**, **gn**, **ps** or **pn**, and before **i** followed by another vowel.

uno spreco (*a waste*); uno zoo (*a zoo*); uno gnocco (*a dumpling*); uno sci (*a ski*); uno ione (*an ion*); uno psicologo (*a psicologist*).

B The feminine form is **una**:

una mela (*an apple*); una pentola (*a saucepan*); una pagina (*a page*)

Una becomes **un'** before a vowel.

un'arancia (*an orange*); un'ala (*a wing*); un'attrice (*an actress*)
BUT
una iena (*a hyena*)

Remember that the masculine form **un** NEVER takes an apostrophe.

⚠ The numeral **uno** (*one*) is the same word as the indefinite article. It therefore agrees in gender with the noun and takes the same forms as above.

un uomo (*one man*); uno sci (*one ski*); una casa (*one house*); un'ape (*one bee*)

C The indefinite article doesn't have a plural. There are, however, forms for *some* and *any*.

➤ *See Unit 20 for* some *and* any.

10 UNIT A, *an*: the indefinite article – *Exercises*

1 Write the indefinite article before the following nouns.

E.g. quadro → quadro

a	_____ attore	k	_____ pentola
b	_____ amico	l	_____ pagina
c	_____ cane	m	_____ ala
d	_____ gatto	n	_____ attrice
e	_____ gnocco	o	_____ iena
f	_____ sci	p	_____ pagina
g	_____ zero	q	_____ ape
h	_____ psicologo	r	_____ zoo
i	_____ xenofobo	s	_____ automobile
j	_____ mela		

2 Write as many nouns as you can for each of the articles below.

E.g. **Una** iena, casa, bambina, pizza, zebra

un   uno   una   un'

3 What are these?

4 Which one of the two forms is right?

E.g. ~~un'albero~~   un albero

a uno zoo   un zoo

b una elica   un'elica

c un attore   un'attore

d un'attrice   un attrice

e un zero   uno zero

f un problema   uno problema

g una psicologa   un psicologa

h uno psicologo   un psicologo

i un album   uno album

11 UNIT The use of the indefinite article

The indefinite article is not translated in the following cases:

A When a role, job, profession, nationality or religion is preceded by **essere** (*to be*) or **diventare** (*to become*) …

Alberto è/è diventato avvocato.	*Albert is/has become a lawyer.*
Cristina è cattolica.	*Cristina is a Catholic.*

… unless qualified by an adjective or followed by an object:

Anna è una segretaria efficiente.	*Anna is an efficient secretary.*
Sono un impiegato delle poste.	*I am a Post Office worker.*

B With expressions starting **Che …** (*What a …*).

Che bel ragazzo!	*What a handsome young man!*
Che peccato!	*What a pity!*

C Before **cento** (*hundred*), **mille** (*thousand*), **mezzo/a** (*half*).

Te l'ho detto mille volte!	*I've told you a thousand times!*
mezz'ora	*half an hour*
mezzo litro di latte	*half a litre of milk*

D However, when *a/an* stands for *every/per*, they are translated by **a** + definite article.

Vado in Italia due volte all'anno.	*I go to Italy twice a year.*
Insegno sei ore al giorno.	*I teach six hours a/per day.*

E Note these expressions: **avere/prendere** (*to have/catch*) …

avere … il mal di gola *a sore throat*; … il mal di denti *a toothache*;
… il mal di testa *a headache*; … il raffreddore *a cold*;
… appetito *an appetite*
prendere … il mal di gola; … il raffreddore
Also: avere l'automobile (*to have a car*); avere fretta (to *be in a hurry*).

F The indefinite article can be used in Italian for emphasis to express words like *such a …* or when a noun is followed by an adjective.

Aveva una fretta!	*He was in such a hurry!*
Ho un raffreddore terribile.	*I have a terrible cold.*

G **Da** is used instead of *as a* in the following kind of expressions.

Mio figlio studia da interprete.	*My son is studying as an interpreter.*
Da bambina ero un maschiaccio.	*As a child I was a tomboy.*

1 Add the indefinite article when needed.

E.g. Cristina è _____ segretaria diligente. → Cristina è una segretaria diligente.

a Alberto è _____ dottore.
b Francesco è _____ segretario.
c Mariangela è _____ professoressa universitaria.
d Cesare è _____ avvocato famoso.
e Umberto è _____ avvocato di successo (*successful*).
f Emanuela è _____ cattolica.
g Andrea è _____ cattolico praticante (*practising*).
h Vittorio è _____ protestante.
i Alessandro è _____ italiano tipico (*typical*).

2 Translate the following into Italian.

a What a pity!
b half a kilo (**chilo**) of apples (**mele**)
c half an hour
d a hundred times
e a thousand times
f six hours a day
g twice a year
h twice a day
i half a pint (**pinta**)
j what a handsome young man!

3 Translate the following into Italian.

a I have (**Ho**) a sore throat.
b I have a headache.
c Andrea has (**ha**) toothache.
d Goffredo has (**ha**) a cold.
e Angela has a terrible cold.
f I am in (**Ho**) such a hurry!
g I have an appetite.
h I have such an appetite!
i Mario has a car.
j As a child I was a tomboy.

4 What would you call these?

a.

b. 1000 LIRE MILLE
BANCA D'ITALIA L0216453

c. SPAGHETTI ½ kg

The gender of nouns (2)

Some nouns seem to have two genders but they are actually different words with different meanings.

A che ora apre il mostro?

MOSTRA

The distinction between masculine and feminine nouns makes sense only for those nouns referring to people and animals. The gender of nouns referring to things is purely a grammatical convention since it is obvious that objects are neither male or female. The following nouns change their meaning, depending on whether they are masculine or feminine.

MASCULINE	FEMININE
l'arco (*arch*)	l'arca (*ark*)
il boa (*boa (snake)*)	la boa (*buoy*)
il camerata (*comrade*)	la camerata (*dormitory*)
il capitale (*capital(money)*)	la capitale (*capital (city)*)
il colpo (*blow*)	la colpa (*fault/guilt*)
il collo (*neck*)	la colla (*glue*)
il fonte (*font (in a church)*)	la fonte (*spring*)
il foglio (*sheet (page)*)	la foglia (*leaf*)
il fosso (*ditch/moat*)	la fossa (*pit/hole*)
il fine (*aim/purpose*)	la fine (*end*)
il manico (*handle*)	la manica (*sleeve/English Channel*)
il modo (*way/manner*)	la moda (*fashion*)
il mostro (*monster*)	la mostra (*exhibition*)
il panno (*cloth*)	la panna (*cream*)
il pianto (*crying/tears*)	la pianta (*plant/plan/map*)
il posto (*place*)	la posta (*post/mail*)
il radio (*radius/radium*)	la radio (*radio*)
il tappo (*cork/plug*)	la tappa (*stage/leg/lap*)
il tasso (*rate/yew/badger*)	la tassa (*tax/fee/duty*)
il visto (*visa/tick/check*)	la vista (*sight/view*)

1 Write the names of these objects (definite article + noun).

2 Complete each phrase with the correct word preceded by the definite or indefinite article as suggested by the English translation.

a _____ di Trionfo (*the Arc de Triomphe*)

b Ho _____ portatile. (*I have a portable radio.*)

c _____ d'interesse è sceso. (*The rate of interest has gone down.*)

d _____ della pentola (*the handle of the saucepan*)

e _____ di carta (*a sheet of paper*)

f _____ è arrivata? (*Has the mail arrived?*)

g Questa bottiglia è senza _____. (*This bottle is without a cork.*)

h Londra è_____ dell'Inghilterra. (*London is the capital of England.*)

i _____ del Tour de France (*the stages of the Tour de France*)

j _____ di fico (*a fig leaf*)

13 UNIT More on the genders of nouns

Some nouns referring to people have only one form, and the gender of the person can be recognized by the article or the following adjective.

Nouns with only one form include:

A Nouns ending in **-ista** and **-cida**

il/la farmacista (*chemist*); un/un'artista (*artist*); il/la violinista (*violinist*); il/la suicida (*suicide*)

B Some nouns of Greek origin ending in **-a**:

il/la collega (*colleague*); il/la pediatra (*paediatrician*); l'atleta (*athlete*)

⚠ The plural forms of the above nouns follow the normal plural pattern.

il farmacista → i farmacisti
la farmacista → le farmaciste
il collega → i colleghi
la collega → le colleghe

C Some nouns ending in **-e**:

il/la nipote (*grandchild/nephew/niece*); il/la parente (*relative*); il/la consorte (*spouse*); il/la cantante (*singer*); un/un'insegnante (*teacher*): un/un'amante (*lover*)

⚠ These nouns ending in **-e** have an identical plural form for both the masculine and the feminine.

il cantante → i cantanti
la cantante → le cantanti

D Nouns like persona (*person*); guida (*guide*); guardia (*guard*) and polizia (*police*) where feminine nouns are applied to either gender:

Quell'uomo è una persona intelligente.	*That man is an intelligent person.*
Il marito è una guida turistica.	*The husband is a tourist guide.*

Remember that nouns ending with an accented vowel have only one form la città → le città (see Unit 6).

E Some names of animals have a male and female form:

cavallo (*stallion*), cavalla (*mare*); cervo (*stag*), cerva (*hind*); bufalo (*bull buffalo*) bufala (*cow buffalo*).

However, the majority only have one gender and thus need to be followed by **maschio** or **femmina** to indicate the animal's sex.

la volpe maschio/il maschio della volpe	*fox*
il leopardo femmina/la femmina del leopardo	*female leopard*

More on the genders of nouns – *Exercises*

1 Add the feminine form to the list of nouns below and give their plural forms.

E.g. il farmacista → i farmacisti; la farmacista → le farmaciste;
il cantante → i cantanti; la cantante → le cantanti

a il ciclista (*cyclist*)
b il turista (*tourist*)
c il violinista (*violinist*)
d l'arpista (*harpist*)
e il pianista (*pianist*)
f l'artista (*artist*)
g il borsista (*grant holder*)
h il ritrattista (*portrait painter*)
i il giornalista (*journalist*)
j il parente (*relative*)

k il collega (*colleague*)
l l'atleta (*athlete*)
m il pediatra (*paediatrician*)
n lo psichiatra (*psychiatrist*)
o lo stratega (*strategist*)
p l'ipocrita (*hypocrite*)
q l'insegnante (*teacher*)
r l'agente (*agent*)
s l'amante (*lover*)

2 Translate the following into Italian.

a The husband is an intelligent person.
b That man is a tourist guide.
c The police are after him (**è sulle sue tracce**).

3 Give the opposite gender form of the animals mentioned below.

E.g. la cavalla → il cavallo

a la cerva
b il maschio del leopardo
c la bufala
d la volpe maschio

e il maschio della zebra
f la femmina del puma
g il rinoceronte maschio

4 Sort these nouns into three groups: masculine, feminine and common gender.

a violinista
b cavalla
c casa
d collega
e gatto
f borsista
g problema
h bufalo
i cerva
j infanticida
k radio

l ritrattista
m maschio della giraffa
n gatta
o femmina del leopardo
p libro
q arco
r posto
s cantante
t posta
u mostra
v zoo

14 UNIT More on the genders and plurals of nouns

Some masculine nouns have a slightly different feminine form, some have a completely different one and others have no plural or no singular form.

A Among the nouns with an irregular feminine form are: eroe/eroina (*hero/heroine*); dio/dea (*god/goddess*); re/regina (*king/queen*); cane/cagna (*dog/bitch*)

B Among masculine nouns with a completely different feminine form are: uomo/donna (*man/woman*); padre/madre (*father/mother*); babbo/papà-mamma (*dad/mum*); marito/moglie (*husband/wife*); fratello/sorella (*brother/sister*); genero/nuora (*son/daughter in law*); celibe/nubile (*bachelor/single* or *unmarried*); maschio/femmina (*male/female*)

C Some nouns keep the same ending in both the singular and plural:
- those ending in an accented vowel:
  bontà (*goodness/kindness*)
- those ending in -**i**:
  tesi, brindisi, analisi, ipotesi, oasi, metropoli
- nouns formed with only one syllable such as **re** and **gru**
- feminine nouns ending in -**ie**:
  serie, specie (BUT moglie → mogli)
- some masculine nouns ending in -**a**:
  gorilla, sosia, lama, cinema
- some feminine nouns ending in -**o**:
  dinamo, radio, auto, foto
- nouns ending in a consonant:
  autobus, gas, bar, film, album, tram

D Some have no singular form: le forbici (*scissors*); gli occhiali (*glasses*) le nozze (*marriage/wedding*); i pantaloni/calzoni (*trousers*)

E Some nouns have no plural form.
- most metals: il rame (*copper*); l'argento (*silver*)
- la fame (*hunger*); la sete (*thirst*); l'uva (*grapes*); la prole (*offspring*)
- groups of people, animals or things:
  un branco (*pack*); la folla (*crowd*); la gente (*people*); il gregge (*flock (sheep)*); la mandria (*herd*); la polizia (*police*); il consiglio comunale (*town council*); la marina (*navy*); l'aviazione (*airforce*)

In English one often says: 'The police are ...', 'The council are ...'; this is not the case in Italian. Unless you are talking about various groups of people or more than one council you say: **La gente è** ... (*The people is* ...).

14 UNIT: More on the genders and plurals of nouns – *Exercises*

1 Give the masculine form of the following:

a la dea
b la regina
c l'eroina
d la cagna

2 Write the opposite gender/article for the nouns below.

E.g. Il padre → la madre

a l'uomo
b la sorella
c la moglie
d il celibe
e la nuora
f il maschio

3 Write the plural form of the following nouns and articles.

E.g. la bontà → le bontà

a la qualità
b la quantità
c la virtù
d la città
e il caffè
f il tè

4 Translate the following words.

a metropolis
b toast (drink/speech)
c hypothesis
d tea
e analysis
f thesis
g oasis

5 Write the plural form of the following nouns.

E.g. La tesi → le tesi

a la metropoli
b il brindisi
c l'analisi (f)
d l'ipotesi (f)
e l'oasi (f)
f la bontà
g la foto
h il re (*king*)
i la serie (*series*)
j la specie (*species*)
k l'auto (f)
l la gru (*crane*)
m la radio (*radio*)
n il sosia (*one's double*)
o la dinamo (*dynamo*)
p il lama (*llama*)
q la moglie (*wife*)
r il cinema
s l'autobus (m)
t il gas
u il bar
v il film
w l'album (m)
x il tram

6 Match the words on either side of *di* (of) and *è* (is) to make a sensible sentence or expression.

E.g. un branco di lupi (*wolves*)

a Un branco		efficiente.
b Una folla	è	Milano.
c La gente	di	lupi.
d La polizia		500 persone.

More on irregular plurals

> *Certain masculine nouns ending in -o form their plural with -a and become feminine in the process.*

A Many of these gender-changing verbs relate to numbers or measurements.

un miglio (*one mile*)
due miglia (*two miles*)
un centinaio (*about one hundred*)
molte centinaia (*many hundreds*)
un migliaio (*about one thousand*)
alcune migliaia (*some thousands*)
un dito (*one finger*)
due dita (*two fingers*)

B In this category also belong a group of words which, while having a feminine plural ending in **-a**, also have a regular plural ending in **-i** with a different meaning.

il braccio (*arm/beam*)   i bracci   (*arms of a chandelier/scales*)
                      le braccia (*of the human body*)

il corno (*horn*)   i corni (*horns = musical instrument*)
               le corna (*horns of animals*)

il membro (*member/limb*) i membri   (*members of a club or commission*)
                      le membra (*members = limbs of the human body*)

il muro (*wall*)   i muri   (*walls of a house*)
              le mura (*walls of a city or a fortress*)

l'osso (*bone*)   gli ossi (*bones, mainly of animals*
             (*i.e. for the dog)*)
             le ossa   (*human bones*)

C Observe these words

il frutto/i frutti (*fruits while on a plant or a tree*)
la frutta/le frutta (*fruits after they have been picked*)
il legno/i legni (*wood of a tree/furniture*)
la legna/le legna (*wood for burning*)

1 Translate the following expressions into Italian.

a one mile

b two miles

c about one hundred persons (_____ **di persone**)

d ten fingers (**dieci** _____)

e about one thousand lire (_____ **di lire**)

f some thousands of miles (**alcune** _____ **di** _____)

g one finger

2 Crossword

ACROSS

3 City walls.

4 Parts of the human body joined to the shoulders.

5 Parts of the human body.

6 Fido buries them.

DOWN

1 The members of a club.

2 The arms of a chandelier.

5 The walls of a house.

7 The bones in the human body.

16 UNIT | Nouns with altered endings

Endings like -ino, -etto, etc. qualify the noun in the same way as an adjective does.

Observe these nouns:

casa   casina/casetta   casona   casaccia   casuccia

A **Casina** means *small house*. The ending **-ino** (**-ina** in the feminine) can be used instead of **piccolo** (*small*). **-Etto** and **-ello**, as well as **-uzzo**, **-icino**, **-olino** and **-erello**, are other endings that can be used in the same way:

> libretto (*small book*); fuocherello (*small fire*); bambinello (*little child*); ossicino (*small bone*); labbruzzo (*small lip*).

All these endings have regular feminine and plural forms. They are added after dropping the final vowel of the root word. While not applied to all nouns, these endings are in common usage and are often heard.

B **Casona** means *large house*. **-one** (**-ona** in the feminine) stands for **grande** (*large*) or **forte** (*strong*)

> un librone (*a large book*)

⚠ The ending **-one** can also be applied to feminine nouns, in which case they become masculine:

> una bottiglia (*a bottle*) → un bottiglione (*a large bottle*)
> una donna (*a woman*) → un donnone (*a tall, large woman*)

C **Casaccia** means *ugly house*. So **-accio/-accia** stand for *ugly, hateful, despicable* and similar:

> una donnaccia (*a despicable woman*)

D **Casuccia** stands for *nice, pretty little house*. **-uccio/-uccia** are terms of endearment and stand for *small, nice, pretty*.

E The value of these endings very much depends on the mood of the person using them. For example, **babbino**, said by a child, is not a small dad, but a dear one; **poveraccio** doesn't mean a poor bad man but a poor old soul.

F Do not confuse this class of nouns with ordinary nouns ending in the same way such as **bottone** (*button*), **limone** (*lemon*) or **bottino** (*booty*).

Names of people can also undergo the same kind of modification.

> Giuseppe → Giuseppino, Pino, Pinuccio, Pinotto, Peppino, Beppe, Beppone, Peppone, Pippo.

1 **Pair the nouns on the left with their altered terms on the right.**

a	tavolo	_____	**1**	cartaccia	_____
b	tesoro	_____	**2**	librone	_____
c	pacco	_____	**3**	elefantino	_____
d	prato	_____	**4**	praticello	_____
e	squadra	_____	**5**	tesoruccio	_____
f	carta	_____	**6**	dentone	_____
g	uomo	_____	**7**	bastoncino	_____
h	bastone	_____	**8**	pacchetto	_____
i	dente	_____	**9**	squadretta	_____
j	elefante	_____	**10**	ometto/omino	_____
k	libro	_____	**11**	tavolino	_____

2 **With the help of the dictionary, find the meaning of each word above.**

3 **What would you call these?**

4 **With the help of the dictionary work out which nouns have been altered by suffixes and which haven't.**

a	limone	**j**	pancione	**s**	barone
b	sermone	**k**	padrone	**t**	finestrella
c	padrino	**l**	uccellaccio	**u**	mulino
d	mandarino	**m**	stradina	**v**	gettone
e	paesino	**n**	torrone	**w**	torrione
f	gonfalone	**o**	boccone	**x**	uccellino
g	stampella	**p**	mattino	**y**	mattone
h	focaccia	**q**	leone	**z**	gattone
i	panciotto	**r**	ideuccia		

17 UNIT | Compound nouns

Compound nouns are those formed by two words: for example
la banconota (banknote) is formed by banco (bank) and nota (note).

A The majority of these nouns form their plurals like other nouns:

il francobollo → i francobolli (*stamps*)

il passaporto → i passaporti (*passports*)

B Where the compound noun is formed by one of the following constructions, both components change into the plural:

noun + adjective	il fabbroferraio (*blacksmith*) → i fabbriferrai	
noun + past participle	la terracotta (*earthenware*) → le terrecotte	

However, in the case of the following constructions, both components stay unchanged:

verb + verb	il saliscendi (*going up and down/latch*) → i saliscendi
adverb + verb	il benestare (*approval*) → i benestare
verb + adverb	il posapiano (*slowcoach*) → i posapiano
verb + noun	il cavalcavia (*flyover*) → i cavalcavia

C No rules apply in the case of compound nouns formed with the word **capo**. When in doubt consult the dictionary:

il caposquadra → i capisquadra	(*foremen/military squads/leaders)/ sports captains*)
il capoverso → i capoversi	(*paragraphs/indentations*)
il capotecnico → i capitecnici	(*chief technicians*)
il capostazione → i capistazione	(*station-masters*)
il capogiro → i capogiri	(*dizzy spells*)
il capofila → i capifila	(*leaders) of a file or line*)
il capolavoro → i capolavori	(*masterpieces*)
il capogruppo → i capigruppo	(*group leaders*)

17 UNIT | Compound nouns – Exercises

1 Crossword

ACROSS
1 door latches
2 earthenware
3 stamps
4 flyover

DOWN
1 blacksmiths
2 banknotes
3 passports
4 approvals

2 Complete the words to give the meanings as shown.

a capo _____ (*masterpieces*)
b capo _____ (*paragraphs*)
c capo _____ (*dizzy spells*)
d capi _____ (*group leaders*)
e capi _____ (*foremen*)
f capi _____ (*chief technicians*)
g capi _____ (*station masters*)
h capi _____ (*leaders of a file (of people)*)

18 UNIT | Descriptive adjectives

These are words that add a quality or a specification to a noun.

A Descriptive adjectives usually agree in gender and number with the noun they qualify, and they usually follow it.

	singular		plural	
Masculine	-o	un uomo onesto *an honest man*	-i	due uomini onesti *two honest men*
Feminine	-a	una ragazza onesta *an honest girl*	-e	due ragazze oneste *two honest girls*
Masculine and Feminine	-e	un vestito semplice *a simple dress* una casa grande *a large house*	-i	due vestiti semplici *two simple dresses* due case grandi *two large houses*

B Adjectives ending in **-e** maintain the **-e** for both the masculine and feminine singular, changing to an **-i** in the plural:

Paul è inglese. Anna è danese.   Mario e Andrea sono intelligenti.
Mario è intelligente. Maria è intelligente.   Giulia e Pina sono intelligenti.

C Where there are two or more nouns of different genders, adjectives take the masculine ending since this has a more 'neutral' value than the feminine form.

Mario e Giulia sono italiani.   *Mario and Giulia are Italian.*

D Some adjectives can be placed either before or after the noun but this can slightly or significantly alter their meaning. Both **un libro vecchio** and **un vecchio libro** mean *an old book* but in the former case the emphasis is on *old*.

un vecchio amico (*an old friend*), un amico vecchio (*a friend who is old*);
un uomo povero (*a man who is poor*), un pover'uomo (*a poor old soul*);
un grand'uomo (*a great man*), un uomo grande (*a large man*)

E Colours follow the noun:

una macchina verde   *a green car*

F When two adjectives describe a noun, one is usually put before and one after.

Indossa un elegante abito blu.   *She is wearing an elegant blue dress.*

G Adjectives of nationality are spelt with a small initial letter.

cinese   *Chinese*

1 Pair the following nouns and their related adjectives and then write down their English equivalents.

E.g. commercio → commerciale *(commerce/commercial)*

a l'economia	**n** l'onestà	**1** artistico	**14** acquatico
b l'industria	**o** la riservatezza	**2** studioso	**15** climatico
c Milano	**p** lo sport	**3** bovino	**16** generoso
d l'America	**q** il peso	**4** industriale	**17** operoso
e gli Stati Uniti	**r** il gusto	**5** spazioso	**18** paziente
f l'Italia	**s** l'aroma	**6** statunitense	**19** onesto
g l'Inghilterra	**t** la pazienza	**7** italiano	**20** sportivo
h lo studio	**u** il clima	**8** presidenziale	**21** aromatico
i la bellezza	**v** la generosità	**9** bello	**22** gustoso
j l'intelligenza	**w** l'opera	**10** inglese	**23** pesante
k l'anno	**x** l'acqua	**11** annuale	**24** riservato
l lo spazio	**y** il bue	**12** americano	**25** economico
m il presidente	**z** l'artista	**13** intelligente	**26** milanese

2 Add the endings to the adjectives so that they agree in number and gender with the noun.

a Alberto è pazient_____ .

b Elena è pover_____ .

c Clelia è una vecchi _____amica.

d Tullio ha un'auto sportiv _____ .

e Bill e Jill sono ingles_____ .

f Francesco è generos_____ .

g Il caffè italian_____ è aromatic_____ .

h Le valige (*suitcases*) sono pesant_____ .

3 Translate the following into Italian.

a the Italian economy

b the English economy

c Paul is (è) rich (**ricco**).

d the annual fee (**retta**)

e the president of the United States

f The room (**stanza**) is spacious.

g Milano is an industrial city.

h an artistic monument (**monumento**)

i an intelligent man

j Filippo is (è) beautiful.

k Clara is (è) beautiful.

l Gino and (**e**) Clara are (**sono**) good.

m Ennio is an old friend.

n an old dress

19 UNIT Demonstrative adjectives and pronouns

The most common demonstrative adjectives are questo (this) and quello (that). They need to agree in number and gender with the noun they qualify.

	Singular		Plural	
	Masculine	Feminine	Masculine	Feminine
this/these	**questo** tavolo	**questa** sedia	**questi** tavoli	**queste** sedie
that/those	**quel** libro **quello** zio	**quella** casa **quella** zia	**quei** libri **quegli** zii	**quelle** case **quelle** zie

A **Questo** has the normal feminine and plural forms. The forms of **quello** 'imitate' those of the definite articles.

> quel libro (*that book*); quello zio (*that uncle*); quella zia (*that aunt*)
> quei libri (*those books*); quegli zii (*those uncles*); quelle zie (*those aunts*).

⚠ Questo and **quello** are shortened before a vowel.

> quest'anno (*this year*); quest'aula (*this classroom*); quell'anno (*that year*);
> quell'enciclopedia (*that encyclopedia*).

The plural forms are not shortened except for **quegli** before i-:

> quegl'italiani *those Italians*

B In the spoken language **questo** (**-a**, **-i**, **-e**) can be shortened to **'sto** (**'sta**, etc.) This gave rise to words like **stamattina** (*this morning*), **stasera** (*this evening*) and **stanotte** (*tonight*).

C **Questo** and **quello** can also be pronouns (when they stand instead of a noun: *this/that one*, *these/those ones*). When used as a pronoun **quello** (and similarly **questo**) takes its usual forms: **quello, quella, quelli** and **quelle**.

> Vuole questo o quello?   *Do you want this or that?*
> Preferisco quelle.   *I prefer those* (f.pl.) *ones.*

1 Complete the sentences below by adding *questo, quest', questa, questi* or *queste*.

   a _____ valigia pesa venti chili.   (*This suitcase weighs 20 kilos.*)

   b _____ scarpe sono troppo strette. (*These shoes are too tight.*)

   c _____ ombrello è mio.   (*This umbrella is mine.*)

   d _____ libri sono pesanti.   (*These books are heavy.*)

   e _____ casa è un po' piccola.   (*This house is a little small.*)

   f _____ esercizi sono facili.   (*These exercises are easy.*)

2 Complete the sentences with *quel, quello, quell', quella, quei, quegli* or *quelle*.

   a _____ valigia pesa venti chili.

   b _____ scarpe sono troppo strette.

   c _____ ombrello è mio.

   d _____ libri sono pesanti.

   e _____ esercizi sono facili.

3 Insert the correct form of *questo* or *quello*.

   a Ti piacciono _____ ?   (*Do you like these shoes?*)

   b Chi vive in _____ ?   (*Who lives in that house?*)

   c Guarda _____ uccelli!   (*Look at those birds!*)

   d _____ cartolina e _____ francobollo   (*this card and this stamp*)

   e Mi scusi, è libero _____ ?   (*Excuse me, is that table free?*)

4 Say the following aloud in Italian.

   a I want (**Voglio**) this one (*m.*).

   b I take (**Prendo**) these (*m.*).

   c I don't want (**Non voglio**) that one (*m.*).

   d I am not taking (**Non prendo**) those (*f.*).

20 UNIT | Indefinite adjectives

Indefinite adjectives are those expressing a vague idea of quantity or quality, e.g. each, some.

A The most common indefinite adjectives are: **ogni** (*each/every*) and **qualche** (*some/any/a few*). **Qualche** must be followed by a singular noun.

ogni volta (*every time*); ogni giorno (*each day*)

Ho qualche libro per te.	*I have some books for you.*
Hai qualche libro per me?	*Have you any books for me?*
Parto tra qualche ora.	*I am leaving in a few hours.*

B *Some* and *a few* are also translated by **alcuni/alcune** followed by a plural masculine or feminine noun, or **di** with the definite article.

Ho alcuni libri per te.	*I have some books for you.*
alcune persone	*some people*
Vorrei delle mele.	*I'd like some apples.*
Ha dei libri sull'ambiente?	*Have you any books on the environment?*

⚠ The form with **di** is particularly used with unmeasured quantities which are usually referred to in the singular.

Vorrei della stoffa blu.   *I'd like some blue material.*

It is not usually used in the negative.

Non ho soldi/amici/tempo.   *I have no (not any) money/friends/time.*

C Note the following expressions:

- **qualunque/qualsiasi** (*whatever/whichever/any* in affirmative sentences).
  a qualsiasi costo   at any cost
  Qualsiasi cosa faccia viene criticato. *Whatever he does he is criticised.*
- **ciascuno** (*each/every*)
  Ciascuna cartolina costa trecento lire. *Each card costs 300 lire.*
- **nessuno** (*no/not...any* in negative sentences)
  Non ho nessuna intenzione di andare. *I have no intention of going.*

⚠ **Ciascuno** and **nessuno** have a masculine and feminine form. Their ending imitates that of the indefinite articles: ciascun/nessun libro ciascuno/nessuno studente ciascun'/nessun'aula (*classroom*)

D **Molto** and **tanto** (*much*), **poco** (*little*), **troppo** (*too much*), **tutto** (*all*), **altro** (*other/another*) always agree in number and gender with the noun they qualify.

Mangia troppi dolciumi.	*She eats too many cakes.*
Tutti i miei amici erano presenti.	*All my friends were present.*
Ho comprato un'altra penna.	*I bought another pen.*

1 How often do you do these things? Choose the right expression from the box to complete each sentence.

E.g. **Devo pagare la spesa ogni giorno.**

---

ogni giorno (*day*)   ogni settimana (*week*)   ogni mese (*month*)
ogni tre mesi (*three months*)   ogni anno (*year*)

Devo pagare (*I must pay*) ...
a ... il lattaio (*the milkman*) _____ .
b ... la bolletta del telefono (*phone bill*) _____ .
c ... la tassa di circolazione (*road tax*) _____ .
d ... la segretaria (*the secretary*) _____ .

2 Replace *qualche* with *alcuni* or *alcune*. Then read both versions aloud.

E.g. qualche libro → alcuni libri

a Hai qualche rivista?   (*Have you some magazines?*)
b Ho atteso qualche ora.   (*I waited a few hours.*)
c Andrò tra qualche giorno.   (*I am going in a few days.*)
d Ha scritto qualche mese fa.   (*S/he wrote some months ago.*)
e Ho comprato qualche regalo.   (*I bought a few presents.*)

3 Translate the following into Italian.

a at any cost
b Whatever he may do he is always happy (**contento**).
c Each book costs 3000 (**tremila**) lire.
d Each sweet (**caramella**) is wrapped (**incartata**).
e I can't see (**Non vedo**) any books.
f The boy hasn't (**non ha**) any friends.
g The girl has (**ha**) many friends.
h Roberto has a lot of money.
i Lauretta eats (**mangia**) too many sweets.
j I have (**Ho**) little time (**tempo**).
k All the girls were absent (**assenti**).

21 UNIT Possessive adjectives and pronouns

MASCULINE		FEMININE		
SINGULAR	PLURAL	SINGULAR	PLURAL	
il mio	**i miei**	**la mia**	**le mie**	*my/mine*
il tuo	**i tuoi**	**la tua**	**le tue**	*your/yours* (**informal**)
il Suo	**i Suoi**	**la Sua**	**le Sue**	*your/yours* (**formal**)
il suo	**i suoi**	**la sua**	**le sue**	*his/her/hers*
il nostro	**i nostri**	**la nostra**	**le nostre**	*our/ours*
il vostro	**i vostri**	**la vostra**	**le vostre**	*your/yours* (**plural**)
il loro	**i loro**	**la loro**	**le loro**	*their/theirs*
il proprio	**i propri**	**la propria**	**le proprie**	*one's*

A Possessive adjectives and pronouns need to agree in gender and number with the noun they qualify rather than with the possessor.

    Maria fa il suo lavoro.   *Maria does her job.*

B The article is NOT used before possessive adjectives referring to relations **mia madre** (*my mother*); **mio padre** (*my father*); **mio fratello** (*my brother*); **mia sorella** (*my sister*) – except when the nouns referring to relations are:
- in the plural: le mie sorelle *my sisters*
- followed by an adjective: la mia sorella maggiore *my eldest sister*
- qualified by a suffix e.g. a diminutive: la mia sorellina *my little sister*
- **mamma** (*mum*), **papà** (*dad*) (in which case they may – though do not need to – be preceded by the article): (il) mio papà, (la) mia mamma.

⚠ • The article is always used before **loro**:
    il loro figlio *their son*
- *mine*, *his*, etc. do not take the article unless some emphasis is required
    Questo libro è (il) mio. *This book is mine.*

C Possessive adjectives are used less in Italian than in English, particularly with personal belongings and when accompanied by reflexive verbs.

    Ho smarrito il passaporto.   *I have lost my passport.*
    Mi lavo le mani.   *I wash my hands.*

⚠ Note these constructions: il giornale di oggi *today's newspaper*
    Questo non è il mio ombrello,   *This is not my umbrella,*
    è quello di Maria.   *it is Maria's.*

➤ See definite articles in Units 7, 8 and 9, reflexive verbs in Unit 47, preposition di in Unit 74.

21 UNIT Possessive adjectives and pronouns – *Exercises*

1 What are these people saying? Fill in the bubbles.

E.g. Questo è il mio giornale. Remember that *questo* has to agree.

2 Supply a suitable article when needed.

a Questo è _____ mio ombrello.

b Quelli sono _____ nostri libri.

c Queste sono _____ sue cartoline.

d Questa è _____ loro penna (*pen*).

e Sono queste _____ tue scarpe (*shoes*)?

f _____ mio ufficio è in via Roma.

g _____ vostre scarpe sono pulite (*clean*)?

h _____ mia madre lavora a Londra.

3 Change the English adjectives or pronouns into their corresponding Italian forms.

a Quelli sono (*our*) libri.

b Questa è (*their*) casa.

c (*My*) ufficio è in via Garibaldi.

d Quei quadri sono (*his*), non (*mine*).

e (*my*) sorella maggiore

f (*her*) fratellino

g (*Your* (informal)) babbo è qui.

h (*Your* (formal)) quadri sono falsi.

4 Translate the following into Italian.

a her book

b their house

c our friends

d This is not today's newspaper, it is yesterday's.

e my sisters

f my little sister

g my eldest brother

22 UNIT | Interrogative adjectives

> Interrogative adjectives are used to ask the identity, the quality or the quantity of the noun they qualify.

Che ...?	What ...?/Which ...?
Quale(-i) ...?	Which ...?
Quanto(-a, -i, -e) ...?	How much ...?/How many ...?

A **Che ...?** is invariable.

Che libro è questo?	*What book is this?*
Che macchina hai?	*What car do you have?*

B **Quale ...?** is both masculine and feminine. Its plural is **quali**.

Quale libro hai scelto?	*Which book did you choose?*
Quali sport preferisci?	*Which sports do you prefer?*

⚠ Before a vowel **quale** drops its final **-e** without taking an apostrophe.

C **Quanto ...?** has masculine, feminine and plural forms.

Quanto tè devo comprare?	*How much tea shall I buy?*
Quanta marmellata hai fatto?	*How much jam did you make?*
Quanti voli ci sono al giorno?	*How many flights are there each day?*
Quante sterline hai?	*How many pounds do you have?*

D **Che** can also be used in exclamations.

Che peccato!	*What a pity!*
Che noia/Che seccatura!	*What a nuisance!*
Che bell'uomo!	*What a handsome man!*
Che vita!	*What a life!*
Che (bella) sorpresa!	*What a (nice) surprise!*
Che notte!	*What a night!*

 ➤ *See interrogative pronouns in Unit 93, questions in Units 94 and 95.*

1 **Ask questions choosing the appropriate adjective** *che, quale,*
quali, quanto, quanta, quanti, quante.

a _____ tipo di musica preferisci? *(What kind of music do you prefer?)*

b _____ figli ha? *(How many children do you have?)*

c _____ sorelle hai? *(How many sisters do you have?)*

d _____ tempo si ferma? *(How long are you staying?)*

e _____ materia preferisci? *(Which subject do you prefer?)*

f _____ materie studi? *(Which subjects do you study?)*

g _____ libro hai letto? *(Which book did you read?)*

h _____ stanza hai pitturato? *(Which room have you decorated?)*

i _____ libri hai scritto? *(How many books have you written?)*

j _____ torta vuole? *(How much cake do you want?)*

2 **Match these answers to the questions in exercise 1.**

1 Preferisco la musica rock.

2 Soltanto una.

3 Mi fermo due giorni.

4 Non molta.

5 Studio matematica e informatica.

6 La camera da letto.

7 Ho letto 'La tempesta'.

8 Ho scritto molti libri.

9 Ho tre figli.

10 Preferisco l'informatica.

3 **What would you say?**

23 UNIT Comparisons

*In English we make comparisons using phrases like **more than** and **as many as**, etc. The same general idea is used in Italian.*

più ... di (che)	*more/—er ... than*
meno ... di (che)	*less ... than*
(tanto) ... quanto ⎫	*as ... as*
(così) ... come ⎭	

A When the comparison is between two things or people (e.g. Anselmo and Giulio) referring to one quality (e.g. **simpatico**), **di** is used.

Anselmo è più simpatico di Giulio. *Anselmo is more pleasant than Giulio.*
Una bici è meno veloce di una moto. *A bike is slower than a motorbike.*

B When the comparison is between two qualities (e.g. **bello** and **simpatico**) referring to one thing or person (e.g. Anselmo), **che** is used.

Anselmo è più bello che   *Anselmo is more handsome than*
  simpatico.   *pleasant.*

C *As ... as ...* is translated by **tanto ... quanto** or **così ... come**. **Tanto** and **così** can be omitted.

Il mio giardino è (così) bello come il tuo. ⎫ *My garden is as beautiful*
Il mio giardino è (tanto) bello quanto il tuo.⎭   *as yours.*

D When a comparison concerns a noun, **tanto ... quanto**, must be used.

Ho tante penne quante te.   *I have as many pens as you.*

⚠ **(Così) ... come** is invariable, whereas both parts of **(tanto) ... quanto** need to agree in number and gender with the noun.

1 Using the words in the box, write sentences comparing Anselmo with Giulio. Then read the exercise aloud.

E.g. Anselmo è più svelto (*faster*) di Giulio.

> simpatico (*pleasant*); bello (*handsome*); intelligente (*intelligent*);
> studioso (*studious*); ostinato (*obstinate*); mascalzone (*wicked*);
> stupido (*stupid*); puntuale (*punctual*); attivo (*active*); orgoglioso (*proud*);
> convincente (*convincing*); prudente (*prudent*); noioso (*boring*)

2 Re-write the same sentences as above using *meno ... di*.

E.g. Giulio è meno svelto di Anselmo.

3 Now choose one of the two men and compare his qualities (or problems) with the help of the pairs of adjectives.

E.g. Giulio è più ostinato che convincente.

a puntuale/attivo **d** studioso/intelligente
b simpatico/bello **e** prudente/noioso
c mascalzone/stupido **f** ostinato/convincente

4 Carla and Cristina are identical twins. Use the adjectives in the box in exercise 1 to say how identical they are. Remember the adjective has to agree with the gender.

E.g. Carla è (tanto) simpatica quanto Cristina. Carla è (così) bella come Cristina.

5 Using *tanto ... quanto* compare Cristina to Carla using the nouns below. Remember the agreements.

E.g. Cristina ha tante penne quante Carla.

a libri (*books*) **d** borse (*handbags*)
b vestiti (*socks*) **e** cassette (*cassettes*)
c paia di scarpe (*pairs of shoes*) **f** dischi (*records*)

6 Match these expressions with their English translation.

a il più possibile **1** as much as possible
b il meno possibile **2** less and less
c il più presto possibile **3** more and more
d sempre più **4** as little as possible
e sempre meno **5** more or less
f più o meno **6** as soon as possible

24 UNIT Superlatives

| il più ... | the most ... /the —est |
| il meno ... | the least ... |

A The relative superlative is obtained by placing **il**, **lo**, **la** or **i** before **più** or **meno** + adjective.

Concetta è la più studiosa (di tutte). *Concetta is the most studious (of all).*

Questo libro è il più interessante *This book is the most interesting*
(di tutti). *(of all)*

L'onestà è la virtù più apprezzata. *Honesty is the most appreciated virtue.*

⚠ When the relative superlative is preceded by a noun, the article goes before that noun and is not repeated immediately before **più** or **meno**.

B The absolute superlative expresses *the most* or *the least* with no comparison. It is formed by dropping the final vowel of the adjective and adding **-issimo**, **-a, -i, -e.**

bello → bellissimo *most/very beautiful*

caro → carissimo *most/very expensive*

Some adjectives do not take **-issimo**.
- those already expressing an idea of superlative such as *colossal, enormous*
- those having an absolutely precise, specific meaning such as *rectangular, annual*, etc.

C A few adjectives ending in **-re** form the superlative by adding **-errimo**.

celebre → celeberrimo *most celebrated*

salubre → saluberrimo *most healthy*

D The following comparatives and superlatives are irregular.

adjective	comparative	relative superlative	absolute superlative
buono *(good)*	**migliore** *(better)*	**il migliore** *(the best)*	**ottimo** *(very good/excellent)*
cattivo *(bad)*	**peggiore** *(worse)*	**il peggiore** *(the worst)*	**pessimo** *(very bad/terrible)*

1 **Add** *il, la, i, le più/meno* **to the sentences below as indicated.**

a Oreste è _____ musicista _____ bravo (*most*).

b Angelo è _____ bello dei miei amici (*most*).

c Ho comprato _____ scarpe _____ costose (*least*).

d Annalisa è _____ simpatica di tutte (*most*).

e Vincenzo è _____ ragazzo _____ onesto che conosco (*most*).

f Benedetta ha _____ macchina _____ veloce di tutte (*least*).

2 **Turn the adjective in each sentence into an absolute superlative. Remember the agreements.**

E.g. **Questo vestito è caro. → Questo vestito è carissimo.**

a Questo vestito è bello.

b Questa musica è piacevole.

c Paolo è orgoglioso.

d Quel quadro ha colori intensi.

e Il libro che leggo è interessante.

f Quell'auto è veloce.

g Mia sorella è intelligente.

h Mio fratello è studioso.

i Il film era noioso.

j Teresa è ostinata.

3 **Sort out the adjectives which take** *-issimo/-errimo* **from those that do not.**

a immenso (*immense*)

b infinito (*infinite*)

c colorato (*coloured*)

d annuale (*annual*)

e celebre (*famous*)

f grande (*large*)

g africano (*African*)

4 **Complete the sentences below adding** *migliore/peggiore, il migliore/il peggiore, ottimo/pessimo.* **Remember all the agreements.**

E.g. **Queste lasagne sono buone ma quelle sono migliori; infatti sono le migliori. Sono ottime!** (Lasagna is used in its plural form in Italian.)

a Questo vino è buono ma quello è _____ ; infatti è _____ . È _____!

b Questi programmi sono cattivi ma quelli sono _____ ; infatti sono _____ . Sono _____!

c Questi studenti sono bravi (*good*) ma quelli sono _____ ; infatti sono _____ . Sono _____!

25 UNIT | Numerals: cardinal numbers

1	uno	16	sedici	100	cento
2	due	17	diciassette	101	centouno
3	tre	18	diciotto	102	centodue
4	quattro	19	diciannove	103	centotré
5	cinque	20	venti	200	duecento
6	sei	21	ventuno	300	trecento
7	sette	22	ventidue	1.000	mille
8	otto	23	ventitré	2.000	duemila
9	nove	30	trenta	10.000	diecimila
10	dieci	40	quaranta	100.000	centomila
11	undici	50	cinquanta	1.000.000	un milione
12	dodici	60	sessanta	10.000.000	dieci milioni
13	tredici	70	settanta	100.000.000	cento milioni
14	quattordici	80	ottanta	1.000.000.000	un miliardo
15	quindici	90	novanta	1.000.000.000.000	un bilione

A Numbers are invariable except for **zero** (*zero*, *nought* and 0 for telephone numbers), which has a plural form (**zeri**), **uno** which follows the same rule as the indefinite article (**un, uno, una, un'**), **mille**, the plural of which is **mila**, and the nouns **milione, miliardo** and **bilione**.

B **Venti, trenta**, etc. drop the final vowel when followed by **uno** or **otto**.
  trentuno, trentotto, quarantuno, quarantotto, novantuno, novantotto.

Ventuno, trentuno, etc. drop their final **-o** before a noun.
  quarantun anni

Tre combined with **venti, trenta, quaranta**, etc. acquires an acute accent on the **-e**: quattrocentoventitré

C Numbers are normally written as one word (**millenovecentonovantanove**). **Milione, miliardo** and **bilione** are written separately: un milione (*one million*)

Thousands are separated by a dot rather than a comma as in English and Italian use a comma for the decimal point: £375,726 = 375.726 sterline
  1.52 *one point five two* = 1,52 uno virgola cinquantadue

In the spoken language, particularly when shopping, there is a tendency to shorten the figures: 3.800 = tremilaotto(cento)

1 Write the numbers below out in full, then read them aloud at least twice.

5 6 7 11 12 13 14 15 16 17 19 20 21 23 27 28 30 36 37 38
100 106 107 121 128 130 133 140 167 176 279 1.576 1.769
2.006 10.876 16.596 17.950 26.700 137.766 678.999 1.500.000
10.758.756
5,8 1,6 3,7 15,9 28,6 74,5 115,9 3.456,98 10.300,53

2 What are the actual prices asked by the greengrocer?

a I pomodori costano tremilaotto al chilo.
b Queste mele costano duemilacinque.
c In tutto spende seimilatré.
d Queste banane costano millesei.
e Le pere costano tremiladue.
f Le fragole costano quattromilasei al cestino (*punnet*).

3 Add the missing vowels to the numbers below.

a vent___
b trent___
c quarant___
d cinquant___
e cinquant___no
f sessant___tto
g cent___tremil___cinquecent___vent___nov___
h mill___nov___cent___novan___nov___
i du___mil___
j mill___nov___cent___sessant___
k duemil___cinquecent___cinquant___cinqu___

26 UNIT Numerals: ordinal numbers

Ordinal numbers (1st, 2nd, 3rd, etc.) indicate a position in an order or a series. They agree in gender and number with the noun.

1st primo	5th quinto	9th nono	100th	centesimo
2nd secondo	6th sesto	10th decimo	1,000th	millesimo
3rd terzo	7th settimo	11th undicesimo	2,000th	duemillesimo
4th quarto	8th ottavo	12th dodicesimo	10,000th	diecimillesimo

A Ordinal numbers from 11th onwards are formed from the cardinal number minus the final vowel + **-esimo**, except for 23rd, 33rd, 43rd, etc. which keeps the vowel:

ventitreesimo, trentatreesimo, quarantatreesimo, cinquantatreesimo

Duemila, **tremil**a, etc. become **duemillesimo**, **tremillesimo**, etc.

B Ordinal numbers agree in gender and number with the noun they precede.

le prime parole (*the first words*); il decimo capitolo (*the 10th chapter*); la quinta sinfonia di Beethoven (*Beethoven's fifth symphony*).

C Ordinal numbers can be written in Roman (II, XI) or as cardinal numbers followed by ° for the masculine and ª for the feminine:

2° = 2nd (m), 10ª = 10th (f)

With monarchs and popes they are usually written in Roman characters and follow the noun but, unlike English, the article is not said:

Enrico VIII (Enrico Ottavo) = *Henry VIII*

⚠ la seconda guerra mondiale (*World War Two*)

D Some Italian streets are named after historical dates using Roman but read as cardinal numbers, e.g. Via XX Settembre (Via Venti Settembre). Below is a list of Roman numerals with their Arabic equivalents.

1 I	11 XI	21 XXI	40 XL	500 D
2 II	12 XII	22 XXII	50 L	600 DC
3 III	13 XIII	23 XXIII	60 LX	700 DCC
4 IV	14 XIV	24 XXIV	70 LXX	800 DCCC
5 V	15 XV	25 XXV	80 LXXX	900 CM
6 VI	16 XVI	26 XXVI	90 XC	1000 M
7 VII	17 XVII	27 XXVII	100 C	2000 MM
8 VIII	18 XVIII	28 XXVIII	200 CC	
9 IX	19 XIX	29 XXIX	300 CCC	
10 X	20 XX	30 XXX	400 CD	

1 **Read aloud in Italian the following ordinal numbers.**

1st 3rd 5th 6th 9th 11th 14th 15th 16th 17th 23rd 154th 33rd 70th
100th 155th 1,000th 1,500th 2,000th 3,000th

2 **Now read aloud the titles of the following popes and monarchs.**

a Papa Paolo VI
b Pio IX
c Leone X
d Giovanni XXIII
e Giovanni Paolo II

f Re Vittorio Emanuele III
g Gustavo XVI
h Giorgio VI
i Enrico IV
j Regina Elisabetta II

3 **Translate the following. Remember the agreements.**

a the 11th chapter (**capitolo**)
b the ninth symphony by Beethoven
c the third man (**uomo**)
d the 17th century
e the second street on the right
(**a destra**)
f the fourth daughter (**figlia**)

g the second son (**figlio**)
h the third leg (**tappa**)
i first gear (**marcia**)
j Fifth Avenue (**strada**)
k the third street on the left
(**a sinistra**)
l the tenth Commandment
(**Comandamento**)

4 **Below are the names of some Italian streets. Sort out those celebrating historical dates and write them down using cardinal numbers, then read the complete list aloud.**

E.g. Via XX Settembre → Via 20 Settembre.

a Via XII Ottobre
b Via Gregorio VII
c Via Napoleone III
d Via Benedetto XIV
e Via Umberto I
f Via XXV Aprile
g Via XXIV Maggio
h Via XXII Marzo

➤ See dates in Unit 29.

27 UNIT | Centuries

A Ordinal numbers are used to name centuries (**secoli**) and are often written in Roman numerals, in which case they usually follow the noun.

il secolo XX/il 20° secolo

B From the 13th century to the 20th century there are alternative expressions equivalent to saying *the twelve hundreds*, etc. in English; centuries are represented by cardinal numbers used as nouns; mille is omitted; and when written in letters the intial letter is capital.

(year 1201–1300)	il Duecento	il secolo XIII	(13°)
(year 1301–1400)	il Trecento	il secolo XIV	(14°)
(year 1401–1500)	il Quattrocento	il secolo XV	(15°)
(year 1501–1600)	il Cinquecento	il secolo XVI	(16°)
(year 1601–1700)	il Seicento	il secolo XVII	(17°)
(year 1701–1800)	il Settecento	il secolo XVIII	(18°)
(year 1801–1900)	l'Ottocento	il secolo XIX	(19°)
(year 1901–2000)	il Novecento	il secolo XX	(20°)

⚠ In English we refer to years as being BC (before Christ) and AD (Anno Domini). In Italian, BC becomes **a.C.** (**avanti Cristo**) and AD becomes **d.C.** (**dopo Cristo**).

Dal X al III secolo a.C. i popoli italici parlavano etrusco.	*From the tenth to the third century BC the Italic peoples spoke Etruscan.*
Giacomo Leopardi è un grande poeta dell'Ottocento.	*Giacomo Leopardi is a great poet of the 1800s.*

⚠ In popular use centuries are calculated, for example, from 1 January 1800 to 31 December 1899.

C *Millennium* is translated by **millennio**.

Il primo millennio è terminato il 31 dicembre 999, il secondo va dal 1° gennaio 1000 al 31 dicembre 1999.	*The first millennium ended on the 31st December 999, the second goes from the 1st January 1000 to the 31st December 1999.*

⚠ In Italian the year 1999 is written **millenovecentonovantanove**.

⚠ In popular use the millennium is calculated, for example, from 1 January 2000 to 31 December 2999.

1 Re-write the dates in the right-hand columns in the form suggested by the headings.

	avanti Cristo	dopo Cristo	secolo (letters)	secolo (Roman)
100 a.C.	**100**			
30 a.C.				
90 d.C.				
1350				
1499				
1875				
1492				
1768				
1650				
1899			l'Ottocento	XIX
1999				
2000				

2 Translate the following into Italian.

a The third millennium goes from the 1st January 2000 to the 31st December 2999.

b Dante is the great poet of the 1200s.

c The present (**attuale**) century is called (**si chiama**) the 20th century.

3 True or false?

a Leonardo da Vinci nacque (*was born*) nel 1452: nel Quattrocento.

b Cristoforo Colombo scoprì (*discovered*) l'America nel 1492: nel XV secolo.

c Guglielmo Marconi inventò (*invented*) la radio nel 1901: nel Novecento.

d Galileo Galilei nacque (*was born*) nel 1564: nel 16° secolo.

e L'Italia fu unita (*was united*) nel 1862: nell'800 d.C.

f Nel 79 d.C. l'eruzione del Vesuvio distrusse (*destroyed*) Pompei: nel I° secolo.

g Nel 1778 Alessandro Volta inventò la batteria elettrica: nell'Ottocento.

28 UNIT Fractions, signs, numbers

A ½ (un mezzo)   ⅗ (tre quinti)   ⅞ (sette ottavi)   ⁹⁄₁₀ (nove decimi)

Mezzo (*half*) agrees with the nouns it refers to: mezzo chilo di pane (*half a kilo of bread*); mezza bottiglia di vino (*half a bottle of wine*)

Mathematical signs

B
+ più	:/÷ diviso
− meno	= uguale a/fa/fanno
× per/moltiplicato	% percento

C Multiple numbers: doppio (*double*); triplo (*treble*); quadruplo (*quadruple*)

D Iterative numbers: una volta (*once*); due volte (*twice*); tre volte (*three times*)

E Collective numbers: **un paio** (*a pair*) generally refers to things: **una coppia** (*a couple*) generally refers to people or animals.

un paio di panini (*a couple of rolls*); una coppia di sposi (*a married couple*); una coppia di cavalli (*a pair of horses*)

Note also the following:

una/mezza dozzina (*a/half a dozen*); una decina (*about ten*); una ventina (*about twenty*); un migliaio (*about a thousand*); un centinaio (*about a hundred*)

una dozzina di uova	*a dozen eggs*
C'era una ventina di persone.	*There were about twenty people.*

F Other expressions to indicate how people or things are divided:

- **ad uno ad uno** (*one by one*), **a due a due/due per due** (*two by two*) etc.
- **uno/due/tre alla volta** (*one/two/three at a time*) etc.
- **ambedue** (invariable), **tutti e due** (with a feminine form) and **entrambi** (with a feminine form), mean *both*.

Entrambe le ragazze sono cinesi.	*Both girls are chinese.*
Ambedue i coniugi sono italiani.	*Both spouses are Italian.*

G Nouns indicating a period of time: biennio (*two years*); triennio (*three years*); quadriennio (*four years*); decennio (*ten years*); ventennio (*twenty years*); bimestre (*two months*); trimestre (*three months*); quadrimestre (*four months*); semestre (*six months*)

Other words and expressions: **gemelli** (*twins*); **bambino trigemino** (*triplet*); **la triplice Alleanza** (*the Triple Alliance*)

28 UNIT | Fractions, signs, numbers – *Exercises*

1 Write these fractions in full and then read them aloud.

a ½

b ⅔

c ¾

d ⅝

e ⅞

f ⅘

g ⁵⁄₁₆

h ¹⁹⁄₃₂

i ⅚

j ⁹⁄₁₀

2 Write *mezzo, mezza* or *mezz'* as appropriate in the spaces.

a _____ litro di latte

b _____ pinta di birra

c _____ bottiglia d'acqua

d _____ mela

e _____ chilo di spaghetti

f _____ chilometro

g _____ ora

h _____ biglietto (*ticket*)

i _____ dozzina di uova

j _____ bicchiere (*m.*)

3 Read aloud the following sums.

E.g. 5 + 5 = 10 → Cinque più cinque fa dieci.
5 – 5 = 0 → Cinque meno cinque fa zero.
5 × 5 = 25 → Cinque per cinque fa venticinque.
5 : 5 = 1 → Cinque diviso cinque fa uno.

a 5 + 12 = 17

b 10 – 6 = 4

c 10 × 10 = 100

d 12 : 2 = 6

e 1.234.567 – 67 = 1.234.500

f 16 + 16 = 32

g 21 – 7 = 14

h 30 × 30 = 900

i 35 : 5 = 7

j 236 + 10 = 246

k 45 – 30 = 15

l 125 × 75 = 9.375

m 136 : 5 = 27,2

n 451 : 8 = 56,37

o 3.826 + 100 = 3.926

p 5.555 – 55 = 5.500

q 332 × 32 = 10.624

r 222:22 = 10,09

s 123 × 231 = 39.483

4 Translate the following into Italian.

a a married couple

b a double whisky

c a couple of bottles

d a couple of shirts

e about ten people

f three at a time

g about twenty kilos

h about a thousand kilometres

i one by one

j Both of them (m.) are English.

k the first semester

l They are (**sono**) twins.

A The days of the week are written with a small initial letter. Note that they are all masculine except for **domenica**, and *on* is not translated except when it means *every*.

I GIORNI DELLA SETTIMANA *(the days of the week)*			
lunedì	*Monday*	venerdì	*Friday*
martedì	*Tuesday*	sabato	*Saturday*
mercoledì	*Wednesday*	domenica	*Sunday*
giovedì	*Thursday*		

Che giorno è oggi? Oggi è lunedì.	*What day (of the week) is it today?* *Today is Monday.*
Ci vediamo martedì.	*See you on Tuesday.*
Ci vediamo martedì prossimo.	*See you next Tuesday.*
Il martedì vado all'università.	*On Tuesdays I go to the university.*
martedì mattina/pomeriggio/sera/ notte/scorso/prossimo	*Tuesday morning/afternoon/evening/ night/last/next*

B Months are also written with a small initial letter.

gennaio	*January*	maggio	*May*	settembre	*September*
febbraio	*February*	giugno	*June*	ottobre	*October*
marzo	*March*	luglio	*July*	novembre	*November*
aprile	*April*	agosto	*August*	dicembre	*December*

Quanti ne abbiamo oggi?	*What day is it today?*
Ne abbiamo tre.	*It's the third.*
Che data è oggi?	*What's the date today?*
È il due luglio.	*It's the second of July.*

C The days of the month are written (and spoken) in cardinal numbers except for the first: il primo maggio, il due, il tre etc. *the first of May, the 2nd, the 3rd etc.*

D Seasons: la primavera (*spring*); l'estate (f.) (*summer*); l'autunno (*autumn*); l'inverno (*winter*)

In can be translated by either **in** or **di**. **Primavera** can also take **a**.

in/di/a primavera *in spring*   in/d'estate *in summer*
in/d'autunno *in autumn*   in/d'inverno *in winter*

1 Translate the following into Italian.

a See you on Monday.

b I will see you next week.

c Every Tuesday I go to the cinema.

d On Wednesdays I go to my Italian lesson.

e I go to the disco on Sundays.

f On Monday afternoons I go to the gym.

g On Saturday mornings I go riding (**vado a cavalcare**).

h On Friday evenings I go to the theatre.

i What day (of the week) is it? It's Thursday.

j What is the date today? It's the first of June.

k What's the date? It's the fifth of July.

2 Say a) today's date, b) the day you were born, c) your favourite month d) your favourite season, e) the season you usually go on holiday.

a Oggi è _____

b Sono nato(-a) il _____

c Il mese che preferisco è _____

d La stagione che preferisco è _____

e Di solito vado in vacanza _____

3 Write these dates in full.

a Il 1.5 è la festa dei lavoratori.

b Il 25.12 è Natale.

c Il 26.12 è Santo Stefano.

d Il 22.11.1963 Kennedy è assassinato a Dallas.

e Il 20.7.1969 la navicella spaziale americana sbarca sulla luna.

f Il 12.4.1961 Yuri Gagarin è il primo uomo lanciato nello spazio.

g Il 4.4.1968 Martin Luther King viene ucciso a Memphis.

h Il 12.10.1492 Colombo arriva in America.

i Il 1.4 è il Pesce d'Aprile.

The adjectives **quello**, **bello**, **grande**, **santo** and **buono** are shortened when used before a noun.

	singular	plural	
m.	quel, quello, quell'	quei, quegli	*that/those*
f.	quella, quell'	quelle	
m.	bel, bello, bell'	bei, begli	*beautiful/nice/*
f.	bella, bell'	belle	*handsome*
m.	gran, grande, grand'	grandi	*large/great*
f.	gran, grande, grand'	grandi	
m.	san, santo, sant'	santi	*saint*
f.	santa, sant'	sante	
m.	buon, buono	buoni	*good*
f.	buona, buon'	buone	

A **Quello** and **bello** imitate the definite article (**il**, **lo**, **la**, **l'**, **i**, **gli**, **le**):
  quel libro (*that book*), quei libri (*those books*)
  quello studente (*that student*), quegli studenti (*those students*)
  bell'uomo (*handsome man*), begli uomini (*handsome men*)
  bella casa (*beautiful house*), belle case (*beautiful houses*)

B **Grande** and **santo** usually become **gran** and **san** before masculine singular nouns starting with a consonant except for **z-** and **s-** followed by consonant.
  un grande santo (*a great saint*); un grand'uomo (*a great man*); un gran successo (*a great success*); una grande casa (*a large house*)

  San Gerolamo, Sant'Angelo, Santo Stefano, Sant'Agnese, Santa Teresa

  una grand'idea (*a great idea*); due grandi libri (*two great books*); due grandi case (*two large houses*)

C **Buono** imitates the indefinite article **un/uno/una/un'**.
  un buon libro (*a good book*); un buono studente (*a good student*); una buona commedia (*a good play*); una buon'idea (*a good idea*)

30 UNIT: Irregular adjectives – *Exercises*

1 Fill in the appropriate form of *quell', quel, quello, quella, quegli*, etc.

a _____ uomo è un genio.

b _____ ragazza viene da Lucca.

c _____ aereo ha 360 posti.

d _____ studenti sono veramente bravi.

e Non ho letto _____ libro.

f Mi piace _____ specchio.

g _____ riviste costano care.

h _____ film è eccellente.

2 Write your comment below the pictures using the correct form of *bello*.

> *E.g.* Che bella ragazza!

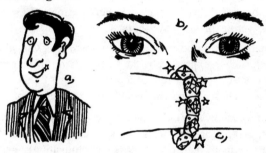

a Che _____ _____ !

b Che _____ occhi!

c Che _____ braccialetto!

3 Enter the right form of *grande*.

> *E.g.* Einstein era un _____ uomo. → Einstein era un grand'uomo.

a un _____ seccatore (*bore*)

b una _____ battaglia (*battle*)

c Le Alpi sono _____ montagne.

d una _____ esperienza

e due _____ errori

f È un _____ peccato (*great pity*).

4 Enter *San, Santo*, etc. correctly.

> *E.g.* _____ Luca è il patrono dei macellai. → San Luca è il patrono dei macellai (*butchers*).

a _____ Cristoforo è il patrono degli automobilisti.

b _____ Tommaso d'Aquino è il patrono dei filosofi.

c _____ Cecilia è la patrona dei musicisti e dei poeti.

d I _____ Cosimo e Damiano sono i patroni dei farmacisti.

e _____ Eligio è il patrono dei gioiellieri (*jewellers*).

f I _____ Francesco e Caterina sono i patroni d'Italia.

g _____ Giuseppe è il patrono dei falegnami (*carpenters*).

31 UNIT | Verbs

The verb is the most important (and most variable) part of speech.
It indicates the action or the state of a person, animal or thing.

A Verbs have different moods which convey the manner in which the action is carried out, since it is important to know whether the action is really happening, or if it depends on a condition, or if it is only probable.

B It is also necessary to know the tense. This indicates the time at which the speaker places the action expressed by the verb (present, past, future). The tense can be simple or compound, the latter being formed by an auxiliary verb (so called because it 'assists' the main verb – usually *to be* or *to have*) followed by the verb expressing the action.

C Equally important is the subject (*I, you*, etc.) which tells you who is doing or undergoing the action expressed by the verb. Italian subject pronouns are seldom used because – with a few exceptions – each of the verbs has a different ending, each one conveying which person it refers to.

D The infinitve of a verb, which in English is preceded by *to*, e.g. *to speak, to see, to leave,* is expressed in Italian by one of three types of ending. They are: **-are** (called verbs of the first type or first conjugation); **-ere** (verbs of the second type or second conjugation); **-ire** (verbs of the third type or third conjugation).

Parlare, vedere, partire are infinitives. The first part (**parl-, ved-, part-**) is known as the 'root' or 'stem'. The second part (**-are, -ere, -ire**) is the ending or suffix.

E To form the right tense and person of a verb involves changing the **-are, -ere** or **-ire** ending and applying another to the stem. For instance, **parl-** has an **-o** added to make **parlo** (*I speak*) or **-avo** added to make **parlavo** (*I was speaking*).

F Most Italian tenses follow a fixed pattern but several do not (like *to be* in English). These irregular verbs will have to be learned separately. They mostly belong to the second type (**-ere**). You will also come across some irregular infinitives ending in **-urre, -arre** and **-orre** like **produrre** (*to produce*), **tradurre** (*to translate*), **proporre** (*to propose*) and **estrarre** (*to extract*): these belong to the **-ere** type, since they come from the old forms **producere, traducere, proponere** and **estraere**.

➤ *See Unit 69 for more on verbs.*

1 **Separate the stem from the ending of these common infinitive verbs.**

E.g. mangiare → mangi/are

a dormire (*to sleep*)
b camminare (*to walk*)
c partire (*to depart*)
d parlare (*to speak*)
e guardare (*to look (at)*)
f vedere (*to see*)
g comprare (*to buy*)
h ascoltare (*to listen to*)
i volare (*to fly*)
j ridere (*to laugh*)
k prendere (*to take*)
l mettere (*to put*)
m vivere (*to live*)
n piangere (*to cry*)
o ballare (*to dance*)
p cantare (*to sing*)
q suonare (*to play*)
r respirare (*to breath*)
s prenotare (*to book*)
t crescere (*to grow*)

2 **Substitute the ending of the verbs in exercise 1 with -o to form the first person singular (io - I).**

E.g. mangiare → (io) mangio

3 **Sort the above verbs into three categories according to their type: first (-are), second (-ere) or third (-ire).**

32 UNIT | The present tense (1)

	PARLARE *to speak*	VEDERE *to see*	PARTIRE *to leave*
(io) *I*	parl-**o**	ved-**o**	part-**o**
(tu) *you (informal)*	parl-**i**	ved-**i**	part-**i**
(lui/lei/Lei)	parl-**a**	ved-**e**	part-**e**
he/she/it; you (formal)			
(noi) *we*	parl-**iamo**	ved-**iamo**	part-**iamo**
(voi) *you (pl. informal)*	parl-**ate**	ved-**ete**	part-**ite**
(loro/Loro) *they; you (pl. formal)*	parl-**ano**	ved-**ono**	part-**ono**

Parla italiano, signora?	*Do you speak Italian, madam?*
Parto.	*I am leaving.*
Vedono il film adesso.	*They are watching the film now.*
Partiamo domani.	*We leave tomorrow.*

⚠ Remember that the subject pronoun is rarely used.

A When using the formal *you*, the third person singular must be used.
Parla italiano, signore?   *Do you speak Italian, sir?*

B The plural form of the formal *you* uses the third person plural, although the second person plural can be safely used:
Parlano italiano, signori? ⎫
Parlate italiano?   ⎬ *Do you speak Italian, gentlemen?*

C Verbs ending in **-iare** do not need the addition of an **-i** in the second person singular and the first plural: tu mangi *you eat* noi mangiamo *we eat*

D Pronunciation. The stress always goes on the stem except for the first and second person plural
p<u>a</u>rlo, p<u>a</u>rli, p<u>a</u>rla, parli<u>a</u>mo, parl<u>a</u>te, p<u>a</u>rlano

E The present tense is also used to express:
- continuous action: Adesso mangio. *I am eating now.*

- the future
Domani parto. *I leave/I am leaving/I am going to leave tomorrow.*

- an action started in the past but still continuing
Abito in Inghilterra da 25 anni. *I have been living in England for 25 years.*

32 Unit

The present tense (1) – Exercises

1 Translate the following into Italian.

a You (*pl informal*) see?

b I do not speak German (**tedesco**).

c They always (**sempre**) speak of you (*formal*).

d She speaks all the time (**sempre**).

e Do you speak English (**inglese**)?

f I see him every day.

g Can you see my glasses (**occhiali**)?

h I have been living here for a year.

i Are you (*informal*) leaving today (**oggi**)?

j They are leaving tomorrow (**domani**).

2 Read the passage then say whether the statements that follow are true (*vero*) or false (*falso*).

studiare *(to study)*	camminare *(to walk)*	allenare *(to train)*
insegnare *(to teach)*	riposare *(to rest)*	dormire *(to sleep)*
informare *(to inform)*	leggere *(to read)*	mantenere *(to keep)*
raccontare *(to tell)*	scrivere *(to write)*	prendere *(to catch/take)*
ritornare *(to return)*	imparare *(to learn)*	ascoltare *(to listen to)*
rientrare *(to go back/home)*		capire *(to understand)*

Paul studia italiano a Firenze, in una classe di studenti stranieri. Il professore parla soltanto italiano e insegna non soltanto la lingua ma li informa anche sulla storia d'Italia e parla d'arte, di musica classica e moderna, di politica e di attualità (*current affairs*). Inoltre (*Also*), racconta molte storielle comiche. Paul abita in una famiglia italiana con altri due studenti stranieri. Dopo la lezione ritorna a casa per il pranzo. Alle tre esce (*he goes out*) a camminare per la città mentre gli altri due studenti studiano o riposano. Alle cinque rientra a casa, legge il giornale e scrive lettere ai suoi amici. La sera guarda la televisione e impara molto perché allena l'orecchio (*trains his listening skills*) soprattutto alla velocità con cui gli Italiani si esprimono (*express themselves*). Prima di andare a dormire (*to go to bed*) fa mezz'ora di jogging per mantenere la forma. La mattina presto studia poi mangia un sandwich e prende un caffè. Alle 8,30 prende l'autobus per l'Istituto Italiano e ascolta la cassetta di canzoni che gli ha dato (*given*) il professore. Capisce quasi tutto anche se (*even if*) impara l'italiano soltanto da un mese.

a Il professore non insegna la lingua.

b Paolo abita in una famiglia straniera.

c Ritorna a casa alle tre.

d Legge il giornale in autobus.

e Scrive lettere a sua madre.

f Gli italiani parlano velocemente.

g Prende il caffè alle 8,30.

h Ascolta la musica in autobus.

i Capisce perfettamente le canzoni.

j Studia l'italiano da 30 giorni.

33 UNIT The present tense (2)

> *There are some verbs that, although regular in their endings, have stems which behave differently.*

A Some verbs of the third type (those ending in **-ire**) have an **-isc** placed between the stem and the ending, except for the first and second persons plural.

FINIRE *to finish*	
fin-**isc-o**	I finish
fin-**isc-i**	you (sing. informal) finish
fin-**isc-e**	he/she/it finishes, you (sing. formal) finish
fin-**iamo**	we finish
fin-**ite**	you finish
fin-**isc-ono**	they/you (plural formal) finish

Among the commonest verbs belonging to this group are:

agire (*to act*); capire (*to understand*); condire (*to season*); costruire (*to build*); guarire (*to heal*); preferire (*to prefer*); proibire (*to forbid*); pulire (*to clean*); restituire (*to give back*); sparire (*to disappear*); spedire (*to send*); unire (*to unite, join*)

⚠ Pay attention when pronouncing these verbs since **-isc** followed by a consonant is pronounced **isk**, but if followed by **-i** or **-e** is pronounced **ish**.

B Some verbs like **cercare** (*to look for, to search*) and **pagare** (*to pay*), in order to preserve the hard sound of the **-c** or the **-g**, add an **-h** before the **-i** or the **-e** of the ending (for this see the future and the conditional):

cercare   cerco, cerchi, cerca, cerchiamo, cercate, cercano
pagare   pago, paghi, paga, paghiamo, pagate, pagano

C Other verbs, like **salire** (*to go up/to get on a bus*, etc.), **spegnere** (*to switch off*), **tenere** (*to keep/to hold*), **rimanere** (*to stay/to remain*) and **scegliere** (*to choose*), have their own irregularities.

salire   salgo, sali, sale, saliamo, salite, salgono
spegnere   spengo, spegni, spegne, spegniamo, spegnete, spengono
tenere   tengo, tieni, tiene, teniamo, tenete, tengono
rimanere   rimango, rimani, rimane, rimaniamo, rimanete, rimangono
scegliere   scelgo, scegli, sceglie, scegliamo, scegliete, scelgono

33 The present tense (2) – Exercises

1 Change the sentences below into the plural form.

E.g. Giorgio finisce di lavorare alle sei → Giorgio e Giovanni finiscono di lavorare alle sei.

a Io finisco di lavorare all'una. Noi …
b Luisa capisce il russo. Luisa e Giacomo …
c Tu preferisci rimanere a casa? Voi …
d Enrico agisce con prudenza. Enrico ed Antonio …
e Mario costruisce una casa. Mario e Giorgio …
f Carla pulisce la casa. Carla e Lia …
g Il gatto sparisce. Il gatto e il cane …
h Ti restituisco il libro domani. Noi …
i Il dottore guarisce il paziente. I dottori …
j Spedisci la lettera? Voi …

2 Write down the correct form of the verb.

E.g. (io) salire → salgo

a (lui) salire
b (noi) salire
c (loro) tenere
d (loro) spegnere
e (io) spegnere
f (tu) tenere
g (loro) tenere
h (noi) tenere
i (voi) scegliere
j (io) rimanere
k (loro) scegliere
l (tu) rimanere

3 Replace the infinitives with the correct form of the verb.

Renzo (a salire) in macchina (*car*) per andare all'università di Brighton dove (b studiare) scienze politiche e (c seguire *(to attend)*) anche un corso di lingua inglese. (d Vedere) un ufficio postale e (e fermare) la macchina per spedire una lettera alla sua ragazza in Italia. (f Spegnere) il motore e (g scendere). Nell'ufficio postale trova due signore italiane che non (h parlare) e non (i capire) l'inglese. Allora lui (j offrire) la sua assistenza poi le signore lo (k ringraziare *(to thank)*) gli (l chiedere) se sa (*if he knows*) dov'è l'Università perché (m avere) un appuntamento con una loro nipote che (n studiare) là. Renzo (o decidere) di accompagnarle; le due signore si (p unire) a lui e (q salire) in auto con lui.

34 UNIT | Subject pronouns

Personal pronouns, which include subject pronouns, are used instead of nouns. I, you, he, etc. are subject pronouns.

SINGULAR		PLURAL	
io	*I*	noi	*we*
tu	*you (sing. informal)*	voi	*you (pl. informal)*
lui (egli); esso	*he; it (m.)*	loro (essi/esse)	*they*
lei (ella); essa	*she; it (f.)*	Loro	*you (pl. formal)*
Lei	*you (sing. formal)*		

A When used, the subject pronoun normally precedes the verb but, unlike English, it is usually omitted.

Vado.   *I am going.*

Subject pronouns are used:

- for emphasis

Io vado.   **I** *am going.*

for an even greater emphasis, it can be placed after the verb.

Vado io!   **I** *am going (not you/you needn't).*

- with **Lei** (the formal you) as a form of courtesy when addressing a person

Lei è inglese?   *Are you English (sir/madam)?*

- when the action, opinion, etc. of one person stands against that of another

Io sono inglese, lui è francese.   *I am English, he is French.*

B **Tu** is used with close friends, children and members of one's family.

C **Egli**, **ella**, **essi** and **esse** are mainly confined to formal written language. **Lui**, **lei** and **loro** are used instead. **Esso** and **essa** can also be used for animals, though they are usually avoided since they sound old fashioned and affected.

D **Lei** (the formal *you*) is often written with a capital letter and used to address adults who are not close friends. It is followed by the third person singular form of the verb.

Lei è inglese, signora?   *Are you English, madam?*

You here is something like *your excellency.*

⚠ The subject pronoun can go at the end of a question. È inglese Lei?

The formal plural **Loro** is also written with the capital letter.

Loro sono tutti inglesi?   *Are you all English?* (lit.: *Are they all English?*)

The rule on its use is more flexible: **voi** can be used without giving offence:

Voi siete tutti inglesi?   *Are you all English?*

34 UNIT Subject pronouns – Exercises

1 **In which of these sentences would you not use the subject pronoun? Delete it when you think it is not needed.**

a Oggi io parto per Napoli. (*Today I leave for Naples.*)

b Lui va a ballare, io vado a teatro. (*He goes dancing, I go to the theatre.*)

c Io esco, ti serve qualcosa? (*I am going out, do you need something?*)

d Loro vanno in vacanza al mare. (*They go on holiday to the seaside.*)

e Io esco e tu? (*I am going out, and you?*)

f La domenica noi ceniamo alle otto. (*We dine at eight on Sundays.*)

g Noi ceniamo alle otto, loro cenano alle sette. (*We dine at eight, they dine at seven.*)

h Io sono inglese. (*I am English.*)

i Io sono inglese e Lei? (*I am English, and you?*)

j Mario ama la musica classica, io amo la musica pop. (*Mario loves classical music, I love pop music.*)

2 **How would you translate these sentences? Remember you need to use the present tense.**

E.g. **Are you going to buy the bananas?** → **Comprate voi le banane?**

a I am answering!

b Are you (*fam. sing.*) answering?

to answer	**rispondere**

c Is he going to answer?

d Are you (*fam. sing.*) going to buy the cards (**cartoline**)?

e Are you (*fam. pl.*) going to buy the cards?

f Yes, we will buy the cards.

3 **Change the following sentences into the plural form.**

E.g. **Lei è inglese, signora?** → **Loro sono inglesi, signore?**

a Lei parla francese, signora?

b Lei vede spesso (*often*) i suoi amici?

c Tu mangi molto?

d Io vedo Mario ogni giorno.

e Lei parte domani, signor Rossi?

35 UNIT | Direct object pronouns

As their name suggests me, him, her, etc. **do not stand for the subject but for the object, that is, for the 'receiver' of the action of the verb.**

SINGULAR		PLURAL	
mi	me	ci	us
ti	you (sing.)	vi	you (pl.)
lo	him; it (m.)	li	them (m.)
la	her; it (f.)	le	them (f.)
La	you (formal)		

A Unlike English, the direct object pronoun precedes the verb.
  Mi vedi? *Do you see me?* Lo vedo. *I see him.* La vedo. *I see her.*

B The singular formal form is **La**, the same as *her*, written with a capital 'L'.
  La trovo molto bene, signor Rossi. *I find you very well, Mr Rossi.*

The plural formal masculine and feminine forms are respectively **Li** and **Le**.
  Li trovo molto bene, signori. Le trovo molto bene, signore.

If the persons addressed are of mixed gender, the masculine form is used.

C Direct object pronouns are added to the end of infinitives, gerunds, past participles and some imperatives. Note the loss of the verb's final vowel.
  Posso presentarLe il signor Marini? *May I introduce you to Mr Marini?*
  Prendilo con te. *Take it with you.*
  Avendolo comprato … *Having bought it …*

D **Lo** and **la** take an apostrophe before a vowel or **h-**: L'amo. *I love it/him/her.*
  L'ho. *I have it.*

Mi, **ti**, **ci** and **vi** are treated similarly, although the full form is more common.
  M'aiuta nei lavori domestici. *He/She helps me with the housework.*

E Past participles must agree with **lo**, **la**, **li** and **le** when they follow **avere**.
  Ho preso il caffè. L'ho preso. *I had the coffee. I had it.*
  Ho preso l'aranciata. L'ho presa. *I had the orangeade. I had it.*
  Ho preso i biglietti. Li ho presi. *I got the tickets. I got them.*
  Ho preso le pillole. Le ho prese. *I took the pills. I took them.*

⚠ When the object is at the beginning of the sentence, **lo**, **la**, **li** and **le** follow it, giving the sentence two objects.
  Le chiavi le hai? *Have you got the keys?* (lit. *The keys do you have them?*)

➤ **See imperatives in Unit 58, gerunds in Unit 66, past participles in Unit 49.**

35 | Direct object pronouns – Exercises

1 Answer the questions or re-write the sentences using the direct object pronoun instead of the noun when needed. Remember to write the correct form of the verb.

E.g. Vedo Giovanni → Lo vedo.
      Prendi le pillole? → Le prendo.

a Vedi quella nave?
b Vedete i miei occhiali?
c La domenica vedo i miei amici.
d Ci vedete?
e Prendo l'autobus (m.).
f Prendi la medicina?
g Prendi i biglietti?
h T'aiuta Marco?
i Vediamo i film alla TV.
j I vostri figli vi aiutano? Sì, …

2 Enter the last vowel of the verb.

E.g. Hai preso il treno? L'ho pres_____ . → L'ho preso.

a Hai preso l'autobus?   L'ho pres_____ .
b Avete preso le mele?   Le abbiamo pres_____ .
c Hanno comprato l'automobile?   L'hanno comprat_____ .
d Gianni ha venduto la casa?   L'ha vendut_____ .
e Hai invitato gli amici?   Li ho invitat_____ .

3 Translate the following into Italian.

a I see her every day.
b I see him every day.
c They see us on Saturdays.
d Marco helps us.
e Federico helps her.
f We buy them (m.).
g We buy them (f.).
h We love them (m.).
i He studies it (f.).
j They know (**conoscono**) us.
k Do you understand (**capisce**) me, sir?
l I do not understand her.
m She doesn't understand (**capisce**) me.
n Do they help you (*plural*)?

36 Unit | Indirect object pronouns

The indirect object pronoun 'receives' the action carried out by the subject: She gave **him** a present. = She gave a present **to him**.

STRESSED		UNSTRESSED
a me	*to me*	mi
a te	*to you*	ti
a lui	*to him*	gli
a lei	*to her*	le
a Lei	*to you (formal)*	Le
a noi	*to us*	ci
a voi	*to you (pl.)*	vi
a loro	*to them*	loro/gli
a Loro	*to you (formal pl.)*	gli

A The stressed form gives emphasis to the pronoun which, as in English, goes at the end of the sentence.

Maria ha fatto un regalo a lui.   *Maria gave a present to him.*

B The more common unstressed form follows the same rules as the direct object pronoun except for **loro**, which is placed after the verb.

Le do il libro.   *I give her the book.*
Do loro il libro.   *I give them the book.*

Nevertheless, nowadays **gli** can be used instead of the more pedantic **loro**, the latter being confined to written or literary use, so **Gli do il libro** can mean either *I give him the book* or *I give them the book.*

C With the exception of **loro**, indirect object pronouns are added to the end of infinitives, gerunds, past participles and some imperatives after the loss of the final vowel.

Voglio parlargli.   *I want to speak to him.*

D As well as *to me, to him, to her,* etc., the indirect pronoun can translate *for me, for him,* etc.

Gli ho fatto una foto.   *I took a picture of him.*
Le ho comprato un profumo.   *I bought (for) her some perfume.*

⚠ English expressions like *I rang him, I told her,* etc. mean *I rang to him, I said to her* and are therefore translated **Gli ho telefonato, Le ho detto**.

➤ See Unit 58 for imperatives, Unit 66 for gerunds and Unit 49 for past particples.

1 **Translate the following using the stressed form.**

E.g. Maria ha fatto un regalo a lui.

a Maria gave a present to me.
b Maria gave a present to you. (*inform. sing.*)
c Maria gave a present to him.
d Maria gave a present to her.
e Maria gave a present to us.
f Maria gave a present to you. (*inform. pl.*)
g Maria gave a present to them.

2 **Re-write the sentences translated in exercise 1 using the unstressed pronoun, including the two possible forms of the third person plural. Then read the eight sentences aloud.**

E.g. Maria gli ha fatto un regalo.

3 **Re-write the following sentences, attaching the unstressed pronoun to the infinitive. Read the sentences aloud several times.**

E.g. Voglio telefonare a te. → Voglio telefonarti.

a Voglio telefonare a lei.
b Voglio telefonare a lui.
c Voglio telefonare a Lei, signor Simoni.
d Voglio telefonare a voi.
e Voglio telefonare a loro.
f Voglio telefonare a Loro, signori.
g Voglio parlare a te.
h Voglio parlare a lei.
i Voglio parlare a lui.
j Voglio parlare a Lei, signora.
k Voglio parlare a voi.
l Voglio parlare a loro.
m Voglio parlare a Loro.

4 **Translate the following into Italian.**

a I give her a book.
b I give him a book.
c I took a picture of them.
d I bought them a chandelier (**lampadario**).
e They bought me a suitcase.
f I told her the truth (**la verità**).

37 UNIT Combined pronouns

When indirect and direct object pronouns occur in the same sentence, they combine in the following way: indirect pronoun + direct pronoun + verb.

INDIRECT OBJECT PRONOUNS			+ DIRECT OBJECT PRONOUNS			
				= COMBINED PRONOUNS		
			+ lo	+ la	+ li	+ le
mi		me	me lo	me la	me li	me le
ti		te	te lo	te la	te li	te le
gli, le, Le		glie	glielo	gliela	glieli	gliele
ci	becomes	ce	ce lo	ce la	ce li	ce le
vi		ve	ve lo	ve la	ve li	ve le
gli		glie	glielo	gliela	glieli	gliele
loro		verb + loro	verb + loro	verb + loro	verb + loro	verb + loro

A Mi, ti, ci, etc. become me, te, ce, etc. Gli and le combine to become glie which is applicable to the masculine, feminine and formal *you* forms.

Ci dai la cassetta?	*Will you give us the cassette?*
Ve la darò domani.	*I will give it to you tomorrow* (lit. *to you it I will give tomorrow*)
Me la vendi?	*Will you sell it* (feminine) *to me?*
Gli hai dato i dischi?	*Did you give him/her/them the records?*
Glieli ho dati ieri.	*I gave them to him/her/them yesterday.*

B If the third person plural loro is used instead of gli, it must follow the verb.
Glielo dirò domani. Lo dirò loro domani. *I will tell them tomorrow.*

C The partitive ne (*some/of it/of them/about it/about them*) combines in the same way as lo, la, li, le.

Me ne manderà una dozzina.	*She'll send me a dozen of them.*
Gliene parlerò domani.	*I will speak to him about it tomorrow.*

D With the verbs potere (*to be able/may/can*), dovere (*must/to have to*) and volere (*to want*) + an infinitive, direct, indirect or combined pronouns can either precede the verb or be attached to the following infinitive.
Lo voglio vedere./Voglio vederlo. *I want to see him.*
Gli devo parlare./Devo parlargli. *I must talk to him.*

1 Answer these questions using the appropriate combined pronouns.

E.g. Mi dai la chiave? → Te la darò domani.

a Mi dai il libro?

b Gli dai la cassetta?

c Le dai il disco?

d Ci dai cinquantamila lire?

e Mi dai le chiavi della macchina?

f Le dai un po' di torta?

g Ci dai le video-cassette?

h Mi dai i pennarelli (*felt pens*)?

2 Answer the questions using *ne*:

E.g. Quanti panini vuole? → Ne voglio due.

Lucia ha nostalgia dell'Italia? → Sì, ne parla spesso.

a Sei sicura (*Are you sure about it*)? Sì, _____ sono sicura.

b Quanti anni ha Mauro? _____ ha venticinque.

c Hai una sigaretta? No, non _____ ho.

d Ha giornali (*newspapers*)? No, _____ _____ _____.

e Ha riviste (*magazines*)? No, _____ _____ _____.

f Quanti caffè prende al giorno? _____ prendo tre.

3 Translate the answers into Italian.

a Quante riviste compra alla settimana? (*I buy three (of them).*)

b Quanti giornali compra? (*I buy two (of them).*)

c Quanti anni ha la sua casa? (lit: *of them it has twenty-five.*)

d Quanto pane vuole? (*I want a chilo (of it).*)

e Quanto salame vuole? (*I want half a chilo (of it).*)

f Quante banane vuole? (*I want six (of them).*)

g Giulia vuole tornare in Italia? (*Yes, she often talks (of it).*)

h Sei sicuro? (*Yes, I am sure of it.*)

4 Write the alternative forms of the direct and indirect pronouns followed by *dovere, potere, volere* + infinitive.

a Lo voglio vedere.

b Gli voglio parlare.

c Le voglio telefonare.

d Vi devo scrivere.

e Ci deve vedere.

f Lo devo leggere.

g Lo posso vedere?

h Gli posso telefonare?

i Ci puoi scrivere?

38 UNIT | Pronouns with a preposition

The use of pronouns preceded by a preposition (with, for, etc.) and the use of ci and vi.

PRONOUNS PRECEDED BY A PREPOSITION OTHER THAN **A**		
SINGULAR		PLURAL
me	*me*	noi *us*
te	*you*	voi *you* (pl.)
lui	*him*	essi
lei	*her*	esse } *them*
Lei	*you* (formal)	loro
esso	*it* (masculine)	
essa	*it* (feminine)	

A These pronouns are used after prepositions (apart from **a**). **Esso, essa, essi** and **esse** refer mainly to objects but are seldom used.

B As can be seen from the above list, these pronouns are very similar to subject pronouns (see Unit 34) except for the first two persons singular.

C'è posta per me?	*Is there any mail for me?*
Vado da lui.	*I am going to him.*
Mi ricordo di lei.	*I remember her.*
Chi viene con Lei, signora?	*Who is coming with you, madam?*
Mario viene con noi.	*Mario is coming with us.*

C Uses of **ci** and **vi**.

Apart from *us/to us,* **ci** can also be an adverb meaning *here* or *there.*

Ci vado ogni giorno.	*I go there every day.*
Ci vengo ogni giorno.	*I come here every day.*
Ci sono dodici mesi in un anno.	*There are twelve months in a year.*
C'è un bar qui vicino?	*Is there a bar near here?*

Additionally it can mean *in it/about it/about them.*

Non ci credo.	*I don't believe in it.*
Ci penso sempre.	*I always think about it/him/her.*

Vi in this context is identical to **ci** but is more used in writing.

➤ *See complete explanation on the use of ci and vi in Unit 70. Reflexive pronouns and reflexive verbs are covered in Unit 47.*

38 UNIT Pronouns with a preposition – *Exercises*

1 Translate the following into Italian.

a Who is coming with you, children?

b Is there a message (**messaggio**) for me?

c There is a letter for them.

d I remember him.

e Is he coming with you (*informal sing.*)?

f Is he coming with you (*formal sing.*)?

g Is he coming with you (*informal pl.*)?

h Is he coming with you (*formal pl.*)?

2 Re-organize the words to make meaningful sentences.

a ricordo mi lui di

b lui da vado

c viene lei con chi?

d Marianna noi con viene

e una c'è per lettera voi

f ricordo di mi lui non

g ricordo non mi lei di

h con viene Gisella noi?

i messaggio c'è per un te

j lei di ricordo mi

k pacco è questo te per

l giornali per lui sono questi

3 Translate into Italian using *ci*.

a Is there a supermarket (**supermercato**) near here?

b I go there every month.

c I come here once a year.

d We always think about them.

e There are seven days in one week.

4 Put these sentences in the right order to form a conversation.

a SUSANNA Non ci credo!

b GIACOMO Ci penso sempre …

c SUSANNA Pensi sempre a lei?

d GIACOMO Ci ho pensato ma ... non ne ho il coraggio.

e SUSANNA Adesso è a casa. Perché non ci vai?

f GIACOMO Tu non ci credi ma è vero.

g SUSANNA Quello io non te lo posso dare!

credere	to believe
pensare	to think

Irregular verbs: *essere*

The English verb *to be doesn't follow the regular pattern: it is irregular in Italian. It is also irregular, as are several other verbs.*

ESSERE *to be*			
(io)	sono	inglese/inglesi	(*English*)
		di Londra	(*from London*)
(tu)	sei	in banca	(*in the bank*)
		in aereo	(*on a plane*)
(lui)/Paolo		in Europa	(*in Europe*)
(lei)/Marianna		in ufficio	(*in the office*)
(Lei)	è	in treno	(*on a train*)
La signora Simoni		in autobus	(*on the bus*)
Il signor Simoni		in barca	(*on the boat*)
		in discoteca	(*at the disco*)
(noi)	siamo	al cinema	(*at the cinema*)
		a teatro	(*at the theatre*)
(voi)	siete	alla mensa	(*in the canteen*)
		alla posta	(*at the post office*)
(loro)		alla partita	(*at the match*)
(Loro)		a Capri	(*in Capri*)
I ragazzi	sono	a Milano	(*in Milan*)
Le ragazze		a scuola	(*at school*)
		a casa	(*at home*)

Siamo a Capri.	*We are in Capri.*
La signora è a casa.	*The lady is at home.*
Chi sono?	*Who are they?*
Sono Paolo e Marianna.	*It is (lit:They are) Paul and Marianna.*
Io sono inglese.	*I am English.*
Loro non sono italiani.	*They are not Italian*
C'è una banca in questa via?	*Is there a bank in this street?*
Dov'è Paolo?	*Where is Paul?*
Dove sono Paolo e Maria?	*Where are Paul and Maria?*

39 Irregular verbs: essere – Exercises

1 Answer the following questions.

E.g. La signora è in treno? → Sì, è in treno.

a Maria è in discoteca?

b Sono in classe i ragazzi?

c Il signor Simoni è in banca?

d Marianna e Paolo sono italiani?

2 Now answer the questions in the negative.

E.g. New York è in Europa? → No, non è in Europa.

a Io sono alla partita?

b Siamo a Capri?

c Marianna e Paolo sono a casa?

d Sei alla mensa?

3 Now write questions.

E.g. Sono a scuola. → Dove sono Paolo e Marianna?

a _____ Simone? È alla partita.

b _____ ? Siamo al cinema.

c _____ ? Siete in auto.

d _____ ? Sei in ufficio.

e _____ una posta in questa via? Sì, c'è.

f _____ banche in questa via? Sì, ci sono.

g _____ supermercati? No, non ci sono/No, non ce (*of them*) ne sono.

4 Fill the spaces in this conversation with the correct form of the verb.

— Scusi, **a** dov'_____ la segreteria?

— Al secondo piano (*floor*).

— Che cosa **b** _____ necessario fare per iscriversi (*enrol*) a questo corso?

— **c** _____ necessario **d** _____ (*to pay*) la tassa d'iscrizione, avere due foto, il passaporto e il suo indirizzo in Italia.

— Quante ore di lezione ci **e** _____ in questo corso?

— Ci **f** _____ trenta ore la settimana.

— **g** _____ _____ lezioni il sabato?

— Il sabato **h** _____ _____ gite ed escursioni.

— E la domenica?

— La domenica **i** _____ _____ uno spettacolo teatrale.

40 UNIT | Irregular verbs: *avere*

The verb avere (to have) is another irregular verb.

AVERE *to have*			
(io)	ho	una macchina nuova	(*a new car*)
		moltissimi amici	(*loads of friends*)
(tu)	hai	un libro da scrivere	(*a book to write*)
		una casa in campagna	(*a house in the country*)
(lui)/Paolo		una barca a motore	(*a motorboat*)
(lei)/Marianna		l'influenza	(*the flu*)
(Lei)	ha	molti soldi	(*a lot of money*)
La signora Simoni		gli occhi azzurri	(*blue eyes*)
Il signor Simoni		una carta di credito	(*a credit card*)
		due biglietti gratis	(*two free tickets*)
(noi)	abbiamo	molti vestiti	(*many clothes*)
		un giardino enorme	(*a large garden*)
(voi)	avete	mal di testa	(*a headache*)
(loro)		moltissimi libri	(*very many books*)
(Loro)		due figli	(*two sons*)
I ragazzi	hanno	uno chalet al mare	(*a chalet by the sea*)
Le ragazze		i capelli biondi	(*blond hair*)

Ha una carta di credito, signora?	*Do you have a credit card, madam?*
Il signor Simoni ha due figli.	*Mr Simoni has two sons.*
Chi ha il mio passaporto?	*Who has my passport?*
Dove hai messo il mio libro?	*Where have you put my book?*
Non ho molti soldi.	*I don't have a lot of money.*
Paolo ha gli occhi azzurri.	*Paul has blue eyes.*
Che barca hanno, Loro?	*What boat do you* (formal) *have?*

⚠ **Avere** is used instead of **essere** in the following expressions.

avere fame (*to be hungry*); avere sete (*to be thirsty*); avere sonno (*to be sleepy*); avere caldo (*to feel hot*); avere freddo (*to feel cold*); avere ragione (*to be right*); avere torto (*to be wrong*).

Hai fame? No, ho sete.	*Are you hungry? No, I am thirsty.*
Tu hai ragione ed io ho torto.	*You are right and I am wrong.*

How old are you? I am … is translated: **Quanti anni hai? Ho .... anni**.

1 **You have just visited the Simoni family in Sorrento and are telling your Italian friend about them. Translate the following into Italian.**

Signor Simoni is writing a book. Signora Simoni has a lot of money and many clothes. They have a son and a daughter. Marianna, their daughter, has blond hair and blue eyes and a boat. She is twenty-three. She has many friends. Paolo, their son, is twenty. He has a new fast (**veloce**) car. They have a large house with an enormous garden. They also (**anche**) have a house in the country. Unfortunately (**Purtroppo**) they always have some (**dei**) problems.

2 **Match the questions with the answers or the two halves of the sentences.**

a Ha i documenti?	**1** No, non li ho.
b Hai fame?	**2** … una casa in campagna.
c Tu hai torto …	**3** Sì, un po', hai un panino (*a roll*)?
d Avete dei problemi?	**4** Sì, in borsa.
e Paolo e Marianna hanno sete.	**5** … e io ho ragione.
f C'è un albergo in questa strada?	**6** Hai dell'acqua minerale?
g I signori Simoni hanno …	**7** Ne abbiamo molti.
h Hai i soldi?	**8** Sì, a duecento metri, a destra.
i Quanti anni hai?	**9** Ne ho trentuno.

3 **Use the information in exercise 1 to form the questions for these answers.**

E.g. Marianna ha molti amici? Sì, ha molti amici.

a _____ ?	Sì, hanno dei problemi.
b _____ ?	Hanno due figli.
c _____ ?	Ne ha venti.
d _____ ?	Ne ha ventitré.
e _____ ?	Sì, ne hanno molti.

41 UNIT | Irregular verbs: *andare, venire* and *uscire*

	ANDARE *to go*	VENIRE *to come*	USCIRE *to go/to come out*
(io)	vado	vengo	esco
(tu)	vai	vieni	esci
(lui)/Paolo (lei)/Marianna (Lei) La signora Simoni Il signor Simoni	va	viene	esce
(noi)	andiamo	veniamo	usciamo
(voi)	andate	venite	uscite
(loro) (Loro) I ragazzi Le ragazze	vanno	vengono	escono

I ragazzi vanno al bar.	*The boys go to the the bar.*
Vai al cinema?	*Are you going to the cinema?*
Chi va a fare la spesa?	*Who is going shopping?*
I signori Rossi vengono stasera?	*Are the Rossis coming this evening?*
Se viene Marianna io vado via.	*If Marianna comes, I go away.*
Da dove viene? Vengo da Pisa.	*Where do you come from? I come from Pisa.*
Vengo con te se non ti dispiace.	*I am coming with you if you don't mind.*
Di solito esco alle sette.	*I usually go out at seven.*
Quando esci?	*When do you go/are you going out?*
Esce dal negozio e gira a destra.	*You go out of the shop and turn right.*

To say where you are from, you can either say **Vengo da …** (*I come from …*) or **Sono di …**

Vengo da Barletta. Sono di Barletta. *I come from Barletta.*

1 **Starting with *Vado a casa*, read out the list of places. Make sure you always include the verb and note the intonation in the questions.**

a		b		c	
Vado a	casa. letto. lezione. scuola. teatro.	Vai al	bar? concerto? cinema? mare? museo?	Maria lui Lei, signora	mensa va alla posta. stazione?

d		e		f	
Andiamo in	albergo. centro. biblioteca. campagna.	Andate in	città? chiesa? farmacia? gelateria?	Vanno	al concerto. al largo. a lezione. in farmacia.

2 **Match the questions and answers.**

a Vai al cinema?	**1** Di solito usciamo alle otto.
b Esci?	**2** Preferisco andare sola.
c Da dove viene, signora?	**3** Ci vanno Renzo e Lucia.
d Vengono stasera i tuoi amici?	**4** No, vado a teatro.
e Vengo con te, ti dispiace?	**5** No, andiamo oggi.
f Uscite alle sette di solito?	**6** Sì, esco.
g Chi va a fare la spesa?	**7** Vengo da Roma, e Lei?
h Andiamo domani?	**8** Vengono domani.

3 **Translate the following into Italian.**
  a Who is going to the chemist?
  b Where do you come from, madam?
  c Where do you come from, Robert?
  d Do you mind if I come with you?
  e I am going out.
  f I am from Rome, and you (*formal*)?
  g I don't usually go with them.
  h Are you going out, Antonio?
  i He goes out every (**ogni**) evening.
  j Are the Rossis going out?

42 Unit Irregular verbs: *fare, bere* and *dire*

Bere *and* dire *are formed as if their infinitive forms were* bevere *and* dicere. Fare *is formed in yet another way.*

	FARE *to do/to make*	BERE *to drink*	DIRE *to say/to tell*
(io)	faccio	bevo	dico
(tu)	fai	bevi	dici
(lui)/Paolo (lei)/Marianna (Lei) La signora Simoni Il signor Simoni	fa	beve	dice
(noi)	facciamo	beviamo	diciamo
(voi)	fate	bevete	dite
(loro) (Loro) I ragazzi Le ragazze	fanno	bevono	dicono

A **Fare** translates *to do* and *to make*. As you know, Italian doesn't use *to do* either in questions or to make the negative form.

To emphasize a verb, as in *I do speak Italian!*, you use expressions like **Certo che** (*certainly*) parlo italiano! or Vedo **bene!** (*I do see!*)
Spero proprio (*really*) di venire!   *I do hope to come!*

Isn't it?, Isn't she?, etc. are translated by **non è vero?**
Does he? Did he? etc. expressing surprise are expressed by **Davvero?** (*Really?*)

B **Fare** is also used in the following expressions: fare uno spuntino (*to have a snack*); fare la coda (*to queue*); fare una passeggiata (*to have a walk*); fare le valigie (*to pack*); fare il biglietto (*to buy the ticket*); fare colazione (*to have breakfast*); fare freddo (*to be cold (weather)*); fare due passi (*to have a stroll*); fare caldo (*to be hot (weather)*); fare una domanda (*to ask a question*)

⚠ **Rifare** (*to do again/to re-make*) is formed in the same way as **fare**.

C **Far fare** or **fare** + infinitive, preceded by the indirect object pronoun (**mi, ti, gli,** etc.), are used to translate *to have something done.*

Mi faccio fare un vestito.   *I'll have a dress made.*
Mi faccio tagliare i capelli.   *I am going to have my hair cut.*

1 Add the missing verb.

E.g. Paolo _____ soltanto vino rosso. → Paolo beve soltanto vino rosso.

a Noi non _____ alcolici.   (*We do not drink alcohol.*)

b Loro _____ sempre le stesse cose. (*They always say the same things.*)

c _____ tutto alla mamma.   (*We tell mum everything.*)

d Serafina _____ una torta.   (*Serafina makes/is making a cake.*)

e La sera _____ quattro passi.   (*We have a stroll in the evenings.*)

f _____ le valigie.   (*I make/am packing the cases.*)

2 Match the two halves of the sentences or a sentence and its response.

a Faccio merenda	**1** acqua?
b Facciamo una passeggiata tutte	**2** non è vero?
c In Italia fanno raramente	**3** la verità.
d Franca fa tre ore di ginnastica al giorno.	**4** uscire.
e Dopo cena (*after dinner*) facciamo	**5** le mattine.
f Lei beve soltanto	**6** la coda.
g Dice che è meglio	**7** ogni pomeriggio.
h Dicono sempre	**8** Davvero!?
i Fa molto caldo oggi,	**9** due passi.

3 Fill the spaces under the pictures.

a _____ molto _____.   **b** Roberta _____ le valigie.   **c** Loro _____ i biglietti.

4 Change the infinitives into the correct person.

La signora Cecilia e la signorina Marcella (**a** fare) molte cose questa mattina: (**b** rifare) i letti, (**c** riordinare) la casa, poi (**d** fare) la spesa. La signora Cecilia (**e** andare) anche (*also*) a (**f** fare) i biglietti per il teatro mentre (*while*) la signorina Marcella (**g** andare) in chiesa, alla Messa, e fa la Comunione, poi (**h** andare) all'ufficio postale e (**i** fare) un vaglia (*postal order*). Quando (**j** ritornare) a casa la signora Cecilia (**k** fare) molte telefonate mentre la signorina Marcella (**l** fare) il minestrone.

Irregular verbs: *dare* and *sapere*

> In Italian two verbs are used to translate *to know*: sapere, which is irregular, and conoscere, a regular verb.

	DARE *to give*	SAPERE *to know*
(io)	do	so
(tu)	dai	sai
(lui)/Paolo (lei)/Marianna (Lei)	dà	sa
(noi)	diamo	sappiamo
(voi)	date	sapete
(loro) (Loro)	danno	sannno

A **Dare** also translates:

- *to hold/have a party*
  Sabato Marta dà una festa.   *On Saturday Marta is giving a party.*

- *to show (film)*
  Che film danno oggi?   *Which film are they showing today?*

- *to perform* (a show, etc.)
  Danno Amleto.   *They're performing Hamlet.*

- **Quanti anni mi dai?** *How old do you think I am?*

⚠ The third person singular of **dare** always carries a grave (**à**) accent.

B **Sapere** is mainly used to express the knowledge of a fact.
     So che Rita sposa John.   *I know that Rita is marrying John.*
     Sai le notizie di oggi?   *Do you know today's news?*

It also means *to know how to do something* (*can you ...?*):
     Sai cucinare?   *Can you cook?*

C **Conoscere** is mainly used for people and places.
     Conosce il professor De Carli?   *Do you know Professor De Carli?*
     Conosce Roma?   *Do you know Rome?*

⚠ Although **conoscere** is a regular verb (**conosco, conosci, conosce, conosciamo, conoscete, conoscono**), you need to pay attention to the pronunciation since **-sc-** is pronounced s*k* if it occurs before **-o** and *sh* before **-e** or **-i**.

1 Fill the blanks with the correct person of the verb *dare*.

a Che cosa _____ al cinema oggi?

b Quando _____ Aida?

c (Noi) _____ un ballo domenica prossima.

d (Tu) mi _____ la macchina?

e I ragazzi _____ una festa sabato prossimo.

f La signora Simoni _____ un banchetto di beneficienza.

g Quanti anni gli _____ ?

h (Voi) mi _____ i vostri documenti?

2 Fill the blanks with the correct person of the verb *sapere*.

a Tu _____ tutto, io non _____ nulla.

b Voi _____ tutto, noi non _____ nulla.

c Lui _____ tutto, loro non _____ nulla.

d (Voi) _____ la novità (*what (just) happened*)?

e (Tu) _____ le ultime notizie?

f (Lei) _____ quattro lingue.

g Come (*How*) (tu) _____ questo?

h (Io) _____ che si è sposato.

3 *Sapere* or *conoscere*? Circle the appropriate verb.

a So/Conosco che Maria ha intenzione di partire per l'Australia.

b So/Conosco l'Italia del Nord piuttosto (*rather*) bene.

c So/Conosco i signori Simoni da moltissini anni.

d So/Conosco che Luisa deve venire la settimana prossima.

e Non so/conosco la verità.

f Eleonora non sa/conosce cucinare molto bene.

4 Translate the following into Italian.

a How old do you think he is?

b What film is on television?

c The Simoni are organizing a party.

d Can you play (**giocare a**) tennis?

e He cannot play cards (**a carte**).

f They know that I cannot (**posso**) go.

g Will you give me your video?

h We do not know the truth.

i She knows Southern Italy well.

j They do not know much.

44 UNIT Irregular verbs: *stare*

As well as *to stay, and to remain,* the verb stare has several other uses.

A **Stare** is also used in the following cases:

* with health and exchanges of courtesies:
  Come sta, signora?
  How are you, madam?
  Oggi non sto molto bene.
  Today I am not very well.

* to translate *to live/reside permanently or temporarily in a place:*
  Luigi sta con lei.
  Luigi lives with her.
  Sto all'albergo.
  I live in the hotel.

* to translate *to be situated*:
  Sta in cima al colle.
  It's on the top of the hill.

	STARE *(to stay/to remain)*
(io)	sto
(tu)	stai
(lui)/Paolo (lei)/Marianna (Lei) La signora Simoni Il signor Simoni	sta
(noi)	stiamo
(voi)	state
(loro) (Loro) I ragazzi Le ragazze	stanno

* followed by **per** + infinitive to translate *to be about to do something*:
  Sto per uscire. *I am about to go out.*
  Michela sta per avere un bambino. *Michela is about to have a baby.*

* followed by the gerund, to forms the continuous form:
  Sta piovendo. *It is raining.*
  In questo momento sto mangiando. *I am eating at the moment.*
  Stavi dormendo? *Were you sleeping?*

B Note the verbal expressions where *to be* is translated by **stare**: **stare attento** (*to be careful*); **stare zitto** (*to be silent*) and **stare fermo** (*to stay still*).
  Perché non stai attento? *Why don't you pay attention/aren't you careful?*
  Paolo non sta mai zitto. *Paul is never quiet.*
  Il bambino non sta mai fermo. *The child is never still.*

C Other uses: **stare in piedi** (*to stand*); **stare alla cassa** (*to be at the till*); **stare a sentire** (*to listen*).

➤ *See Unit 66 for the gerund.*

44 UNIT Irregular verbs: *stare* – *Exercises*

1 Match the questions and answers.

a Perché non stai attento quando ti parlo?

b Come sta sua figlia?

c Com'è il tempo (*weather*)?

d Con chi abita Renato?

e Desidera sedersi?

1 Sta piovendo.

2 Sta con sua madre.

3 Perché sto leggendo in questo momento.

4 No grazie, sto in piedi.

5 Sta bene grazie, e la sua?

2 Using the information on the opposite page, give the other half of the questions/answers below.

a _____ ?   Bene grazie, e Lei?

b _____ ?   Sto all'albergo Regina.

c Hai notizie di Michela?   Sta _____ .

d Com'è il tuo bambino?   È molto bello ma _____ .

e _____ ?   Oggi non sto molto bene.

3 Enter the correct form of *stare*.

a Come _____ , Annamaria?

b Come il _____ signor Gazzolo?

c Oggi noi non _____ molto bene.

d _____ piovendo in questo momento.

e Loro _____ in piedi perché non c'è posto a sedere.

f Paolo _____ alla cassa.

g Voi _____ sempre (*always*) in via Garibaldi?

h Noi _____ sempre in casa.

4 Translate the following into Italian.

a Are you (*inform. sing.*) staying in today?

b They are about to eat.

c Is the child sleeping?

d She is at Claridges.

e They are not paying attention.

f Marianna is never quiet.

g He never listens to anybody (**nessuno**).

89

45 UNIT Irregular verbs: *volere, potere, dovere*

Particular attention should be given to these three irregular verbs since they are constantly used.

	VOLERE *to want/to wish*	POTERE *can/to be able/may*	USCIRE *must/to have to*
(io)	voglio	posso	devo
(tu)	vuoi	puoi	devi
(lui)/Paolo (lei)/Marianna (Lei) La signora Simoni Il signor Simoni	vuole	può	deve
(noi)	vogliamo	possiamo	dobbiamo
(voi)	volete	potete	dovete
(loro) (Loro) I ragazzi Le ragazze	vogliono	possono	devono

A **Volere, dovere** and **potere** are usually followed by an infinitive.

Voglio parlare al direttore.	*I want to speak to the manager.*
Puoi fare tutto quello che vuoi.	*You can do all you want.*
Devo partire.	*I must leave.*

B **Volere** may be followed by an object.

Voglio una Ferrari rossa.	*I want a red Ferrari.*

C The interrogative **Vuoi ...?/Volete ...?** (*Do you want ...?*) can also translate *Will you ...?* while **Posso ...?/Possiamo ...?** can mean *May I ...?/May we ...?*. **Devo ...?, Dobbiamo ...?** (*Must I ...?/Must we ...?*) can mean *Shall I ...?/Shall we ...?*

Vuoi/Volete venire in vacanza con me?	*Will you come on holiday with me?*
Posso/Possiamo venire con te?	*May I/we come with you?*
Devo/Dobbiamo venire anche noi?	*Shall I/we come as well?*

A **Il potere** (*the power*), **il volere** (*the will*), **il dovere** (*the duty*): these three words are nouns.

➤ See Unit 56 for the translation of ought.

45 Irregular verbs: *volere, potere, dovere* – Exercises

1 Match each question with an appropriate answer.

a Vuole parlare al mio collega?
b Vuoi un gelato al limone?
c Volete aprire la porta?
d Puoi venire da me domani?
e Può chiudere il finestrino?
f Potete stare zitti, per favore?
g Dobbiamo venire subito?
h Devo farlo oggi?

i Dovete pagare il conto (*bill*)?
j A chi deve il suo successo?

1 Lo devo ai miei genitori.
2 No, potete venire domani.
3 Sì, è urgente.
4 Certamente, signora.
5 No, voglio parlare al direttore.
6 Sì, lo paghiamo prima di andare via.
7 Certo, ci scusi
8 No, lo voglio alla fragola (*strawberry*).
9 Ci dispiace, non possiamo aprirla.
10 Posso ma non voglio.

2 Answer the questions in the negative.

E.g. **Vuoi venire con me?** → **No, non voglio.**

a Può farlo subito?
b Puoi prestarmi centomila lire?
c Posso venire con te?
d Potete andare oggi?
e Possiamo chiudere la finestra?
f Carlo e Maria possono stare qui?
g Volete andare in treno?

h Vuoi venire in discoteca?
i Puoi telefonare tu?
j Ida può fare la babysitter stasera?
k Il suo successo, lo deve a lui?
l Potete darmi una mano?
m I signori vogliono il conto?
n Signora, vuole uscire con me?

3 Insert the appropriate form of volere, dovere or potere.

a Noi non _____ fare quest'esercizio. (**potere**)
b Chi _____ leggere questo brano (*passage*)? (**volere**)
c Loro _____ ascoltare la radio. (**volere**)
d Marianna e Paolo _____ guardare la televisione. (**volere**)
e Noi non _____ vedere bene la lavagna (*board*). (**potere**)
f Lei non _____ parlare così, signore. (**dovere**)
g A chi _____ rivolgerci (*apply to/turn to*) noi? (**dovere**)
h Io _____ soltanto lavorare. (**dovere**)
i Tu _____ studiare di più. (**dovere**)

46 UNIT Transitive/intransitive and active/passive verbs

A few words on some technical terms to help identify some kinds of verbs.

A Transitive verbs imply an object. The action they express 'transits' from the subject to the object: **Leggo un libro** (*I read a book*). Even if I had only said *I read*, it would be understood that I (subject) read something (object). *To read* is therefore a transitive verb.

Intransitive verbs do not imply an object. With these verbs, the action stays with (or goes back) to the subject: **(Io) esco** (*I am going out*).

A simple test to see whether a verb is transitive or intransitive is to see if it can be followed by something that 'answers' the question *what?* or *who?*: **leggo** (*I am reading*) is transitive because I can ask *reading what?* and get the answer *a book, a magazine*, etc. Whereas if I say **Il bambino dorme** (*The child sleeps*), the answer *sleeps what/who?* doesn't make sense. **Dormire** (*to sleep*) is therefore intransitive.

B Some verbs can be transitive or intransitive according to the way they are used. **Salgo le scale** (*I am going up the stairs*). The question *going up what?* is answered by *the stairs*, so **salire** in this case is transitive; **Salgo in camera** (*I am going up to my room*). This doesn't answer *what?* or *who?* and it is therefore intransitive.

C A verb, according to how it is related to the subject, can be either active or passive. The active form is when the subject carries out the action: **Battisti** (subject) **canta la canzone** (*Battisti is singing the song*). The passive form is when the action is carried out by the object: **La canzone è cantata da Battisti** (object) (*The song is being sung by Battisti*). The meaning of the two forms is identical, although Italian tends to use the passive form far less than English.

⚠ As in English, the passive form is rendered by **essere** (*to be*) and the past participle, which agrees with the subject in gender and number.

D With simple tenses, **venire** can be used instead of **essere** to give the same meaning:

    Il Chianti viene prodotto in Italia. *Chianti is produced in Italy.*

E Some common passive constructions use **si** (*one*) + third person singular or plural of the verb: Si parla italiano qui. *Italian is spoken here.*
Si, unlike the English *one*, is much used in Italian.

➤ *See impersonal verbs in Unit 53.*

1 Sort out which are transitive and which are intransitive verbs.
vedere dormire avere essere mangiare finire capire studiare imparare
piovere.

2 Sort out the sentences with transitive and intransitive verbs.
Take care – some transitive verbs may be used intransitively.
  a Il sole tramonta.
  b Maria mangia una pesca.
  c L'autobus è partito.
  d Sono salita in camera.
  e Ho salito le scale.
  f Piove.
  g Angelo dorme.
  h Il costo del pane è aumentato.
  i Il governo ha aumentato le tasse.
  j Vincenzo studia il latino.

3 Which sentences are active and which are passive?
  a Io recito una poesia.
  b La poesia è recitata da me.
  c L'auto viene fabbricata in Italia.
  d L'Italia produce pasta, olio e vino.
  e La scheda telefonica è usata da molte persone.
  f La carta di credito viene emessa (*issued*) dalla banca.

4 Re-write these sentences using *si* + third person singular (or plural when you refer to something plural).
  E.g. **L'inglese è parlato qui. → Qui si parla inglese/Si parla inglese qui.**
  a Il vino viene tenuto in cantina (*kept in the cellar*).
  b Il traffico aereo è controllato dalla torre (*by the tower*).
  c Sono richieste ottime referenze.
  d I libri usati vengono venduti.

47 UNIT | Reflexive verbs

A In this verbal form, the subject and the object are the same person.

(io)	mi	lavo	*I wash myself*
(tu)	ti	lavi	*you wash yourself*
(lui)/(lei)/(Lei)	si	lava	*he/she washes him/herself/ you wash yourself (formal)*
(noi)	ci	laviamo	*we wash ourselves*
(voi)	vi	lavate	*you wash yourselves*
(loro/Loro)	si	lavano	*they wash themselves/ you wash yourselves (formal)*

B As in English, these are ordinary verbs but unlike English, they are preceded (rather than followed) by the reflexive pronoun.

Reflexive pronouns behave like all the other direct and indirect object pronouns and are identical to them, except for the third persons singular and plural (**si**):

Mario si rade.	*Mario is shaving (shaves himself).*
Teresa si veste.	*Teresa is getting dressed (dressing herself).*
Lui si lava.	*He washes/is washing (himself).*
Loro si lavano.	*They wash/are washing (themselves).*

C The reflexive infinitive is formed by replacing the final vowel of an ordinary infinitive with **-si**: **lavare** (*to wash*) → **lavarsi** (*to wash oneself*).

D Like **lavarsi** and **radersi**, several verbs are reflexive both in Italian and in English: **farsi male** (*to hurt oneself*), **divertirsi** (*to enjoy oneself*).

The English verbal form *to get* + past participle or adjective usually corresponds to an Italian reflexive verb:

sposarsi	(*to get married*);	arrabbiarsi	(*to get angry*);
abituarsi	(*to get used*);	annoiarsi	(*to get bored*);
prepararsi	(*to get ready*);	seccarsi	(*to get annoyed*);
vestirsi	(*to get dressed*);	stancarsi	(*to get tired*);
abbronzarsi	(*to get a tan*);	preoccuparsi	(*to get worried*)

Here are some common Italian reflexive verbs which are not reflexive in English: **chiamarsi** (*to be called*), **accorgersi** (*to realize*), **svegliarsi** (*to wake up*), **alzarsi** (*to get up*), **sentirsi** (*to feel*), **rivolgersi (a)** (*to apply to*).

Marianna si trucca.   Ciccio non si alza presto.

1 Take the correct verb from the box and change its ending to complete Marianna's description of her daily routine with her flat mate Ciccio. Don't forget that the reflexive pronoun is attached at the end of the infinitive.

> svegliarsi *(to wake up)* alzarsi *(to get up)* vestirsi *(to get dressed)* radersi *(to shave)* lavarsi *(to wash)* pettinarsi *(to comb)* prepararsi *(to get ready)* abbronzarsi *(to get a tan)* truccarsi *(to put on make-up)* mantenersi in forma *(to keep fit)* lavarsi i denti *(to brush one's teeth)* stancarsi *(to get tired)* arrabbiarsi *(to get angry)* annoiarsi *(to get bored)* preoccuparsi *(to worry)* spazzolarsi i capelli *(to brush one's hair)*

(a *I wake up*) e subito (b *I get up*) e (c *I wash*). Alle sette e mezzo faccio colazione e poi (d *I brush my teeth*) con cura. (e *I put on my make-up*), (f *I get dressed*) e (g *I comb my hair*). Alle otto esco da casa e prendo l'autobus per l'ufficio. Ciccio, che divide con me il mio appartamento in città, (h *wakes up*) alle undici perché fa il pianista in un nightclub e ritorna a casa alle tre di mattina. Lui non (i *gets up*) subito (*at once*), sta a letto a leggere il giornale e ad ascoltare la radio.

All'una (j *he gets up*), (k *washes*), (l *shaves*), (m *brushes his teeth*) e poi (n *he brushes his hair*) e (o *gets dressed*). Alle due esce e va in palestra per (p *to keep fit*), dopo la palestra va a 'Il Solarium' per (q *to get tanned*). Ciccio è molto simpatico: non (r *gets angry*) e non (s *gets bored)* mai. È sempre molto calmo, non (t *gets worried*) mai. Ciccio è il suo soprannome, infatti (u *he's called*) Federico Tranquillo.

48 UNIT The use of reflexive verbs

A Italian tends to use a reflexive verb to indicate possession when referring to parts of the body, clothing and other personal effects because it is usual to say, for example, *the leg* or *a leg* rather than *my leg* as in English.

Luigi si è rotto una gamba sciando.   *Luigi broke his leg while skiing.*
Devo lavarmi i capelli.   *I must wash my hair.*

B The reflexive form is also used to express reciprocal action and to translate expressions like *each other*, *one another*.

Si telefonano ogni giorno.   *They ring each other every day.*
Si incontrano.   *They meet (each other).*
Dovete rispettarvi.   *You must respect one another.*

C Other uses. Observe these examples:

L'autobus si è fermato.   *The bus stopped (lit. itself).*
Maria ha fermato l'autobus.   *Maria stopped the bus.*
La porta si è aperta.   *The door opened (lit. itself).*
Maria ha aperto la porta.   *Maria opened the door.*

D Some verbs can be used reflexively or non-reflexively:

Ho dimenticato il passaporto/Mi   *I forgot the passport.*
   sono dimenticata il passaporto.
Ho riposato un'ora. Mi sono   *I had an hour's rest.*
   riposata un'ora.

E Reflexive pronouns preceded by a preposition are translated:

sé/se stesso,	-a	*oneself*	noi/noi stessi,	-e	*ourselves*
me/me stesso,	-a	*myself*	voi/voi stessi,	-e	*yourselves*
te/te stesso,	-a	*yourself*	sé/se stessi/se stesse,	-e	*themselves*
sé/se stesso,	-a	*him/herself*			

Quella ragazza è piena di sé.   *That girl is full of herself.*
Devi credere in te stesso.   *You must believe in yourself.*

F Note this use of **stesso** (*oneself*).

Andrò io stesso.   *I will go myself.*
Ha deciso lui stesso.   *He himself decided.*

1 Cross out the possessive adjective when not needed.

E.g. Devo lavarmi i ~~miei~~ capelli.

a Vuoi cambiarti la tua giacca?

b Mi metto (*put on*) il mio vestito.

c Voglio farmi tagliare (*cut*) i miei capelli.

d Ti sei lavato le tue mani?

e Luigi si è tagliato un dito (*cut his/a finger*).

f Ho dimenticato la mia patente (*driving licence*).

g Ieri ho visto tuo figlio.

2 Marianna and Francesco do several things together every day. (Bisticciarsi (*to quarrel*) can be used also non reflexively: bisticciare.) Translate the following.

a They ring each other.

b They meet each other.

c They kiss each other.

d They see each other.

e They speak to each other.

f They quarrel (with each other).

3 Now it's your turn. Every day you and your partner do the same things as Francesco and Marianna: Tutti i giorni noi ...

4 Translate the following into Italian.

a The train stopped at Lucca.

b The window opened.

c Giulia opened the window.

d That man is full of himself.

e The car stopped and the door opened.

f The alarm (**allarme**) stopped the train.

g Giulia doesn't believe in herself.

h She herself went.

5 Complete the passage by writing the Italian forms of the reflexive verbs.

Ciccio (**a** *stops*) al Bar dello Sportivo alle sei. Poi ritorna a casa a (**b** *to get ready*) per andare al lavoro. Marianna esce dal lavoro alle sei e (**c** *stops (herself)*) in centro per fare un po' di spesa. Marianna e Ciccio non (**d** *see each other*) spesso: soltanto il sabato e la domenica quando, con Francesco e Margherita, vanno fuori a (**e** *to enjoy themselves*).

49 UNIT | The past participle

The past participle is an extremely useful part of the verb because, as in English, it is added to the auxiliaries to be and to have to make other tenses.

A These three examples use the auxiliary verb *to have* + the past participle.
ho parlato (*I have spoken*); ho venduto (*I have sold*); ho finito (*I have finished*)

Spoken, sold and *finished* are past participles. You form the past participle in the following way: **-are**, **-ere** and **-ire** become **-ato**, **-uto**, **-ito** respectively.
parlato (*spoken*); studiato (*studied*); imparato (*learned*); andato (*gone*); mangiato (*eaten*); dato (*given*); stato (*been*); avuto (*had*); venduto (*sold*); conosciuto (*known*); ripetuto (*repeated*); creduto (*believed*); partito (*left/departed*); udito (*heard*); sentito (*felt/heard*); capito (*understood*); bollito (*boiled*).

B All **-are** verbs have a regular past participle except **fare**. Most **-ere** and a few **-ire** past participles are irregular. The most common are:

aprire → aperto (*opened*)	nascere → nato (*born*)
bere → bevuto (*drunk*)	offrire → offerto (*offered*)
chiudere → chiuso (*closed/shut*)	permettere → permesso (*allowed*)
correre → corso (*run*)	prendere → preso (*taken/caught*)
dire → detto (*said/told*)	rimanere → rimasto (*remained*)
essere → stato (*been*)	rompere → rotto (*broken*)
fare → fatto (*done/made*)	scendere → sceso (*gone/come down*)
leggere → letto (*read*)	scrivere → scritto (*written*)
mettere → messo (*put*	venire → venuto (*come*)
muovere → mosso (*moved*)	vivere → vissuto (*lived*)

⚠ Although **vedere** has a regular and an irregular past participle, the latter is more common: **veduto** and **visto**.

C The past participle can often be used as an adjective or as a noun:
un attore ben conosciuto   *a well-known actor*
Il ferito è in condizioni stazionarie. *The injured man is in a stable condition.*

⚠ Some past participles are spelt exactly as some nouns with a completely different meaning: **letto** (*bed*), **corso** (*avenue*), **dato** (*datum*).

The past participle – Exercises

1 **Write the regular past participles of the infinitives below, then read aloud both forms.**

E.g. parlare → parlato

a parlare b vendere c camminare d capire e studiare f riposare g ascoltare h ritornare i mangiare j continuare k salire l imparare m costruire n guarire o pagare p cercare q pulire r andare s sapere t stare u volere v potere w dovere x avere.

2 **Write the irregular past participles of the infinitives below, then read them aloud.**

E.g. leggere → letto

a venire b rompere c offrire d correre e fare f mettere g bere h prendere i vedere j rimanere k aprire l essere m chiudere n scrivere o nascere p muovere q leggere r dire s scendere t vivere.

3 **Write an N next to a word in bold when used as a noun, an A when used as an adjective and a V when used as a verb.**

a Ho il **permesso** di uscire.

b Ho **permesso** a Marina di uscire.

c **Chiuso** al pubblico.

d Il **fatto** è che io non voglio andare.

e Ho **fatto** una torta di mele.

f Voglio **riso** (*rice*) bollito.

4 **Translate into Italian.**

a The shop is closed.

b The chemist is open.

c I have seen the film twice.

d I have written a letter.

e I have taken the liberty (**libertà**) of coming.

f I have made a cake (**torta**).

g She has lived well.

h I have allowed Marina to go out.

i I have read the book.

j I have walked three kilometers.

50 UNIT | The perfect tense

An important tense to learn. In Italian, it is called passato prossimo and it is used to talk about something that happened in the past.

A It is formed by the present tense of **avere** or **essere** + past participle.

Ho parlato. *I spoke.*   Sono partita. *I left (f).*

	PARLARE *to speak*	PARTIRE *to leave*
(io)	ho parlato	sono partito/partita
(tu)	hai parlato	sei partito/partita
(lui)/Paolo (lei)/Marianna (Lei)	ha parlato	è partito/partita
(noi)	abbiamo parlato	siamo partiti/partite
(voi)	avete parlato	siete partiti/partite
(loro) (Loro)	hanno parlato	sono partiti/partite

B **Essere** is used instead of **avere** mainly (but not always) with verbs of motions or with verbs expressing a change in position or condition. Here are the most common verbs taking **essere**: andare, venire, arrivare, partire, scendere, salire, nascere, morire, fuggire, scappare, correre, ritornare, uscire, diventare, arrossire, stare, rimanere.

Mario è partito ieri.   *Mario left yesterday.*
Siamo usciti.   *We went out.*

⚠ **Camminare** takes **avere**.

Other cases in which **essere** is used are:
- with reflexive verbs: Mi sono molto meravigliata. *I was very surprised.*
- with impersonal verbs: È stato necessario lavorare. *It was necessary to work.*

C Agreements. With essere, the past participle needs to agree in gender and number with the subject

Rosella è partita ieri.   *Rosella left yesterday.*

This doesn't happen with **avere** unless the perfect is preceded by an object pronoun.

Abbiamo comprato due dischi. Li   *We have bought two records. We*
abbiamo comprati.   *have bought them.*

1 This is an extract from Marianna's diary. Change the verbs in the present tense into the perfect.

E.g. Sono andata in vacanza ...

(**a** Sono) in vacanza con Paolo, Liana e Francesco. Questa mattina Liana e Paolo (**b** vanno) al mare mentre (*while*) Francesco ed io (**c** andiamo) a Portofino a piedi; (**d** impieghiamo) circa 50 minuti. (**e** Arriviamo) a Portofino e (**f** facciamo) il giro dei negozi, poi (**g** ci sediamo) in piazza, all'aperto, al tavolino di un bar e (**h** prendiamo) un cappuccino con un sandwich. (**i** Osserviamo) i turisti, gli yachts ormeggiati nel porticciolo. Alle undici (**j** decidiamo) di prendere un battello per Camogli dove (**k** arriviamo) all'ora di pranzo. (**l** Andiamo) al ristorante la Camogliese e (**m** mangiamo) trenette col pesto e pesce alla griglia; (**n** beviamo) vino bianco delle Cinque Terre e (**o** prendiamo) un espresso. Poi (**p** paghiamo) il conto e (**q** andiamo) a visitare alcuni amici che abitano in collina. (**r** Parliamo) di un po' di tutto: di chi (**s** nasce), di chi (**t** muore), di chi (**u** si sposa) e di chi (**v** divorzia). Dopo di che (*after which*) (**w** andiamo) in giardino e (**x** raccogliamo) fiori e pomodori. Alle sei (**y** facciamo) un po' di spesa nei negozi locali, quindi (**z** prendiamo) il treno per ritornare a Santa Margherita dove (**aa** troviamo) Paolo e Liana abbronzatissimi. (**bb** Ceniamo) (*dine*) e poi (**cc** andiamo) in una discoteca alla moda e (**dd** balliamo) fino alle tre del mattino.

2 Translate the following into Italian.

a I have been on holiday with Claire.
b We took the boat to San Fruttuoso.
c We have been walking all day.
d We did some shopping.
e We went to a disco.
f We drank a coffee and went out.
g They caught the train.
h They returned home last week.
i She arrived at Portofino.
j The thief (ladro) escaped.
k I ran home.
l Alessandro was born in 1978.
m They stayed only one day.
n I ran one mile.

3 Write an account of one day in your holiday to send to the Annual Foreign Language Students Award.

51 | UNIT | The use of the perfect

The Italian perfect tense can be used to translate the English perfect and simple past tenses.

A The Italian perfect tense (**passato prossimo**), as well as translating the English perfect (*I have spoken, I have gone*), is used – particularly in spoken Italian – to express an action started and ended in the past expressed in English by the simple past (*I spoke, I went*).

Ho capito. *I have understood/I understood.*
Avete fatto la spesa? *Have you done the shopping? Did you do the shopping?*
Anna è arrivata in tempo. *Anna has arrived on time. Anna arrived on time.*

B The perfect tense is also used to translate *I have been* …
ho camminato (*I have been walking*)
ho guardato (*I have been looking*)
ho vissuto (*I have been living*)

Ho camminato tutto il giorno.	*I have been walking all day.*
Ho vissuto a Roma per sei mesi.	*I have been living in Rome for six months.*

⚠ The object pronoun precedes the auxiliary.

Ho bevuto il caffè in fretta.	*I drank the coffee in a hurry.*
L'ho bevuto in fretta.	*I drank it in a hurry*

C With **dovere**, **potere** and **voler**e, the choice between the use of **essere** or **avere** depends on the following infinitive.

Sono dovuto partire (since **partire** takes **essere**) (*I had to leave*) but **ho dovuto camminare** (since **camminare** takes **avere**) (*I had to walk*).

1 Enter the correct auxiliary verb.

a Renzo _____ dovuto tornare indietro.

b Clara _____ voluta restare a Roma.

c Claudia non _____ potuto telefonare.

d Flavia non _____ potuta restare.

e I Simoni _____ voluto invitare Maria.

f Non _____ potuti andare al mare.

g (Noi) _____ guardato la partita di calcio alla TV.

2 Translate the following into Italian.

a I had to walk two miles.

b They had to leave early.

c Have you (*informal singular*) spoken to the (**al**) doctor?

d Did you go out yesterday evening?

e We watched the football match on TV.

f I saw him yesterday.

g They told her at once (**subito**).

h She rang him from (**da**) Naples (**Napoli**).

i They spoke to the (**al**) president.

j We have been living in India for three years.

3 Re-write Marianna's diary changing the verbs into the perfect tense.

E.g. Arrivo ieri sera ... → Sono arrivata ieri sera ...

(**a** Arrivo) ieri sera da Firenze dove (**b** passo) dieci giorni fantastici. Durante questo periodo (**c** ho) l'opportunità di visitare la città e i suoi dintorni. Alla Galleria dell'Accademia (**d** vedo), tra le altre cose, il David di Michelangelo. Il Palazzo degli Uffizi è la mia meta preferita (*my favourite destination*). Lì (**e** posso) ammirare moltissimi quadri: una collezione ineguagliabile (*matchless*). (**f** Ho) l'opportunità di esplorare vari posti intorno alla città come Fiesole da dove si gode (*one enjoys*) una splendida vista di Firenze. Inoltre (*also*) (**g** ho) l'opportunità di andare in altre città della Toscana come Lucca e Arezzo. A Lucca (**h** visito) la casa dove (**i** nasce) Puccini, il compositore de 'La Bohème'. Ad Arezzo, una bellissima città, (**j** posso) ammirare la chiesa di San Francesco, costruita nel XII secolo, con i suoi famosi affreschi di Piero della Francesca.

52 UNIT | The imperfect tense

The imperfect, also called the past descriptive, is the tense used to describe events which happened in the past.

The imperfect is a relatively easy tense to conjugate, with no irregular forms, except for **essere**.

	PARLARE	VENDERE	FINIRE	ESSERE
(io)	parlavo	vendevo	finivo	ero
(tu)	parlavi	vendevi	finivi	eri
(lui/lei/Lei)	parlava	vendeva	finiva	era
(noi)	parlavamo	vendevamo	finivamo	eravamo
(voi)	parlavate	vendevate	finivate	eravate
(loro/Loro)	parlavano	vendevano	finivano	erano

A The imperfect is used to describe:
- a situation in the past:
  Era povero.   *He was poor.*
- a repeated or habitual action carried out in the past (*I used to ...*):
  Prendevo il treno tutti i giorni.   *I took the train every day.*
  Leggevo molto.   *I used to read a lot.*
- an action going on while something else happened or was happening (*I was ...ing*); often the word **mentre** (*while*) introduces these sentences.
  Scrivevo quando il campanello   *I was writing when the door bell*
    ha suonato.   *rang.*
  Mentre uscivo è arrivata la posta.   *The mail arrived while I was*
         going out.

B The compound tense of this verb, called the pluperfect, is formed by the imperfect of **essere** or **avere** + the past participle.

ero partito/a *I had left*, etc.   avevo parlato *I had spoken*, etc.
eri partito/a   avevi parlato
era partito/a   aveva parlato
eravamo partiti/e   avevamo parlato
eravate partiti/e   avevate parlato
erano partiti/e   avevano parlato
    L'autobus era partito.   *The bus had left.*
    Avevo visto quel film.   *I had seen that film.*
    Gli avevano parlato.   *They had spoken to him.*

1 **Change the verbs in italics into the Italian imperfect form.**

a Quando *I was* un teenager *I wanted* una Ferrari rossa.

b *I used to play* le mie canzoni preferite al pianoforte ma non *was* molto brava.

c D'estate *I used to go* alla spiaggia ogni giorno.

d *I would swim* per ore ed ore.

e *I used to eat* continuamente.

f Mentre *I was studying, I listened* la radio, e *ate* torte.

g Prima di cena *I used to go out* con i miei amici.

h *We spoke* di tutto: teatro, musica, filosofia …

i Alle otto *I would return* a casa per la cena.

2 **Read the passage then change the present tense into the imperfect.**

I miei nonni (**a** abitano) in una casa in collina. D'estate, quando (**b** iniziano) le vacanze, (**c** vado) a vivere con loro per una settimana o due. La casa (**d** è) a soli venti minuti di distanza dal centro della cittadina ma lassù (*up there*) (**e** c'è) un'atmosfera molto diversa: in centro (**f** si può) uscire e subito (**g** ci sono) i negozi e molte persone a cui parlare o da salutare (*to greet*). (**h** Basta) scendere una scala per trovarsi immediatamente al mare che, dalla finestra di casa, (**i** si vede) proprio vicino. La casa dei nonni (**j** è) isolata, circondata (*surrounded*) da grandi muri come le poche ville nel vicinato. (**k** C'è) soltanto un negozio che (**l** vende) un po' di tutto. (**m** Si vede) pochissima gente nella stradina che (**n** conduce) (*leads*) in quella zona: le macchine non (**o** possono) entrare. (**p** C'è) molto silenzio specialmente dopo il pranzo quando i nonni (**q** vanno) a riposare. (**r** Si sentono) soltanto le cicale (*cicadas*). Io (**s** gioco) con il gattino oppure (*or*) (**t** osservo) le lucertole (*lizards*) che, sui muri di cinta, (**u** si scaldano) (*warm up*) al sole.

3 **Write at least ten sentences on what you used to do during the summer holidays when you were seven.**

4 **Change the imperfect into the pluperfect.**

E.g. Andavo al cinema. → Ero andata al cinema.

a Avevo il raffreddore.

b Il treno partiva alle otto.

c Mangiavo poco.

d Scrivevo una lettera.

e Dicevo tutto a mia madre.

f Studiavo molto.

g Imparavo molto.

h Parlavamo di letteratura.

53 | UNIT | Impersonal verb constructions

Impersonal verbs do not have a subject. They are verbs used only in the third person.

You can test to see if a verb is impersonal by trying to use other subject pronouns with it. **Piove** (*it's raining*) is impersonal because you can't say *I am raining*, *you are raining*, etc.

The following verbs belong in this group.

A **bisognare/essere necessario/occorrere** + infinitive (*to be necessary*)
  Bisogna/è necessario/occorre   *It's necessary to pay taxes.*
        pagare le tasse.

⚠ Do not confuse **bisogna** with **avere bisogno di ...** (*to have need of*):
  Ho bisogno di un nuovo paio di scarpe. *I need a new pair of shoes.*

B **volerci** + noun (*to be needed/to take*) (with expressions of time):
  Ci vuole un sacco di pazienza.   *A lot of patience is needed.*
  Quanto ci vuole?   *How long does it take?*

⚠ When **volerci** has a plural object, the third person plural must be used:

  Quante ore ci vogliono?   *How many hours does it take?*

C **bastare** + infinitive or noun (*to suffice/to be enough*)
  Per superare l'esame basta studiare. *It is enough to study to pass the exam.*
  Basta un litro.   *One litre is enough.*

⚠ When **bastare** is followed by a plural object, the third person plural must be used:
  Bastano duecento grammi di pasta. *Two hundred grams of pasta is sufficient.*

D **piacere** + noun or infinitive (*to like*). This verb is dealt with in the next unit.

E Verbs concerning the weather such as
  piovere (*to rain*); piovigginare (*to drizzle*); nevicare (*to snow*); grandinare (*to hail*); lampeggiare (*to be lightning*); tuonare (*to thunder*); rasserenarsi (*to clear up*)

  Oggi piove.   *It is raining today.*
  Si è rasserenato.   *It has cleared up.*

➤ See Unit 54 for the use of piacere.

1 Choose between *bisogna* and the right person of *avere bisogno di* and complete the following sentences.

a _____ pagare le tasse (*to pay taxes*).

b Io _____ un ombrello nuovo.

c _____ divertirsi quando si può.

d Marcello _____ di una vacanza.

e _____ lavorare per vivere.

f Noi _____ una macchina nuova.

g _____ cambiare (*to change*) treno a Verona.

h _____ prenotare (*to book*) i posti (*the seats*).

2 Choose between *ci vuole* or *ci vogliono* and complete the following sentences. Read the whole sentence each time.

E.g. **Per andare all'estero _____ il passaporto.** → **Per andare all'estero ci vuole il passaporto.**

Per andare all'estero …

a _____ la valigia.

b _____ molti soldi.

c _____ il biglietto.

Per guidare la macchina …

d _____ la patente.

e _____ molti litri di benzina.

f _____ il libretto di circolazione.

Per cucinare questo piatto …

g _____ 200 grammi di funghi.

h _____ una cipolla (*onion*).

i _____ due carote.

3 With the help of the words in brackets, answer these questions choosing between *basta* or *bastano*.

E.g. **Quanto sale (*salt*)? (un grammo)** → **Ne (*of it*) basta un grammo.**
Quante carote? (due) → **Ne (*of them*) bastano due.**
È difficile superare l'esame? → **No, basta studiare.**

a Quanto zucchero? (due cucchiaini)

b Quanto vino? (mezzo bicchiere)

c Quanti funghi? (cento grammi)

d È difficile imparare? (studiare)

e È difficile da trovare? (avere la carta stradale)

54 UNIT | The use of *piacere*

The Italian verb piacere (to like) behaves differently from its English equivalent. Only the third person singular and plural (piace and piacciono) are used.

A In Italian, **piacere** is used in the same way as *to be pleasing*; it is therefore constructed impersonally (only in the third persons singular and plural).

Mi piace la musica.	*I like music (Music is pleasing to me).*
Mi piacciono i fiori.	*I like flowers (Fowers are pleasing to me).*

In other words, what in English is the subject in Italian becomes an indirect object: indirect object (**mi**, **ti**, **gli**, **ci**, **vi**, etc.) + **piacere** + subject.

Piacere can be followed by an infinitive, in which case the third person singular is used.

Mi piace camminare.	*I like walking.*

A The negative **non** precedes the pronoun:

Non mi piace spettegolare.	*I don't like gossiping.*

A **Dispiacere** means *to be sorry* and is used in the same way as **piacere**.

Mi dispiace molto.	*I'm very sorry.*

B The stressed pronoun is used for emphasis.

A me piace questo libro.	*I like this book.*

It must also be used when two objects are involved.

A lui piace ma a me no.	*He likes it but I don't.*

If there is a noun or a name instead of **mi**, **ti**, **gli** etc. the following construction must be used.

A Paolo piace il polo.	*Paul likes polo.*
Agli italiani piace l'espresso.	*Italians like espresso coffee.*

C **Piacere** has an irregular present: **piaccio**, **piaci**, **piace**, **piacciamo**, **piacete**, **piacciono** (past participle: **piaciuto**). When conjugated normally, without the indirect object pronoun, it means *I am liked*, *you are liked*, etc.

D The perfect is formed with **essere**.

Vi è piaciuta la mostra?	*Did you like the exhibition?*

A *What would you like?* in a bar or a restaurant is translated by **Che cosa prende?** When shopping, *I would like* is translated by **vorrei**.

> *See indirect object pronouns in Unit 36 and the perfect tense in Unit 50.*

54 UNIT The use of *piacere* – Exercises

1 Fill in the blanks.

a Mi _____ molto la storia.

b Vi _____ sciare?

c Ti _____ la musica pop?

d I tuoi dischi non mi _____ .

e A Paolo _____ le tagliatelle.

f Agli inglesi _____ visitare i musei.

g A me _____ i fiordalisi, a Cristina _____ le rose.

h Non ci _____ quel profumo.

2 Match the two halves of the sentences.

a A Pavarotti …	**1** … piace cantare.
b Ai gatti piace …	**2** … la gita?
c Il vino dolce …	**3** … non mi piacciono per niente.
d Agli inglesi …	**4** … il pesce.
e Agli italiani piacciono …	**5** … gli spaghetti.
f Agli studenti …	**6** … non mi piace.
g Ti è piaciuta …	**7** … piace il tè.
h Le zanzare …	**8** … piacciono le vacanze.

3 Translate the following into Italian.

a Mario likes strawberries (**fragole**).

b Anna and Paolo like Italian cars.

c I like reading Italian magazines.

d She likes swimming.

e I would like two rolls.

f Do you like walking (*informal*)?

g Does she like spaghetti?

h Did you like the book (*informal*)?

i Did Paolo and Lucia like the film?

j What will you have (*formal*)?

4 What do Cristina and Marco like or dislike?

E.g. **A Cristina non piace il calcio, a Marco piace la televisione.**

55 UNIT The future tense

	PARLARE (to speak)	LEGGERE (to read)	PARTIRE (to leave)	ESSERE (to be)	AVERE (to have)
(io)	parlerò	leggerò	partirò	sarò	avrò
(tu)	parlerai	leggerai	partirai	sarai	avrai
(lui/lei/Lei)	parlerà	leggerà	partirà	sarà	avrà
(noi)	parleremo	leggeremo	partiremo	saremo	avremo
(voi)	parlerete	leggerete	partirete	sarete	avrete
(loro/Loro)	parleranno	leggeranno	partiranno	saranno	avranno

A The future is used to express:
- an action still to happen: Presto gli scriverò. *I will write to him soon.*
- a probability or a hypothesis: Paolo sarà fuori. *Paul must be out.*
  Avrà perso il treno. *He may have missed the train.*

B The present tense is often used, particularly in the spoken language, to indicate an action that is going to happen in the future, when English would use the continuous form. Domani gli parlo. *Tomorrow I am going to speak to him.*

⚠ When *to be going to* expresses intention, it can be translated by **intendere** or **avere intenzione di** + infinitive.

Ho intenzione di/Intendo partire domani. *I am going to leave tomorrow.*
To indicate an action about to happen, Italian uses **stare per**.
Sto per uscire. *I am going out (I am about to go out).*

Avere, andare, venire, dovere, potere, volere, vedere and **rimanere** have a slightly shortened future form: **avrò…**; **andrò…**; **verrò…**; **dovrò…**; **potrò…**; **vorrò…**; **vedrò…**; **rimarrò…**

C The future perfect is formed using the future of **essere** or **avere** + past participle. Avrò finito questo libro per settembre. *I will have finished this book by September.*

⚠ Note these constructions:
Se/Quando andrò a Roma ti telefone. *If/When I go to Rome, I will ring you.*
Che cosa prendi? Prendo … *What will you have? I will have …*

1 Change these sentences into the future tense. Add *domani* or *tra poco* (in a short time) to either the beginning or the end of your answer.

E.g. Oggi esco. → Domani uscirò.
Gli parlo. → Gli parlerò domani.

a Leggo il libro.
b Il treno parte.
c L'autobus arriva.
d Studio la lezione.
e Vado a piedi.
f Rimango a casa.
g Le telefono.
h La vedo.

2 Answer these questions by transforming the English into Italian.

a Dov'è il gatto?	*It must be in the garden.*
b Quanto costerà il suo computer?	*It must cost at least (**almeno**) £900.*
c Quanti anni avrà Vera?	*She must be (**Ne**) twenty-three.*
d Antonio non è arrivato.	*He must have missed the train.*
e Hai visto i miei occhiali?	*No. They may be in the car.*

3 Below is a list of things you want to do when you are in the Seychelles. Change the verb from the present to the future tense.

Quando andrò alle Seychelles …

a nuoto almeno due ore al giorno.
b mi abbronzo moltissimo.
c leggo molti libri sulla spiaggia.
d faccio nuove conoscenze.
e prendo a nolo una barca.
f scrivo ai miei amici.
g non guardo le notizie alla TV.
h non leggo i giornali.

4 Complete the future perfect sentences by translating the words in italics.

a Presto *I will have finished* di imparare d'italiano.
b Entro domani Nina *will have left*.
c Quando tu ritornerai Paolo *will have cooked* una cena con i fiocchi.
d Quando *they will have arrived* vorranno riposare.

56 UNIT The conditional tense

> The conditional is used to imply a condition or a possibility. It is also used for polite requests.

	PARLARE (to speak)	SCRIVERE (to write)	FINIRE (to finish/end)
(io)	parl**erei**	scriv**erei**	fin**irei**
(tu)	parl**eresti**	scriv**eresti**	fin**iresti**
(lui/lei/Lei)	parl**erebbe**	scriv**erebbe**	fin**irebbe**
(noi)	parl**eremmo**	scriv**eremmo**	fin**iremmo**
(voi)	parl**ereste**	scriv**ereste**	fin**ireste**
(loro/Loro)	parl**erebbero**	scriv**erebbero**	fin**irebbero**

A The following verbs have a slightly shortened stem/ending combination in the conditional. The first person singular is given to indicate the pattern: **avere → avrei; essere → sarei; andare → andrei; venire → verrei; dovere → dovrei; potere → potrei; volere → vorrei; vedere → vedrei; rimanere → rimarrei**

Dovresti studiare di più.   *You should study more.*

B The conditional present is used in the same way as in English to express a wish, request, opinion or intention.

Vorrei andare in vacanza.   *I'd like to go on holiday.*
Io direi di sì.   *I would agree.*
Aldo verrebbe ma non può.   *Aldo would come, but he can't.*

C As in English, the conditional present is often linked with the conjunction **se** (*if*), which in Italian requires the imperfect subjunctive.

Andrei in vacanza se potessi.   *I would go on holiday if I could.*

D *Ought to* is translated by **dovrei, dovresti**, etc. or **bisognerebbe**

Dovresti essere contento.   *You ought to be glad/happy.*
Bisognerebbe dirglielo.   *One ought to tell him.*

E The difference between **mi piacerebbe** and **vorrei** is that the former is a mere wish: **Mi piacerebbe imparare il cinese** (*I'd like/love to learn Chinese*), whereas the latter is more positive and must be used when you are asking for directions, information or something in a shop, office, etc.

➤ *See imperfect subjunctive in Unit 61.*

1 **Answer the questions using the correct person of the verb.**

E.g. **Perché non parli? (ho mal di gola). → Parlerei ma ho mal di gola.**

a Perché non studi? (sono stanca)

b Perché non scrivete? (non abbiamo tempo)

c Perché non finite? (è troppo tardi)

d Perché non partono? (non hanno i soldi)

e Perché non guardano la TV? (hanno altro da fare)

f Che fa tuo fratello, viene? (non ha tempo)

g Che fanno i tuoi genitori, partono? (non vogliono lasciarmi sola)

h Che fa tuo zio, non lavora? (non trova un posto)

i Che fanno i tuoi figli, non escono? (piove)

j Che fa Luca, non scrive? (è malato)

k Che fanno i tuoi nipoti, non telefonano? (non hanno abbastanza soldi)

2 **Respond to these sentences using *bisognerebbe* + infinitive, then read them aloud.**

E.g. **Ci vogliono molti soldi. → Sì, bisognerebbe avere molti soldi.**
Bisogna partire. → Sì, bisognerebbe partire.

a Ci vuole molta pazienza.

b Bisogna riposare.

3 **Answer these questions.**

E.g. **Hai fatto il compito? (non ho capito la spiegazione) → L'avrei fatto ma non ho capito la spiegazione.**

a Hai comprato il quadro? (non avevo i soldi)

b Hai parlato a Giorgio? (non l'ho visto)

4 **Translate the following into Italian.**

a I'd like a beer and a roll.

b I'd love to go on holiday.

c You (*inform. sing.*) ought to tell him.

d I couldn't do it.

e He wouldn't do it.

This tense is formed from the present conditional of essere or avere plus the past participle of the verb.

	ESSERE	AVERE
(io)	sarei stato/a	avrei avuto
(tu)	saresti stato/a	avresti avuto
(lui/lei/Lei)	sarebbe stato/a	avrebbe avuto
(noi)	saremmo stati/e	avremmo avuto
(voi)	sareste stati/e	avreste avuto
(loro/Loro)	sarebbero stati/e	avrebbero avuto

	PARLARE	VENDERE	PARTIRE
(io)	avrei parlato	avrei venduto	sarei partito/a
(tu)	avresti parlato	avresti venduto	saresti partito/a
(lui/lei/Lei)	avrebbe parlato	avrebbe venduto	sarebbe partito/a
(noi)	avremmo parlato	avremmo venduto	saremmo partiti/e
(voi)	avreste parlato	avreste venduto	sareste partiti/e
(loro/Loro)	avrebbero parlato	avrebbero venduto	sarebbero partiti/e

The conditional perfect is used:

- to express an intention, a possibility or a request made in the past:
  Avrei voluto fare domanda.   *I would have liked to apply.*

- with verbs like *to imagine, to feel, to believe, to think,* etc. when the main clause is in the past and the dependent clause refers to a later time (still in the past).
  Credevo che sarebbe venuto.   *I believed/thought that he would come.*

- to express uncertainty of some news not confirmed as a fact that happened in the past:
  La signora X avrebbe assassinato   *Apparently Mrs X killed the porter.*
  il portiere.

⚠ The conditional perfect is often linked with an *if* clause which requires the pluperfect subjunctive:

L'avrei comprato se avessi avuto   *I'd have bought it if I had had*
i soldi.   *the money.*

I/you etc. had better … is translated: **farei/faresti meglio a** + infinitive.
I'd rather is translated by **preferirei**.

➤ *See subjunctive in Unit 61.*

The conditional: perfect tense – *Exercises*

1 Match the two halves of the sentences.

a Sarei andata al Cairo ma …   1 … di essere trattato in tale maniera.

b L'avrei comprato ma …   2 … è andato in Venezuela.

c Sarei andato a piedi ma …   3 … non volevo lasciarlo solo.

d Sarei uscita ma …   4 … non c'erano posti sull'aereo.

e Il maggiordomo (*butler*) …   5 … avrebbe ucciso (*killed*) la contessa.

f Avrei voluto vederlo ma …   6 … pioveva a dirotto (*pouring with rain*).

g Non avrei mai immaginato …   7 … non era in buone condizioni.

2 Change the two tenses in each sentence into the past. (See the subjunctive in Unit 61.)

E.g. **Canterei ma ho mal di gola. → Avrei cantato se non avessi avuto mal di gola.**

Studierebbe ma è troppo stanco. → Avrebbe studiato se non fosse stato troppo stanco.

a Finirei ma è troppo tardi.

b Verrebbe ma non ne ha il tempo.

c Scriveremmo ma siamo malati.

d Guarderemmo la TV ma abbiamo altro da fare.

e Telefonerebbero ma non hanno abbastanza soldi.

3 Complete the answers to these questions.

E.g. **Perché non l'hai letto? → L'avrei letto ma non l'avevo con me.**

a Perché non l'hai mangiato?   _____ era finito.

b Perché non gli hai telefonato?   _____ non avevo monete.

c Perché non l'hai voluto?   _____ costava troppo.

4 Translate the following into Italian.

a I would have liked a tea, but there was only coffee.

b They would have sold the house but they had no offers (**offerte**).

c We would have left, but the plane was booked up.

d She should have arrived yesterday.

e You had better come.

f I would rather not see her.

58 UNIT Imperatives

The imperative mood (modo imperativo) expresses a wish or a command that something be done.

	PARLARE	VENDERE	DORMIRE	ESSERE	AVERE
(tu)	parla	vendi	dormi	sii	abbi
(lui/lei/Lei)	parli	venda	dorma	sia	abbia
(noi)	parliamo	vendiamo	dormiamo	siamo	abbiamo
(voi)	parlate	vendete	dormite	siate	abbiate
(loro/Loro)	parlino	vendano	dormano	siano	abbiano

A This tense does not have the first person singular (*I*).

The second and third persons singular of **-are** verbs have their own form.

Parla!	*Speak!*
Parli più lentamente, signora.	*Speak more slowly, madam.*
Lui parli, noi lo ascoeteremo.	*Let him speak, we'll listen.*

All the other persons are borrowed from the present indicative or, in the case of the formal *you* (third person singular and plural), from the present subjunctive. The use of the subjunctive makes the formal *you* more of an exhortation rather than a command, but particularly with this tense, much depends on the tone of one's voice or on the context of what is being said:

Vada avanti dritto.	*Go straight on.*
Abbia pazienza!	*Bear with me!/Please do not bother me.*

B The negative for the second person plural (**tu**) uses the infinitive preceded by **non**.

Non vendere la casa, Paolo!	*Do not sell the house, Paul!*

All the other forms take **non** before the affirmative form.

Non venda la casa, signora.	*Do not sell the house, madam.*
Non uscite ragazzi!	*Do not go out, boys!*

C The object pronoun is attached to the end of the infinitive except for the formal *you* when it precedes the imperative.

Comprala. *Buy it.* Non comprarla. *Do not buy it.*
Parlategli. *Speak to him.* Non parlatele. *Do not speak to her.*
Gli parli, signora. *Speak to him, madam.* Glielo scriva. *Write (it) to him.*
Andiamoci. *Let's go there.* Non andiamoci. *Let's not go there.*

➤ *See Unit 59 for irregular imperatives and Units 60–63 for subjunctive.*

1 Replace the names or nouns with the appropriate indirect object pronoun.

E.g. Manda il pacco a Marianna. → Mandale il pacco.

Telefona la notizia a Paolo. → Telefonagli la notizia.

a Scrivi la lettera a Marcello.

b Racconta tutto a Goffredo.

c Venda la macchina a Susanna.

d Compri un nuovo computer a Sandro.

e Consigli (*advise*) a Renzo di stare a casa.

f Parlate del fatto al presidente.

g Mandate i documenti al sindaco (*mayor*).

h Regala la collana ad Anna.

2 Using the sentences you have written above, change the direct object pronoun to the appropriate pronoun *lo, la, li, le, ci* or *ne*.

E.g. Mandaglielo. Telefonagliela.

3 Write down the negative form of the sentences in exercise 1.

E.g. Non mandare il pacco a Marianna.

Non telefonare la notizia a Paolo.

4 Write the the negative form of exercise 2.

E.g. Non mandarglielo. Non telefonargliela.

5 Translate into Italian in the second person singular (*tu*).

E.g. Speak to him! → Parlagli!

a Be polite (**gentile**)!   e Have faith (**fede**)!

b Buy!   f Sell!

c Sleep!   g Be (**avere**) patient!

d Walk!   h Eat!

6 Re-write the exercise above in the third person singular (*Lei*).

E.g. Gli parli!

7 Re-write the exercise in the first person plural (*noi*).

E.g. Parliamogli!

8 Re-write it in the second person plural (*voi*).

E.g. Parlategli!

9 Now re-write it in the third person plural (*Loro*).

E.g. Gli parlino!

Irregular imperatives

	ANDARE	STARE	DARE	FARE	DIRE
(tu)	va'	sta'	da'	fa'	di'
(lui/lei/Lei)	vada	stia	dia	faccia	dica
(noi)	andiamo	stiamo	diamo	facciamo	diciamo
(voi)	andate	state	date	fate	dite
(loro/Loro)	vadano	stiano	diano	facciano	dicano

⚠ va' = vai, sta' = stai, da' = dai, fa' = fai.

A When the second person singular is followed by a pronoun, the first consonant of the pronoun is doubled except for the **-g** in **gli**.

Dammi quel libro, per favore.	*Give me that book, please.*
Dammelo, per favore.	*Give it to me, please.*
Fammi un favore.	*Do me a favour.*
Facci un caffè.	*Make us a coffee.*
Dagli una mano.	*Give him a hand.*

B *Go/come and see, go/come and take/buy*, etc. are translated by the verb of motion in the imperative form + **a** (*to*) + infinitive.

Vieni a prendere un caffè.	*Come and have a cup of coffee.*
Vai a comprare il dolce.	*Go and buy the cake.*

C The future imperative is formed by the future of the indicative mood as in English.

Farai come dico io!	*You will do as I say!*
Andrai domani!	*You will go tomorrow!*

1 Translate into Italian using the second person singular.

E.g. **Stai attento/a!**

a Give her the book!

b Go away (**andare via**)!

c Tell the truth (**verità**)!

d Pay attention (**fare attenzione**)!

e Be quick (**fare presto**)!

2 Change the Italian version of the sentences above into the third person singular (*Lei*).

E.g. **Stia attento/a.**

3 Match the two columns bearing in mind that you use the *tu* form with Marianna and Paul and the *Lei* form with her parents.

E.g. **Ho detto a Marianna: 'Vieni domani'.**

a Ho detto a Marianna: 1 'Vada tranquillo, io sto attenta a tutto.'

b Ho detto a Paul: 2 'Sta' attento!'

c Ho detto al signor Simoni: 3 'Prestami (*lend me*) la tua borsa.'

d Ho detto alla signora Simoni: 4 'Mi faccia un favore.'

4 Below is a list of orders, polite requests or suggestions; to whom would you say them?

a Vada via o chiamo la polizia!   1 *someone you are interviewing*

b Mi dia il menù, per favore!   2 *someone bothering you*

c Non mi faccia perdere tempo!   3 *someone threatening you*

d Sta' attento!   4 *the barman (in Italy)*

e Mi faccia un caffè.   5 *your partner making coffee*

f Mi dica una cosa!   6 *your daughter going out*

g Dimmi tutto!   7 *someone in danger*

h Fa' un caffè anche per me.   8 *your child crossing the road*

i Vai in farmacia con questa ricetta. 9 *waiter in restaurant*

j Stia attento!   10 *your friend coming from a very exciting meeting.*

5 Write appropriate forms of the imperative for the following situations.

a A policeman asks a motorist to show him (**fare vedere**) her documents.

b A client asks the waiter to give her a clean glass.

c Alessandro tells his children not to make noise.

d A man asks a group of people to do him a favour.

60 UNIT | The subjunctive mood

Rarely used in English, this mood is used more in Italian, although at times it may be expressed by the future or the present indicative as in English.

A The subjunctive does not express a fact but a probability, a possibility, an uncertainty, a desire, a curse or an exhortation which often depends on an action expressed in the main clause: *We insist* (main clause) *that she go* (dependent clause). This verb often depends on the conjunction **che** (*that*). Also, since the first three persons singular have the same form, the subject pronoun is often used (to avoid confusion). This mood has two simple tenses (present and imperfect) and two compound tenses (perfect and pluperfect).

B The present subjunctive

	PARLARE	VENDERE	PARTIRE	FINIRE	ESSERE	AVERE
che io	parli	venda	parta	finisca	sia	abbia
che tu	parli	venda	parta	finisca	sia	abbia
che lui/lei/Lei	parli	venda	parta	finisca	sia	abbia
che noi	parliamo	vendiamo	partiamo	finiamo	siamo	abbiamo
che voi	parliate	vendiate	partiate	finiate	siate	abbiate
che loro/Loro	parlino	vendano	partano	finiscano	siano	abbiano

Spero che Renza telefoni presto.   *I hope (that) Renza will ring soon.*
Digli che venga.   *Tell him to come.*

C The subjunctive is used with conjunctions like **a meno che** (*unless*); **affinché** (*so that*); **benché/sebbene/quantunque** (*although*); **malgrado/ nonostante** (*in spite of*); **a patto che/purché/a condizione che** (*as long as*); **prima che** (*before*); **senza che** (*without*); **nel caso che** (*in case of*); **supposto che** (*supposing*).

Benché abbia l'influenza Marco   *Marco wants to go out although* vuole uscire.   *he has the flu.*

D When the subject in the main clause expressing hope, fear, desire, command, etc. is the same as the dependent clause, the construction is verb + **di** + infinitive.

Suppongo di avere ragione.   *I suppose I am right.*

E The perfect subjunctive is formed by the present subjunctive of **avere** or **essere** + the past participle of the verb.

Immagino che sia partito.   *I imagine he has left.*
Immagino che lui abbia perso il treno. *I imagine (that) he has missed the train.*

➤ See Unit 61 for more on the subjunctive, Units 85 and 86 for conjunctions and Unit 49 for past participles.

1 Change the verb in bold into the right form of the present subjunctive.

a Spero che lui mi **vendere** i biglietti per la partita di calcio.

b Suppongo che lei **avere** ragione.

c Penso che loro **partire** la settimana prossima.

d Lo aiutano sebbene non lo **meritare**.

e Spera che i Rossi gli **vendere** la villa.

f Voglio uscire prima che **piovere**.

g Nonostante io **mangiare** moltissimo non ingrasso.

h Credo che la festa **avere** luogo domani.

2 Change the verb in bold into the correct form of the perfect subjunctive.

E.g. **Credo che lui partire ieri.** → **Credo che sia partito ieri.**

a Spero che loro **comprare** un'auto nuova.

b Lo aiutano sebbene non lo **meritare**.

c Nonostante io **mangiare** moltissimo non sono ingrassata.

d Credo che la festa **avere** luogo ieri.

e Immagino che lei **vendere** le azioni (*shares*).

3 Bearing in mind rule D on the opposite page, correct the wrong sentences below.

a Credo che io abbia l'influenza.

b Immagino che lui abbia vinto al lotto.

c Malgrado io provi (*try*) non riesco a crederci (*I cannot believe it*).

d Erica crede che lei sia intelligentissima.

e Patrizio immagina che lui sia bellissimo.

f Lo aiuto a condizione che smetta di fumare.

4 Translate the following into Italian.

a I believe that he is honest.

b I suppose that I have a cold.

c Although I spoke to her, she wouldn't listen.

d I think that he has already (**già**) dined (**cenato**).

e I demand (**Esigo**) that you finish now.

f In the event (**caso**) that you leave for London, take an umbrella with you.

61 UNIT The imperfect subjunctive

The initial vowel of the three regular verb endings is the same as the initial vowel of the three infinitives: -are/-assi, -ere/-essi, -ire/-issi.

	PARLARE	VENDERE	PARTIRE	ESSERE	AVERE
che io	parlassi	vendessi	partissi	fossi	avessi
che tu	parlassi	vendessi	partissi	fossi	avessi
che lui/lei/Lei	parlasse	vendesse	partisse	fosse	avesse
che noi	parlassimo	vendessimo	partissimo	fossimo	avessimo
che voi	parlaste	vendeste	partiste	foste	aveste
che loro/Loro	parlassero	vendessero	partissero	fossero	avessero

A The pluperfect subjunctive is formed by the imperfect subjunctive of **essere** or **avere** + the past participle of the verb:

Mario credeva che io fossi partita. *Mario thought that I had left.*
Era importante che Mario fosse informato. *It was important that Mario should be informed.*

B If the verb in the main clause is in the past or in the conditional, it is followed by the imperfect subjunctive.

Pensavo che partisse. *I thought that he was leaving.*
Vorrei che tu fossi qui *I wish you were here.*
Temevo che non venisse. *I feared he wouldn't come.*
Ritornerebbe se avesse i soldi. *He/She would return if he/she had the money.*

C As you can see in the examples above, the two actions happen at the same time. When the action of the subordinate clause occurs *before* that of the main clause e.g. *I thought* (main clause) *he had left* (subordinate clause), it is rendered by the pluperfect subjunctive.

Pensavo che fosse partito. *I thought that he had left.*
Immaginavo che lo avessero trovato. *I imagined that they had found it.*

D It may happen that a past action with no connection at all with the present has a present tense in the main clause.

Immagino che gli Etruschi fossero un popolo felice. *I imagine that the Etruscans were a happy people.*

⚠ *I wish …!* can also be translated by **Magari fossi …!**

Magari fossi ricco/-a! *I wish I were rich!*

122

1 Change the verb in bold to the correct form of the imperfect subjunctive.

a Speravo che lui mi **vendere** i biglietti per la partita di calcio.

b Supponevo che lei **avere** ragione.

c Pensavo che loro **partire** la settimana prossima.

d Lo aiutavano sebbene non lo **meritare**.

e Sperava che i Rossi gli **vendere** la villa.

f Volevo uscire prima che **piovere**.

g Nonostante io **mangiare** moltissimo non ingrassavo.

h Credevo che la festa **avere** luogo domani.

2 Change the verb in bold to the correct form of the pluperfect subjunctive. Remember that the main clause tells about something that happened in the past and the dependent clause (subjunctive) about something that happened before that.

E.g. Speravo che loro comprare una macchina nuova. → Speravo che loro avessero comprato una macchina nuova.

a Non ero ingrassata nonostante io **mangiare** moltissimo.

b Immaginavo che loro **vendere** le azioni.

c Credevo che la festa **avere** luogo ieri.

d Lo avevano aiutato sebbene non lo **meritare**.

e Avevano supposto che lui **partire**.

3 Match the two halves of the sentences.

a Se fossi in te …   1 se li avessi.

b Se Marcello avesse mangiato di più …   2 fossi partito in treno.

c Non avrei mai immaginato …   3 che fossero così scorretti.

d Avrei voluto …   4 fosse il suo compleanno.

e Credevo che domani …   5 adesso sarebbe più grasso.

f Pensavo che il professore …   6 cambierei casa.

g Supponevo che tu …   7 che loro venissero.

h Ti darei volentieri i libri …   8 mi avrebbe aiutato a scrivere. una lettera all'Ambasciatore.

4 Translate the following into Italian.

a What would you do if you were (**in**) me?

b If I were (**in**) you, I would buy a piano.

c I thought that the neighbours (**vicini**) were in (**a casa**).

d The students thought that the professor would help them.

62 UNIT The use of the subjunctive

The subjunctive is mainly used:

A when the verb in the main clause is in the conditional mood (in which case the imperfect or the pluperfect subjunctive is used).

Andrei in vacanza se ne avessi il tempo.	*I would go on holiday if I had the time.*
Sarei andato/a in vacanza se ne avessi avuto il tempo.	*I would have gone on holiday if I had had the time.*

B with verbs or expressions conveying personal opinion or something not certain, such as: **credere, immaginare, parere/sembrare** (*to seem*), **pensare, ritenere** (*to think/to deem*), **supporre; può darsi/può essere** (*may be*), **si dice** (*it is said*), **è possibile, è impossibile, è probabile, è improbabile.**

Si dice che sia un buon professore.	*He is said to be a good teacher.*
Si diceva che fosse un buon professore.	*It was said that he was a good teacher.*

⚠ With verbs expressing personal opinion, the subjunctive is not necessary if one is well convinced of one's own opinion.

Penso che Dio esiste. *I think God exists.*

C with verbs or expressions of hope, will or fear such as: **sperare, volere, desiderare, preferire, augurarsi, avere paura/temere** (*to fear*), **insistere**.

Mi auguro che tu abbia ragione. *I hope that you are right.*

D with verbs expressing feeling such as: **far piacere, dispiacere, essere lieto/a, essere spiacente/rincrescere** (*to be sorry*).

Sono lieto che lui abbia accettato il posto.	*I am glad that he has accepted the job.*

E with verbs expressing judgment such as: **è necessario, bisogna, conviene, è bene, è male, è pericoloso, è giusto, è ingiusto, è stupido, è incredibile, è un peccato** (*it's a shame*), **è importante, è strano** (*it's strange*).

È strano che si comporti così. *It's strange that he should behave so.*

F with conjunctions or expressions like: **benché/sebbene/quantunque** (*although*), **malgrado/nonostante** (*in spite of*), **a patto che/a condizione che/purché** (*as long as*), **a meno che** (*unless*), **prima che, nel caso che, supposto che**.

Benché abbia ragione tace. *Although she is right, she keeps silent.*

1 Translate the following into Italian.

⚠️ *Should* in this context is not a conditional verb, but stands for the subjunctive. The bureaucratic-sounding phrase *I demand that he reply at once* becomes in ordinary English speech *I demand that he should reply at once.*

a They insisted that we should leave at once (**subito**).

b I fear that the child has caught a cold.

c I feared that the child had caught a cold.

d She is anxious (**Ci tiene molto**) that he should finish the job.

e It is necessary that you should catch the next train.

f It is right that you should leave.

g It is strange that they should behave like that.

h Although they were right, they didn't complain.

2 Match the two halves of the sentences.

a È giusto che …	**1** … finisca i compiti prima di uscire.
b Mi fa piacere che voi …	**2** … prima che sia troppo tardi.
c Cogli (*take*) l'opportunità …	**3** … tu chieda scusa.
d È meglio che Mario …	**4** … superino (*pass*) l'esame.
e È ingiusto …	**5** … abbiate accettato l'invito.
f È necessario che …	**6** … che gli studenti siano promossi se non hanno studiato.

3 Decide which verb or expression below can take either: *che abbia ragione* or *che avesse ragione* and which can only take *che avesse ragione.*

> **E.g.** Penso (*now*) che abbia ragione (*now*).
> Penso (*now*) che avesse ragione (*then*).

a Mi sembra …

b È facile …

c È improbabile …

d È impossibile …

e Ritengo …

f Pensavo …

g Sembrava …

h È possibile …

i Immagino …

j Credevo …

63 UNIT Irregular subjunctives

	STARE (to stay)		DARE (to give)		FARE (to make/do)	
	present	imperfect	present	imperfect	present	imperfect
che io	stia	stessi	dia	dessi	faccia	facessi
che tu	stia	stessi	dia	dessi	faccia	facessi
che lui/lei/Lei	stia	stesse	dia	desse	faccia	facesse
che noi	stiamo	stessimo	diamo	dessimo	facciamo	facessimo
che voi	stiate	steste	diate	deste	facciate	faceste
che loro/Loro	stiano	stessero	diano	dessero	facciano	facessero

	ANDARE (to go)		DOVERE (to have to)		POTERE (can/may)	
	present	imperfect	present	imperfect	present	imperfect
che io	vada	andassi	debba	dovessi	possa	potessi
che tu	vada	andassi	debba	dovessi	possa	potessi
che lui/lei/Lei	vada	andasse	debba	dovesse	possa	potesse
che noi	andiamo	andassimo	dobbiamo	dovessimo	possiamo	potessimo
che voi	andiate	andaste	dobbiate	doveste	possiate	poteste
che loro/Loro	vadano	andassero	debbano	dovessero	possano	potessero

	VOLERE (to want)		VENIRE (to come)		DIRE (to say)	
	present	imperfect	present	imperfect	present	imperfect
che io	voglia	volessi	venga	venissi	dica	dicessi
che tu	voglia	volessi	venga	venissi	dica	dicessi
che lui/lei/Lei	voglia	volesse	venga	venisse	dica	dicesse
che noi	vogliamo	volessimo	veniamo	venissimo	diciamo	dicessimo
che voi	vogliate	voleste	veniate	veniste	diciate	diceste
che loro/Loro	vogliano	volessimo	vengano	venissero	dicano	dicessero

	TOGLIERE (to remove)		TENERE (to keep/hold)		USCIRE (to go out)	
	present	imperfect	present	imperfect	present	imperfect
che io	tolga	togliessi	tenga	tenessi	esca	uscissi
che tu	tolga	togliessi	tenga	tenessi	esca	uscissi
che lui/lei/Lei	tolga	togliesse	tenga	tenesse	esca	uscisse
che noi	togliamo	togliessimo	teniamo	tenessimo	usciamo	uscissimo
che voi	togliate	toglieste	teniate	teneste	usciate	usciste
che loro/Loro	tolgano	togliessero	tengano	tenessero	escano	uscissero

1 **Which verbs are in the present subjunctive and which in the imperfect subjunctive?**

a Voglio che tu stia attento.

b Vorrei che voi steste più attenti.

c Credo che stiano sempre a casa.

d Credevo che stessero sempre a casa.

e Vorrei che deste una mano a Pietro.

f Spero che facciano presto.

g E se facessimo un bella gita …?

h Mario non vuole che sua moglie vada al mare.

i Vorrebbe che andasse in montagna.

j Credo che Pina debba lavorare giorno e notte per mantenere la famiglia.

k Se dovessi scegliere tra i due sceglierei il primo.

l Spero che tu possa guarire presto.

m Se fossi in te non lo farei.

2 **Put the verb in brackets into the Italian subjunctive.**

a Vorrei che i miei figli (*stayed*) a casa di più.

b Sarei molto contenta se ti (*removed*) le scarpe quando entri in casa.

c Credo che Marietta (*goes out*) con Filippo.

d Credevo che Marietta (*went out*) con Filippo.

e Mi crederesti se ti (*I told*) che ho dimenticato il passaporto a casa?

f Sarebbe meglio se il gatto (*was kept*) in casa la notte.

3 **Translate the following into Italian.**

a I want you to go out more.

b I think they want to move (**cambiare casa**).

c I thought he would come.

d I think he keeps it in the desk.

e If they had to choose, they would go to France.

f She wanted him to give her a hand.

g I hope you go tomorrow (**domani**).

h I hope he goes.

64 UNIT | The past definite tense

Also called past historic, this tense is mainly used instead of the perfect in formal writing such as documents, newspapers and books.

A The Italian past definite translates verb forms like *I went*, *I did*, *I spoke* which express actions started and ended in the past. More recently, the perfect (*I have been*, *I have done*, *I have spoken*) has been adopted in Italian to convey the meaning of both tenses, at least in the spoken language and in informal writing. Nevertheless you should at least be aware of the existence of the past definite in order to be able to recognize it when you read.

	PARLARE	VENDERE	PARTIRE	FINIRE
(io)	parlai	vendei/vendetti	partii	finii
(tu)	parlasti	vendesti	partisti	finisti
(lui/lei/Lei)	parlò	vendè/vendette	partì	finì
(noi)	parlammo	vendemmo	partimmo	finimmo
(voi)	parlaste	vendeste	partiste	finiste
(loro/Loro)	parlarono	venderono/vendettero	partirono	finirono

-Ere verbs have an alternative first and third person singular and third person plural. Both forms are correct, though the first form is preferable when the verb stem ends in **-t**: **potei/potè/poterono** rather than **potetti/potette/potettero**.

B A large number of verbs have an irregular past definite. Here are few of the most common ones.

essere: fui, fosti, fu, fummo, foste, furono
avere: ebbi, avesti, ebbe, avemmo, aveste, ebbero
dire: dissi, dicesti, disse, dicemmo, diceste, dissero
dare: diedi/detti, desti, diede/dette, demmo, deste, diedero/dettero
stare: stetti, stesti, stette, stemmo, steste, stettero
fare: feci, facesti, fece, facemmo, faceste, fecero
venire: venni, venisti, venne, venimmo, veniste, vennero
bere: bevvi, bevesti, bevve, bevemmo, beveste, bevvero
potere: potei, potesti, potè, potemmo, poteste, poterono
volere: volli, volesti, volle, volemmo, voleste, vollero
dovere: dovetti, dovesti, dovette, dovemmo, doveste, dovettero
nascere: nacqui, nascesti, nacque, nascemmo, nasceste, nacquero

⚠ The use of **essere** and **avere** is mainly confined to the compound tense (past anterior): Dopo che ebbe finito partì. *After he had finished, he went.* The past definite of **essere** is also used to form the passive.

Il palazzo fu costruito nel 1800.   *The building was built in 1800.*

1 **Answer the questions with the help of the information in brackets.**

E.g. Chi fu Dante? (Il padre della lingua italiana). → **Dante fu il padre della lingua italiana.**

a Dove e quando nacque Garibaldi? (a Nizza nel 1807)

b Quando dovette fuggire in Sud America? (dopo che ebbe partecipato ad un attentato (*attack*) per conquistare Genova)

c Che cosa fece quando ritornò? (partecipò alla lotta per l'Unità d'Italia)

d Dopo l'Unità d'Italia fu premiato? (non volle nessun riconoscimento)

e Che cosa fece? (si ritirò a Caprera dove visse (*lived*) fino alla morte)

f Quando morì? (nel 1882)

2 **Add the missing verbs to the passage below.**

Garibaldi, patriota italiano, **a** _____ a Nizza nel 1807. Si unì al movimento 'Giovane Italia' e **b** _____ condannato a morte per aver partecipato ad un attentato per conquistare Genova. Fuggì in Sud America e **c** _____ in Italia nel 1849 ma dovette fuggire un'altra volta. Dopo avere lavorato a New York, **d** _____ in Italia nel 1854. Nel 1859 tornò a combattere per la libertà d'Italia e nel 1860 si **e** _____ all'isola di Caprera dove **f** _____ fino alla morte.

3 **Change the infinitives into the past definite.**

Quando Lusardi (**a** uscire) di casa (**b** iniziare) a piovere a dirotto (*pouring*) ma era troppo tardi per tornare indietro a prendere l'ombrello. (**c** Pensare) che se fosse tornato a casa avrebbe potuto prendere anche il suo libro da leggere sul treno. (**d** Fermarsi) sotto la pioggia, a metà strada tra casa sua e la stazione. La pioggia (**e** diventare) grandine e (**f** cominciare) a lampeggiare. Nel frattempo però Lusardi aveva deciso di tornare indietro. È (**g** ritornare). (**h** Cominciare) a camminare velocemente. Sua moglie gli aveva detto di prendere l'ombrello ma lui non (**i** volere) ascoltarla perché era sicuro che non sarebbe piovuto. Quando finalmente (**j** arrivare) alla stazione il treno era là, fermo al binario nove. Lusardi non (**k** potere) fare il biglietto e (**l** salire) sul treno. Il treno era un rapido e non si (**m** fermare) in nessuna stazione. Ogni tanto si vedeva una stazione con il nome scritto sul muro, grande, ma non poteva leggerlo perché il rapido sfrecciava (*was darting*) tanto rapidamente che era impossibile leggerlo. Dopo tre ore e mezzo di viaggio il rapido (**n** arrivare) a destinazione e finalmente (**o** potere) leggere il nome della stazione: Milano. (**p** Essere) preso dallo sconforto (*he felt dejected*) perché lui credeva di avere preso il treno per Roma.

65 UNIT | Which past tense?

The perfect, the imperfect and the past definite can sometimes be found in the same sentence. This unit shows the three tenses working together.

A While the imperfect expresses an action either going on or repeated in the past (= what was happening or used to happen), the perfect and the past definite express an action that started and ended (either at once or within a period of time) in the past (= what happened).

In everyday speech you can safely use the perfect instead of the past definite but the former should express an action bearing some connection with the present while the latter should express an action completely removed from it:

Paolo è nato nel 1975. *Paul was born in 1975.* (he is still living – perfect).
Michelangelo nacque nel 1475. *Michelangelo was born in 1475.* (dead a long time – past definite).

You say: Ho appena comprato questo libro. *I've just bought this book.*
You could say: Ho comprato questo libro tre anni fa. *I bought this book three years ago.* (you still have it, maybe you are re-reading it now, or it is part of your library, a fact that bears some relation with the present, even if you had bought it thirty years ago)
but you can equally say: Comprai questo libro tre anni fa. *I bought this book three years ago.* (here the emphasis is on the starting and ending of the action which happened three years ago).

When referring to distant events or historic facts and telling stories, the past definite is a must. Observe the verbs in this passage where the past definite (past action) interacts with the imperfect (background action) and the perfect (ended action but still 'current').

Si alzò dalla scrivania e si avvicinò al pianoforte. Non riusciva più a scrivere, pensò. Osservò la stanza: i fiori erano appassiti, i mobili avevano accumulato un velo di polvere. Cominciò a suonare pensando agli ultimi avvenimenti che avevano tanto cambiato la sua vita. Non si accorse che intanto faceva buio. Suonò per ore. A tarda notte si alzò dal pianoforte e salì in camera a fare le valigie. Da quel giorno non ha più scritto nulla.

He rose from his desk and approached the piano. He could not write a word, he thought. He slowly surveyed the room: the flowers had withered, the furniture had gathered a thin layer of dust. He started playing, thinking about the recent events that had changed his life so much. He did not realize it was getting dark. He played for hours. In the middle of the night he got up from the piano and went up to his room to pack. From that day he has written nothing.

1 Put the infinitives in brackets into the perfect, pluperfect or imperfect as appropriate.

Ieri mattina la sveglia (**a** suonare) alle sei e mezzo. Siccome (**b** essere) sabato (io) (**c** decidere) di restare a letto almeno un altro paio d'ore ma, non appena (**d** premere) il bottone per fermare l'allarme, il telefono (**e** cominciare) a squillare: (**f** essere) una mia vecchia amica che non vedo da vent'anni. Mi (**g** telefonare) per chiedermi un'informazione per lei molto importante. Mentre (noi) (**h** parlare) il campanello (**i** suonare): (**j** essere) il lattaio che (**k** rompere) una bottiglia di latte e (**l** volere) qualcosa per pulire lo scalino della porta d'ingresso (*doorstep*). Dopo di ciò (**m** fare) un tazza di tè e mentre (**n** tornare) a letto con l'intento di dormire almeno un'altra ora (**o** arrivare) l'autoimmondizie (*dust cart*) dopo di che una squadra (*gang*) di uomini con il trapano pneumatico (**p** cominciare) a perforare una sezione di strada. Il resto della giornata (**q** essere) molto tranquillo: nessuno (**r** telefonare), nessuno mi (**s** visitare) nemmeno il postino.

2 Can you remember a day when something amusing or remarkable happened to you? If not, invent one! Write about it and then read it aloud.

3 Change the present tense in the following story into the imperfect or the past definite as necessary.

⚠ Irregular past definite:
perdere: persi, perdesti, perse, perdemmo, perdeste, persero

Cenerentola (**a** è) una bella ragazza, buona di carattere ed operosa. (**b** vive) con la matrigna e due sorellastre che la (**c** maltrattano (*ill-treat*)). (**d** Fa) i lavori più umili che la matrigna e le sorellastre le (**e** ordinano) di fare.

Un giorno Fata Turchina le (**f** offre) l'opportunità di partecipare al ballo del principe. La fata le (**g** raccomanda) di lasciare la festa per mezzanotte e Cenerentola (**h** accetta). Quando il principe la (**i** vede) (**j** s'innamora) di lei. A mezzanotte Cenerentola (**k** lascia) il palazzo ma nella fretta (**l** perde) una scarpetta. Grazie alla scarpetta il principe (**m** ritrova) Cenerentola, la (**n** sposa) e (**o** vivono) felici e contenti.

66 UNIT Words ending in *-ing* (1): the gerund

Not all English words ending in -ing have the same function: some function as verbs, some as nouns and others as adjectives.

A When an *-ing* word is used as a verb it is known as the gerund. This is formed by replacing the infinitive endings **-are**, **-ere**, and **-ire** with **-ando**, **-endo** and **-endo** respectively.

PARLARE	VENDERE	PARTIRE	ESSERE	AVERE
parlando	**vendendo**	**partendo**	**essendo**	**avendo**

The gerund has only one form and it doesn't have to agree with the subject.

Partendo alle otto potrei arrivare   *(By) Leaving at 8 o'clock I could*
  prima.   *arrive earlier.*

Irregular gerunds: dire → dicendo, fare → facendo, bere → bevendo

B The compound tense is formed by **essendo** or **avendo** + past participle …

Essendo partita alle otto sono   *Having left at 8 o'clock I arrived*
  arrivata prima.   *earlier.*

… but it is not greatly used, and expressions like these are favoured:

Siccome (*Since*) sono partita alle otto sono arrivata presto.
Sono arrivata presto perché sono partita alle otto.

⚠ Object pronouns are added to the end of the gerund.

Avendolo comprato, decisi di usarlo.   *Having bought it, I decided to use it.*

C The gerund expresses the manner in which an action happens.

Ascolto spesso la musica scrivendo   *I often listen to music when writing.*
Facendo così avrai una carriera   *In doing so you'll have a fast*
  veloce.   *career.*

It is also used to translate *by, while, in, since, after,* etc. + *-ing* …

Avendo finito il compito sono   *After having finished my homework,*
  uscito.   *I went out.*

… but equally you can say: Dopo che avevo finito il compito sono uscito.

D The progressive tense is formed by **stare** + gerund.

Non mi parlare adesso, sto leggendo.   *Do not speak to me now, I am reading.*

Andare + gerund gives a progressive form which expresses an unfolding or the repetition of an action.

La situazione andava peggiorando.   *The situation was worsening.*

1 Change the infinitives in brackets to gerunds.

a Non si risolvono i problemi (parlare).

b (Sbagliare) s'impara.

c Si è comprato la casa (lavorare) sodo (*hard*).

d (Continuare) così ti prenderai un esaurimento nervoso.

e (Avere) perso il treno chiamò un tassì.

f (Essere) arrivato in ritardo dovette rinunciare alla colazione.

g (Dire) così s'avviò (*set off*) verso la stazione.

h (Fare) così potrai risolvere i tuoi problemi.

2 Replace *dopo, mentre, siccome* + verb with the gerund.

E.g. Siccome sono arrivata in anticipo (*early*) non ho trovato nessuno.
→ **Essendo arrivata in anticipo non ho trovato nessuno.**

a Siccome non era stanco è andato a piedi.

b Siccome i negozi erano chiusi è andato al ristorante.

c Dopo aver comprato i biglietti sono tornato a casa.

d Dopo avere commesso tale gaffe preferì tacere per il resto della serata.

e Mentre attraversava la strada inciampò e cadde (*he stumbled and fell*).

f Mentre usciva di casa decise di prendere l'ombrello.

3 Answer the questions in the continuous form.

E.g. Che cosa stai facendo? (stirare una camicia). → **Sto stirando una camicia.**

a Che cosa stai scrivendo? (scrivere una lettera a Ronaldo)

b Che cosa stai leggendo? (leggere un articolo su Sting)

c Che cosa sta mangiando Andrea? (mangiare una bistecca alla fiorentina)

d Che cosa stai ascoltando? (ascoltare il Requiem di Verdi)

e Che cosa sta facendo Marcello? (riparare la lavatrice (*washing machine*))

f Che cosa sta bevendo Michele? (bere un doppio whisky con ghiaccio)

g Che cosa stanno dicendo? (raccontare una barzelletta)

h A che cosa state giocando? (a scacchi (*chess*))

4 Match the two halves of the sentences.

a La sua salute (*health*) …	**1** … va crescendo di ora in ora (*growing by the hour*).
b Va in giro (*about*) …	
c Che cosa …	**2** … il suo carattere va peggiorando.
d Col passare degli anni …	**3** … va migliorando.
e Il livello dell'acqua …	**4** … cianciando (*gossiping*).
	5 … vai dicendo (*talking about*)?

67 Unit Endings in *-ing* (2): present participle

This part of the verb translates those -ing ending verbs which have an adjectival or a nominal function.

A The present participle in Italian is formed by replacing **-are**, **-ere** and **-ire** with **-ante**, **-ente** and **-ente** respectively.

PARLARE	CONTENERE	PARTIRE	ESSERE	AVERE
parlante	contenente	partente	essente/ente	avente/abbiente

⚠ **Essente** is very rarely used; **abbiente** can mean *s/he who owns* (i.e. someone rich). The plural is formed by changing the last vowel (**-e**) into an **-i**.

B The present participle is very rarely used in Italian except:

- as an adjective:
  acqua bollente (*boiling water*); l'anno seguente (*the following year*)

- when it stands for a relative clause (*which*):

  Le uova sono un cibo nutriente   *Eggs are a nourishing food.*
  (= che nutre).

  Il treno proveniente da Roma è in   *The train (coming) from Rome is*
  arrivo sul secondo binario.   *arriving on platform two.*

  When in doubt, it is safer to use a relative clause:

  Sto leggendo una relazione   *I am reading a report concerning*
  riguardante (= che riguarda)   *(= that concerns) the school.*
  la scuola.

C Some Italian present participles have the value of a noun.
  cantante (*singer*); insegnante (*teacher*); amante (*lover*); studente (*student*); concorrente (*competitor*); dipendente (*employee*); dirigente (*manager*); emigrante (*emigrant*).

D Many nouns which include an *-ing* form in English are expressed differently in Italian: canna da pesca (*fishing rod*); casa di cura/clinica (*nursing home*); carrozza letto (*sleeping car*); piscina (*swimming pool*); carrozza ristorante (*dining car*); sala da pranzo (*dining room*); lavatrice (*washing machine*); salotto (*sitting room*); macchina da cucire (*sewing machine*); sala d'aspetto (*waiting room*).

E Verbal nouns such as: *fishing, swimming, drinking, writing, travelling, reading, painting,* etc. are rendered in Italian by the infinitive.
  Mi piace scrivere. *I like writing.* Vado a nuotare. *I am going swimming.*

➤ *See also the gerund in Unit 66 and the infinitive in Unit 31.*

1 **Replace the relative clause with a present participle/adjective.**

a (una persona) **che ama**

b il treno **che proviene** da Roma

c una ragazza **'che brilla'**

d una signora **che sorride**

e una storia **che diverte**

f una situazione **che non si conclude** (inconc…)

g il sole **che nasce**

h la luna **che cala**

2 **Now identify which of the groups of adjectives below correspond to each of your answers in exercise 1.**

a allegra/gaia/felice/serena

b decrescente/declinante

c sorgente/che ha inizio

d senza risultato

e dilettevole/spassoso

f splendente/scintillante/sfavillante

g affezionata/appassionata/innamorata

h in arrivo

3 **Translate the following using present participles/adjectives.**

a Paolo is always (**sempre**) smiling.

b Francesco is a rich man.

c Is this the train from Rome?

d It was an amusing film.

e Do you know Maria's lover?

f Giovanni is a brilliant student.

g the rising sun

h the waning moon

4 **Translate the following using the present participles/nouns from the opposite page.**

a Francesco is an important manager.

b During (**Durante**) the last century, many Italian emigrants went to America.

c Both contestants are very good.

d Our competitors are loosing their clients.

e He is an acquaintance of mine.

f My washing machine is not working (**non funziona**).

g I want a new fishing rod for Christmas.

68 UNIT Words ending in -ing (3): the infinitive

A -ing verbs are translated with an infinitive when:

- an -ing form has the function of a noun. In this case, the infinitive may even be preceded by the definite article.

  (L') aiutare gli amici è lo scopo della sua vita.

  Helping his friends is the main purpose of his life.

- after a preposition, in which case the preposition is followed by the definite article.

  Con l'andare del tempo si dimenticano molte cose.

  With the passing of time one forgets many things.

- with the prepositions **prima di** (*before*); **senza** (*without*); **oltre a** (*besides*); **invece di** (*instead*) and **dopo** (*after*).

  Le telefonò prima di uscire.

  He rang her before going out.

  Parlò senza alzare la testa.

  He spoke without raising his head.

⚠ In this case, **dopo** is followed by the infinitive of **avere** or **essere**:

  Dopo avere cenato pagò il conto e uscì.

  After having dined, she paid and went out.

To express purpose (*in order to*), **per** is used:

  Lavora per comprarsi una casa.

  He works (in order) to buy himself a house.

B *To go* + -ing is often translated by **andare a** + infinitive.

  Vado a ballare tutte le domeniche.   *I go dancing every Sunday.*

  Il sabato vado a pescare.   *I go fishing on Saturdays.*

  Il venerdì vado a nuotare.   *I go swimming on Fridays.*

C Here is a list of English verbs + preposition + -ing verb which in Italian need to be followed by an infinitive.

  to be used to (essere abituato a); *to be tired of* (essere stanco di); *to be on the point of* (essere sul punto di); *to thank for* (ringraziare di); *to think of* (pensare di); *to succeed in* (riuscire a); *to look forward to* (non vedere l'ora di).

➤ See present participle in Unit 67, gerund in Unit 66 and prepositions in Units 71–81.

1 Choose a suitable verb from the box to complete these sentences:

a Il _____ civile impone delle regole (*rules*) ben precise.

b (Il) _____ ad alta voce non è molto socievole.

c (Lo) _____ più di quanto si ha non è molto saggio.

d (Il) _____ troppo non giova alla salute (*doesn't help health*).

e (Il) _____ è nocivo (*damaging*) alla salute.

f _____ con poca luce stanca la vista (*sight*).

g Il _____ alcolici fa male al fegato.

h _____ è necessario per vivere bene.

divertirsi	fumare	leggere	parlare
vivere	lavorare	spendere	bere

2 Choose a suitable verb from the box to complete these sentences.

venire	giocare	avere studiato	uscire	pensare
tornare	continuare	dire	vedere	essere arrivato

a Invece di _____ domani perché non vieni oggi?

b Invece di _____ a lamentarti perché non fai qualcosa?

c Non devi parlare senza _____ .

d Uscì senza _____ nulla.

e Vive senza _____ nessuno.

f Oltre a _____ a pallacanestro fa anche molto nuoto.

g Prima di _____ ricordati di telefonare all'idraulico (*plumber*).

h Prima di _____ a casa devo andare in banca.

i Dopo _____ _____ per tanti anni è andato a fare il cameriere.

j Dopo _____ _____ ha cenato ed è andato a letto.

3 Translate the following into Italian.

a He studies (in order) to become a lawyer.

b They save (**risparmiano**) to buy a new car.

c They go swimming every day.

d Marianne and Paul go fishing when they can.

e I'm tired of repeating the same things.

f They did not succeed in convincing him (**convincerlo**).

69 UNIT | Infinitives ending in -urre/-orre/-arre

Some infinitives end in -urre, -orre and -arre. These belong to the second conjugation (-ere).

A Verbs ending in **-urre** come from the old form ending in **-ucere**.

produrre (*to produce*); tradurre (*to translate*); ridurre (*to reduce*); dedurre (*to deduce*); introdurre (*to introduce/insert*); riprodurre (*to reproduce*).

Verbs ending in **-orre** come from the old form ending in **-enere**:

porre (*to place/put/lay*); comporre (*to compose*), esporre (*to expose/exhibit*); disporre (*to dispose/arrange*); proporre (*to propose*).

Verbs ending in **-arre** come from the old form ending in **-aggere**:

trarre (*to draw*); contrarre (*to contract*); attrarre (*to attract*); distrarre (*to distract*); estrarre (*to extract*).

B These verbs have regular endings but slight variations in their stems. Each of the three groups behaves in the same way.

infinitive	PRODURRE	PORRE	TRARRE
present indicative	produco, produci, produce, produciamo, producete, producono	pongo, poni, pone poniamo, ponete, pongono	traggo, trai, trae, traiamo, traete, traggono
future indicative	produrrò, produrrai, produrrà, produrremo, produrrete, produrranno	porrò, porrai, porrà, porremo, porrete, porranno	trarrò, trarrai, trarrà, trarremo trarrete, trarranno
past definite	produssi, producesti, produsse, producemmo, produceste, produssero	posi, ponesti, pose, ponemmo, poneste, posero	trassi, traesti, trasse, traemmo, traeste, trassero
present subjunctive	produca, etc.	ponga, ponga, ponga, poniamo, poniate pongano	tragga, tragga, tragga, traiamo, traiate, traggano
imperfect subjunctive	producessi, etc.	ponessi, ponessi, ponesse, ponessimo, poneste, ponessero	traessi, traessi, traesse, traessimo, traeste, traessero
conditional	produrrei, etc.	porrei, porresti, porrebbe, porremmo, porreste, porrebbero	trarrei, trarresti, trarrebbe, trarremmo, trarreste, trarrebbero
imperative	produci, etc.	poni, ponga, poniamo, ponete, pongano	trai, tragga, traiamo, traete, traggano
past participle	prodotto	posto	tratto
gerund	producendo	ponendo	traendo

69 UNIT · Infinitives ending in -urre/-orre/-arre – Exercises

1 Change the verb in brackets to the corresponding Italian one.

a La FIAT (*produces*) il maggior numero di auto in Italia. La Topolino, la più piccola utilitaria italiana, fu (*produced*) nel 1936.

b Ho (*placed*) le scatole l'una sull'altra. Se ci fosse stato più spazio le avrei (*placed*) una accanto all'altra

c Goffredo (*draws*) ispirazione dalla natura per i suoi quadri. I suoi studenti (*draw*) esempio dalle sue opere. Lui ha (*exhibited*) le sue opere alla Galleria d'Arte Moderna. I suoi allievi di solito (*exhibit*) nell'Aula Magna dell'università.

2 Write out the following verbs.

a the present tense of **comporre**
b the past definite of **attrarre**
c the imperative of **tradurre**
d the present tense of **tradurre**
e the past participles of: **riprodurre, introdurre, ridurre, posporre, disporre, proporre, contrarre, attrarre.**

139

70 UNIT Uses of *si, ci* and *vi*

A Si

- Reflexive (third person singular and plural) and reciprocal pronoun.

  Mario si è rotto una gamba.   *Mario broke his leg* (reflexive).

  Si amano molto.   *They love each other a lot* (reciprocal).

Si becomes **se** before direct object pronouns **lo, la, li** and **le** and before **ne**:

  Si lava la faccia. = Se la lava.   *He washes his face./He washes it.*

The reflexive form of **andare** is **andarsene** (*to go away/off*).

  Vorrei che se ne andasse.   *I wish her to go away.*

  Devo andarmene.   *I must be going.*

The above form can be used with other verbs to give an emphatic meaning to the action expressed by the verb:

  Si è mangiato la torta.   *He ate the cake (all by himself).*

  Se l'è mangiata tutta.   *He ate it all.*

- Impersonal pronoun: Si dice che sia ricco. *He is said to be rich.*
- Passive constructions: Qui non si fa credito. *Credit is not allowed here.*

B Ci/Vi

- Direct and indirect object pronouns meaning *us, to us/you, to you* (plural).

  Ci vieni a trovare?   *Will you come and see us?*

  Vi ho scritto molte lettere.   *I wrote (to) you many letters.*

⚠ All direct object pronouns can be added to **ecco: eccoci, eccomi, eccolo**, etc.

- Reflexive pronouns (ourselves/yourselves):

  Ci siamo divertiti.   *We enjoyed ourselves.*
- Instead of **si** to make the impersonal form when the verb is reflexive.

  Quando ci si sveglia la mattina … *When one wakes up in the morning …*
- Reciprocal pronouns (*each other*).

  Ci telefoniamo ogni giorno.   *We ring each other every day.*
- Adverb: **qui/qua** (*here*); **là/lì** (*there*).

  Ci sono stata.   *I have been there.*

⚠ **Vi** can be used instead of **ci** although it's usually confined to writing.

- In spoken Italian you will hear people adding **ci** before **avere**.

  Ci ho tre figli.   *I have three sons.*
- With **credere** and **pensare**: Non ci credo. *I do not believe (in) it.*

1 Match the two halves of the sentences.

a Devo andarmene perché …   **1** … una donna molto potente.

b Si è mangiato …   **2** … vecchi per imparare.

c Se li è mangiati …   **3** … appartamenti.

d Si dice che lei sia …   **4** … l'un l'altro.

e Non si è mai troppo …   **5** … tedesco e spagnolo.

f Si affittano (*to let*) …   **6** … tutti.

g I nostri studenti si rispettano …   **7** … si è fatto tardi.

h Qui si parla inglese, francese, …   **8** … due porzioni di ravioli.

2 Change the noun (and article) used as an object to the correct pronoun.

E.g. **Si lava la camicia da solo.** → **Se la lava.**

a Si fa il letto da solo.

b Si fa la spesa da solo.

c Si prepara la cena da solo.

d Si stira i pantaloni da solo.

3 Translate the following into Italian.

one of them **ne**   *often* **spesso**

⚠ The adverb *only* (**soltanto/solamente**) goes after the verb.

a We got sun-tanned.

b When are you coming to see us?

c We introduced (ourselves).

d Have you ever (**mai**) been to Rome? Yes, I've been there three times.

e Here you (*inform. pl.*) are!

f We met on holiday.

g I do not believe it!

h I sent a fax (**fax**) to you (*inform. pl.*) yesterday.

i Is there a bank here (**qui**)?

j There is one in Via Roma.

k Are there public toilets here?

l There is one in that bar.

m We help each other a lot.

n Do you see each other often?

o No, we only meet once a year.

4 Change the *you* plural form of the reflexive verbs into *ci si* to make the sentence impersonal.

E.g. **Se vi alzate troppo tardi vi dovete vestire in fretta.** →
   Se ci si alza troppo tardi ci si deve vestire in fretta.

a In estate **vi abbronzerete** di più se mangerete (se si mangiano) molti pomodori.

b Per avere i capelli lucidi **sciaquatevi** (*rinse*) i capelli con acqua e aceto (*vinegar*).

c Se **vi preoccupate** troppo a causa degli esami rischiate (si rischia) di imparare di meno.

71 UNIT | Infinitives with or without a preposition

Sometimes a verb is followed by an infinitive, and the two verbs either follow each other directly or are linked with the prepositions a or di.

A Observe these three sentences:

Mi piace uscire.	*I like **going** out.*
Intendo uscire.	*I intend **to go** out.*
Devo uscire.	*I must **go** out.*

In each sentence, there are two verbs one after the other; all the English verbs in bold appear to have different forms (*going, to go, go*). In Italian, the second verb is usually an infinitive which may just follow the previous verb or be linked to it by a preposition (usually **a** or **di**).

Ho iniziato a studiare arte.	*I have started to study art.*
Cerca di capire.	*Try to understand.*

B Infinitives may also follow nouns and adjectives:

Sono sicuro di superare l'esame.	*I'm sure to pass the exam.*
Non ha l'opportunità di viaggiare.	*He doesn't have the opportunity to travel.*

⚠ Some verbs can be linked by the prepositions **con** (*with*) or **per** (*for/in order to*).

Ha finito con l'accettare le loro condizioni.	*He ended up by accepting their conditions.*
Venne da me per chiedere un'informazione.	*She came to ask for some information.*

C Below is a list of common verbs which do not need any preposition when followed by an infinitive.

amare (*to love/like*); ascoltare (*to listen to*); bastare (*to be enough*); bisognare (*to be necessary*); desiderare (*to wish/want*); detestare (*to detest*); dovere (*must/to have to*); fare (*to do/make*); guardare (*to look at*); importare (*to matter*); occorrere (*to be necessary*); odiare (*to hate*); osare (*to dare*); potere (*to be able to*); preferire (*to prefer*); sapere (*to know/know how to do something*); sentire (*to hear/listen to*); servire (*to serve/be of use*); vedere (*to see*); volere (*to want*)

Sai nuotare?	*Can you swim?*
Amo dipingere.	*I love painting.*

➤ *See infinitives + a and di in Unit 72, prepositions da, a, per and con in Units 80, 75, 78 and 73.*

1 **Below is a list of activities, sports and pastimes that you may like or dislike. Make a sentence for each one of them.**

E.g. **Mi piace nuotare. Non mi piace giocare a rugby.**

giocare a tennis	andare in bicicletta	leggere
visitare i musei	visitare le gallerie d'arte	viaggiare
giocare a carte	giocare a pallacanestro (*basketball*)	studiare l'italiano
andare a pesca	andare in discoteca	ascoltare la musica
dipingere	giocare a scacchi (*chess*)	dormire
ballare	cavalcare (*horse riding*)	scrivere

2 **Match the two halves of the sentences.**

a Come osi …
b Bisogna lasciarlo …
c Per superare gli esami …
d Detesto dover …
e Mi piace sentire …
f Vorrei …
g Non serve …
h Dovresti …

1 … vedere quanto è bello.
2 … piangere (*cry*) sul latte versato.
3 … sapere dove ho messo gli occhiali.
4 … cantare gli uccelli.
5 … fare tutto in fretta.
6 … basta studiare.
7 … fare come desidera.
8 … dire una cosa simile?

3 **Solve the crossword.**

1 desiderare intensamente
2 (*orizzontale*) sentire avversione verso qualcuno o qualcosa
2 (*verticale*) essere necessario
3 essere obbligato
4 avere il coraggio di compiere un'azione
5 essere sufficiente

4 **Now fill the blanks below using the verbs from the crossword. Change the tense as necessary.**

a Mi spiace di _____ dirti ciò.
b _____ mandare quel pacco oggi stesso.
c Gino _____ vedere i film di fantascienza (*science fiction*).
d Non ha _____ rispondere.
e Ha _____ comprarmi quel disco.
f Per avere un'informazione _____ chiedere al vigile.

72 UNIT Verbs taking *a* and *di*

Some of the most common verbs take a preposition when they occur before an infinitive.

A verb + **a** + infinitive

affrettarsi a (*to hasten to*); aiutare a (*to help to*); autorizzare a (*to authorize to*); avere ragione a (*to be right to/in -ing*); avere torto a (*to be wrong to/in -ing*); cominciare a (*to start to*); continuare a (*to continue to/to go on -ing*); convincere a (*to convince (someone) to*); costringere a (*to force (someone) to*); esitare a (*to hesitate to*); fare meglio a (*to do better to*); imparare a (*to learn to*); impegnarsi a (*to undertake to*); incitare a (*to urge to*); incoraggiare a (*to encourage to*); indurre a (*to induce to*); invitare a (*to invite to*); mettersi a (*to set out to*); obbligare a (*to oblige to*); ostinarsi a (*to persist in -ing*); persuadere a (*to persuade to*); prepararsi a (*to get ready to*); provare a (*to try to*); rinunciare a (*to renounce to*); seguitare a (*to keep on -ing*); servire a (*to serve to/to be used for + -ing*); tardare a (*to be late in -ing*); tenerci a (*to keep on -ing*); venire a (*to come to/come and*)

⚠ The preposition **a** acquires a consonant before a vowel.

Si fermò ad osservare il panorama. *She stopped to see the view.*

B verb + **di** + infinitive

accettare di (*to accept*); accorgersi di (*to realise*); avere bisogno di (*to need to*); avere intenzione di (*to intend to*); avere paura di (*to be afraid to*); avere vergogna di (*to be ashamed to*); avere voglia di (*to feel like -ing*); cercare di (*to try to*); cessare di (*to stop -ing*); chiedere di (*to ask (someone) to*); consigliare di (*to suggest -ing*); credere di (*to believe*); decidere di (*to decide to*); dire di (*to tell (someone) to*); essere contento di (*to be happy to*); essere sicuro di (*to be sure of -ing*); essere stanco di (*to be tired of -ing*); essere stufo di (*to be sick and tired of -ing*); fingere di (*to pretend to*); finire di (*to finish -ing*); giurare di (*to swear to*); immaginare di (*to imagine*); non veder l'ora di (*to look forward to -ing*); pensare di (*to think of -ing*); permettere di (*to allow to*); pregare di (*to beg to*); pretendere di (*to claim to*); proibire di (*to forbid to*); promettere di (*to promise to*); proporre di (*to propose/suggest -ing*); raccomandare di (*to urge (someone) to*); rendersi conto di (*to realise*); ricordare di (*to remember to*); rifiutarsi di (*to refuse to*); sentirsela di (*to be willing to/have the strength of -ing*); sopportare di (*to bear -ing*); smettere di (*to give up -ing*); sognare di (*to dream of -ing*); sopportare di (*to bear to*); sperare di (*to hope to*); tentare di (*to try/attempt to*); vantarsi di (*to boast of/about -ing*); vietare di (*to forbid to*)

1 Add the preposition *a* or *di* as appropriate, then try to finish the story making use of the verbs on the opposite page.

Renzo pensava **a** _____ prendersi una vacanza. Sua moglie lo aveva incoraggiato **b** _____ raggiungerlo al mare ma lui si era impegnato **c** _____ fare degli affari (*business*) molto importanti per la sua ditta e tardava **d** _____ prendere una decisione. D'altra parte (*On the other hand*) non voleva rinunciare **e** _____ riposarsi un po' dopo un lungo inverno di lavoro senza pausa. 'Se ti ostini **f** _____ lavorare così, ti ammalerai' gli diceva sua moglie nel tentativo (*attempting*) di persuaderlo **g** _____ desistere. Però lui ci teneva talmente (*so much*) **h** _____ suo lavoro che seguitava ad andare in ufficio anche il sabato. Certo sua moglie aveva ragione **i** _____ insistere e anche il dottore che gli aveva consigliato **j** _____ lavorare di meno, però lui sognava di comprare una bella casa per la sua famiglia e tentava **k** _____ rimandare il riposo ed i divertimenti al futuro. Fermò la macchina e scese per comprare un rivista. 'D'altra parte' – pensava, seguitando **l** _____ ragionare su questo argomento 'se andassi al mare, sarei obbligato **m** _____ passare molto tempo sulla spiaggia, sotto l'ombrellone mentre io preferirei di gran lunga (*by far*) essere in montagna'. Si rendeva conto **n** _____ essere esagerato nella sua ostinazione **o** _____ trovare scuse e non vedeva l'ora **p** _____ trovare una soluzione o perlomeno un compromesso. E la soluzione la trovò quando …

2 Using the verbs on the opposite page, translate into Italian.

⚠ Remember the agreements in gender and number.

a Teresa is learning to play the piano.
b Paul is very keen on playing tennis.
c I am looking forward to seeing you.
d We are sick and tired of translating these exercises.
e They were sure to be right.
f Remember to write a card to uncle.
g You'd do better to accept their invitation.
h I intend to buy a sport car.
i You are right in wanting to enjoy yourselves.
j I am afraid of catching a cold.
k They refused to give her any advice (**alcun consiglio**).
l I feel like going to a party.

73 UNIT | Prepositions

Prepositions locate, in position or time, a person/object in relation to another person/object. They are words like with, at, to, by, from, of, about, etc.

A Since Italian prepositions are not always translated with their nominal English counterparts, it is important to learn their use. In Italian it is sometimes possible to choose between two prepositions to convey the same meaning: Sono a casa/Sono in casa. *I am at home.*

⚠️ When the definite article follows **di**, **a**, **da**, **in**, **su** it combines with it, e.g. **a + il = al**. **Con** may combine, but modern Italian tends to combine it mainly with **il** (= **col**) if at all.

B **Con** (*with*)

Vado a Roma con Paolo.	*I am going to Rome with Paul.*
un tè con latte ma senza zucchero.	*a tea with milk but without sugar.*

Con also translates *by* when associated with means of transport.

Vado a Roma con l'aereo/con il treno/con il pullman.	*I am going to Rome by air/train/coach.*

⚠️ In this context, **in** can also be used: **in aereo/in treno/in pullman**.

C Other uses of **con** are when it conveys the meaning of:

• *cause*
   Con questo caldo è difficile lavorare. *It's difficult to work in this heat.*
• *against* (particulary with words like *fighting, at war* etc.)
   È come lottare con i mulini a vento. *It is like fighting against windmills.*
• *out of*
   Ho fatto queste tende con un vecchio copriletto. *I made these curtains out of an old bed cover.*
• *in spite of*
   Con tutti gli amici che ha è andato solo. *In spite of the many friends he has, he went by himself.*
• *to*
   È sempre molto gentile con me. *He is always very kind to me.*
   con mia grande sorpresa. *to my great surprise.*

Useful expressions: prenderla con calma *to take it easy*;
prendersela con calma *to dawdle over something*

➤ *See Unit 76 for the preposition in, Units 71 and 72 for infinitives after prepositions.*

73 UNIT Prepositions – *Exercises*

1 Rearrange the words to make meaningful sentences.

a lavorare difficile con rumore (*noise*) questo è

b prendo zucchero due caffè cucchiaini (*teaspoon*) il con di

c è arrivato Paolo madre sua l'automobile con di

d Marianna loro è con gentile stata

e Eleonora di ha andare la sua deciso con al cinema amica

f ha l'invito con accettato sorpresa mia grande

g dovrebbero a imparare calma con prendersela

h al con cinema lui andata ieri sono

2 Add either *a(d)*, *di* or *con*, to the sentences below.

a Devi affrettarti _____ andare.

b Crede sempre _____ avere ragione.

c Sono stata in Corsica _____ la nave traghetto (*ferry boat*).

d Faresti meglio _____ studiare di più.

e Vieni al cinema _____ me?

f Ho il passaporto _____ me.

g Prendo un bicchiere di latte _____ un panino.

h _____ il freddo che faceva ho dovuto comprarmi un berretto di lana.

i Dovresti prendertela _____ più calma.

j Mi piace molto il pesce _____ le patate fritte.

3 Translate the following into Italian.

a Thank you for coming (**per essere venuta**) in this weather.

b meat with chilli (**peperoncino**)

c In 1915, Italy was at war against Germany.

d He made this table out of second hand (**usato**) wood.

e In spite of all their problems, they managed to stay together.

f He had been so kind to them that they couldn't refuse the favour.

g They are kind to her.

h To their great surprise, he left his job.

i She should learn to take it calmly.

j In Italy, civil servants (**gli impiegati pubblici**) dawdle over forms (**pratiche**) of this kind.

74 UNIT The preposition *di*

di +	il	lo	la	l'	i	gli	le
	del	dello	della	dell'	dei	degli	delle

Parlano di sport.	*They are talking about sport.*
Da questa finestra c'è una bella vista della città.	*From this window there is a lovely view of the town.*

A **Di** + article is used to express the partitive *some* or *any*.

'Ha del pane?'	*'Have you any bread?'*
'Ho del pane bianco e del pane integrale.'	*'I have some white and some brown bread.'*

B **Di** is also used to indicate:
* possession: i giocattoli dei bambini *the children's toys*
* specification: l'arrivo dei passeggeri *the arrival of the passengers*
* denomination: la città di Venezia *the city of Venice*
* origin: Sono di Genova. *I am from Genoa.*

> **△** *Where you are from* is expressed by either **Sono di** … or **Vengo da** …

* authorship (*by*): un libro di Rea *a book by Rea*
* content: una tazza di tè *a cup of tea*
* what something is made of: una cravatta di seta *a silk tie*
* ailments: Soffre di lombaggine. *He suffers from lumbago.*
* comparisons: Mio padre è più grande del tuo. *My father is bigger than yours.*
* time: di giorno *during the day*; di notte *during the night/at night*; di mattina/di sera *in the morning/evening*; di sabato *on Saturdays*; di ora in ora *hour by hour*; di giorno in giorno *day by day*
* after **qualcosa** and **niente** + adjective
  Vorrei qualcosa di meno caro. *I'd like something less expensive.*
  Non c'è niente d'interessante alla TV. *There is nothing interesting on TV.*

C Note these phrases and expressions:

di solito	*usually*
Mi è caduto di mano.	*It fell from my hands.*
È il più grande cantante del mondo.	*He is the greatest singer in the world.*

➤ See the partitive in Unit 20 and infinitives after prepositions in
Units 71 and 72.

1 Write the combined preposition and articles *del, dello, della* etc. in the blanks.

a L'amica _____ mamma ha telefonato da Miami.

b Da questa finestra c'è una bella vista _____ mare (*m.*).

c La gente _____ zona è molto simpatica e interessante.

d Vorrei _____ carciofi (*artichokes*), _____ zucchini (*courgettes*) e _____ mele.

e L'arrivo _____ nave (*f.*) è il 18 agosto.

f L'inizio _____ spettacolo è alle 21.15.

g Questo è un quadro _____ famoso pittore italiano Grignani.

h Quello che vedi laggiù è lo yacht _____ signora Marini.

i Il quoziente d'intelligenza _____ miei studenti è generalmente alto.

j Suda molto a causa _____ clima (*m.*) caldo e umido.

2 Re-write the sentences with the preposition *di* if it is needed.

E.g. un paio scarpe → un paio di scarpe

a un vestito seta

b un bicchiere rotto

c un bicchiere vino

d Il mio giardino è più piccolo tuo.

e Hai visto niente interessante?

f Sono inglese.

g Soffre gotta (*gout*).

h la città romana

i la città Firenze

j Ti consiglio scrivergli.

k un tavolo legno

l la scrivania Giorgio

m Ho deciso venire.

n Sono Londra.

o una scatola (*tin*) pomodori

3 Translate the following into Italian.

a hour by hour

b Is there anything interesting on TV?

c I would like something better.

d I bought the complete (**l'intera**) works of Shakespeare.

e the bus route (**itinerario**)

f a marble statue

g Actors work at night and sleep during the day.

4 Match the two halves of the sentences.

a Mio marito mi ha regalato …

b Vorrei qualcosa …

c Ti vedo ringiovanire …

d Sono …

e È l'uomo più famoso …

1 … di Liverpool.

2 … di giorno in giorno.

3 … del mondo.

4 … una collana di perle.

5 … di più economico.

75 UNIT | The preposition *a*

The preposition *a* can mean *to, at, in, on*. It combines with the definite article.

a +	il	lo	la	l'	i	gli	le
	al	allo	alla	all'	ai	agli	alle

Ho dato il libro a Roberto.   *I gave the book to Roberto.*

A **A** is used with:

- position. When referring to cities, towns, villages and small islands, **a** expresses both a motion toward a place (e.g. **vado a ...**) or being in a place (e.g. **sono a ...**).

Vado a Pisa. *I am going to Pisa.*   Vado a Capri. *I am going to Capri.*

Sono a Pisa. *I am in Pisa.*   Abito a Capri. *I live in Capri.*

Also: a casa (*home/at home*); al mare (*at/to the seaside*); a cena (*at/to dinner*); al ristorante (*at/to the restaurant*); al bar (*at/to the bar*); all'aperto (*in the open air*); alla stazione (*at/to the station*); al porto (*at/to the port*); all'aeroporto (*at/to the airport*); alla televisione (*on television*); al cinema (*at/to the cinema*); a teatro (*at/to the theatre*)

- time: alle sei (*at six*); a mezzogiorno (*at midday*); a mezzanotte (*at midnight*); all'alba (*at dawn*); al tramonto (*at sunset*)

- age:

A vent'anni ha preso moglie.   *He married at twenty.*

- manner:

Mi piace la pasta al pomodoro.   *I like pasta with tomato sauce.*

Non parlare a voce alta/bassa.   *Do not speak in a loud/low voice.*

  un uovo alla coque   *a boiled egg*

Ho preso un libro a caso.   *I took a book at random.*

  all'italiana   *Italian style*

Non parlare ad alta voce, parla a   *Do not speak aloud, speak softly.*
  bassa voce.

- means:

Anna va a cavallo io vado a piedi.   *Anna rides, I go on foot.*

Questo ricamo è fatto a macchina.   *This embroidery is made by machine.*

B In Italian, **ascoltare** (*to listen to*), **guardare** (*to look at/to watch*), **additare** (*to point at*) and **fissare** (*to stare at/to gaze at*) are not followed by a preposition.

Ascolto la radio.   *I listen to the radio.*

Guardo il panorama.   *I look at the view.*

➤ *See infinitives after prepositions in Units 71 and 72.*

75 UNIT The preposition *a* – Exercises

1 What are these people doing?

a Il bambino sta andando _____ . **b** Il tassì sta andando _____ .
c La famiglia sta andando _____ .

2 Translate the following into Italian. The sentences all refer to a woman.

a I live in London and I spend (**passo**) my holidays in Capri.
b The day before yesterday I went to the airport at eleven.
c I left at 16.50 and arrived in Naples at 18.50 local time (**ora locale**).
d In Naples I took a taxi to go to the port to get the boat.
e My friends had given me the keys of their flat so I went to their home.
f After a shower (**doccia**) I went to dinner at the restaurant.
g I ordered spaghetti with clams (**vongole**) and grilled (**alla griglia**) fish.
h Yesterday I got up at dawn to go (**per andare a fare**) on an excursion.
i I spent all morning walking up hills in the sun.
j At midday I returned to Marina Grande and sat in a bar with a cool beer.
k I was glad to find a seat (**un posto**) in the shade and just sit there looking at the people passing by.

3 Write the missing prepositions *con, di* and *a* in the blanks. In some cases you will need to combine them with the article. Then read the passage aloud slowly and clearly.

Quando vado in Italia, visito sempre nuovi posti. Due anni fa sono andata in Toscana: **a** _____ Siena, **b** _____ Lucca, **c** _____ Vinci e **d** _____ isola d'Elba. Quando ero **e** _____ Siena ho fatto un'escursione **f** _____ Monteriggioni, una cittadina costruita nel 1200 sulla cima **g** _____ una collina e circondata da mura **h** _____ quattordici torrioni. **i** _____ Lucca ho visitato la casa **j** _____ Puccini, il compositore **k** _____ 'Boheme'. **l** _____ Vinci sono stata **m** _____ Museo Leonardiano. **n** _____ isola d'Elba sono stata **o** _____ Marciana Alta e da lì, **p** _____ la funivia (*cable car*) sono salita fino **q** _____ Monte Capanne da dove si gode una vista bellissima.

76 UNIT | The preposition *in*

A

in +	il	lo	la	l'	i	gli	le
	nel	nello	nella	nell'	nei	negli	nelle

In is used with:

- position (both movement toward (**vado in ...**) and being in (**sono in ...**) for regions, counties, countries, continents and large islands)

Vado/Sono in Lombardia/	*I'm going to/I'm in Lombardy,*
in Cornovaglia/in Grecia/	*Cornwall, Greece,*
in Europa/in Sicilia.	*Europe, Sicily.*

Also: in città (*in/to the town*); nel parco (*in/to the park*); in campagna (*in/to the country*); in ufficio (*in/to the office*); in montagna (*in/to the mountains*); in chiesa (*in/to church*)

- time (seasons and centuries)
  in primavera *in spring*; in estate *in summer*; In autunno iniziano le scuole. *Schools start in autumn*; nel 1999 *in 1999*; nel XXI Secolo *in the 21st century.*

Also: in anticipo/in ritardo/in orario *early/late/on time*

⚠ With seasons you can also use **di**: d'estate (*in summer*).

- means (transport and payment)
  in autobus *by bus*; in bicicletta *by bike*; pagare in contanti *to pay cash*
- manner:
  essere in pericolo *to be in danger*; essere in abito da sera *to be in an evening dress*; carne in umido *stewed meat*

B Other expressions to learn:

essere debole/bravo in matematica *to be weak/good at maths*; in omaggio *complimentary*; un biglietto in omaggio *a complimentary ticket*; in apparenza *apparently*; di quando in quando *now and again*; stare in piedi *to stand*; alzarsi in piedi *to stand up*; Siamo in tre/quattro. *There are three/four of us.*

| Maria Schiaffino in Bianchi | *Maria Bianchi neé Schiaffino* |

(**in** here means *married to* since in official documents the wife's surname is that of her father)

➤ *See use of the definite article in Units 7, 8 and 9.*

1 Match the two halves of the sentences.

a Questa bicicletta l'ho pagata ...

b Vado in ufficio in ...

c Io prendo carne ...

d Era in pericolo ...

e Le signore hanno ricevuto ...

f Un tavolo per quante persone?

g Abbiamo dovuto viaggiare ...

h Durante l'ovazione il pubblico ...

i Di tanto in tanto ...

1 ... in piedi.

2 Siamo in quattro.

3 ... una rosa in omaggio.

4 ... di vita.

5 ... in umido con patate.

6 ... si è alzato in piedi.

7 ... in contanti.

8 ... autobus.

9 ... vado a trovarla.

2 Translate the following into Italian.

a When I am in Italy, I often go to Tuscany.

b When I used to live in Cornwall, I used to go to France every year.

c I have not decided whether (**se**) to go to Sicily or to Elba.

d I live in town.

e This afternoon I am going to town.

f My sister went to live in the country.

g The Simoni family is in the mountains.

h Francesco is jogging (**sta facendo il jogging**) in the park.

i My Italian course starts in winter.

j In 1999 I will go to Australia.

k My train arrived on time.

l I take my holidays in the summer.

77 UNIT | The preposition *su*

Su *translates* on, about, over. *It combines with the definite article.*

A

su +	il	lo	la	l'	i	gli	le
	sul	sullo	sulla	sull'	sui	sugli	sul

Su translates:

• *on, onto*

Il libro è sul tavolo.	*The book is on the table.*
La casa è costruita sulla roccia.	*The house is built on the rock.*
Firenze è sull'Arno.	*Florence is on the (river) Arno.*
La camera dà sulla spiaggia.	*The room looks onto the beach.*

• *over*

| L'aereo vola su Roma. | *The plane is flying over Rome.* |
| Metti qualcosa sulle spalle. | *Put something over your shoulders.* |

• *about, around/roughly*

una donna sulla trentina	*a woman of about 30 (years old)*
pesare sui 60 chili	*to weigh around 60 kilos*
Ha scritto un saggio sulla guerra.	*She wrote an essay about the war.*

B Note also these expressions:

su due piedi	*there and then*
sul momento	*at first*
fatto su misura	*made to measure*
fare sul serio	*to be in earnest*
sette su dieci	*seven out of ten*
essere sul punto di fare qualcosa	*to be about to do something*
fare promesse su promesse	*to make one promise after another*
commettere errori su errori	*to make mistake after mistake*

⚠ *on television* = **alla televisione**

1 Match the two halves of the sentences.

a L'elicottero sta volando sulla …   1 … giardino.
b Ha una casetta sul …   2 … tavolo.
c I piatti sono sul …   3 … costa.
d La finestra dà sul …   4 … monte.
e Aveva un bellissimo scialle (*shawl*) sulle …   5 … misura.
f Mi sono fatta fare un vestito su …   6 … spalle.
g È un uomo sulla …   7 … cinquantina.
h Ha scritto un libro sugli …   8 … punto di partire.
i Ero sul …   9 … Zulù.
j Non posso decidere su …   10 … due piedi.

2 Answer the questions.

E.g. **Che cosa c'è sulla rivista? → Sulla rivista c'è una penna.**

a Dov'è il telefono?   b Dov'è la penna?   c Che c'è sul televisore?
d Che cosa cè scritto sulla rivista?   e Che cosa hai visto alla televisione?

3 Translate the following into Italian.

a The lighthouse (**faro**) is on the rock.   d My colleague writes essays
b Rome in on the river Tiber (**Tevere**).   on psychology.
c My teacher is about fifty years old.   e My shoes are made to measure.

4 Fill the blanks with the expressions in the box.

Non mi sembra che mio figlio studi **a** _____ . Nove volte **b** _____
ritorna a casa con un brutto voto. Anche in classe è svogliato e disattento,
infatti il suo professore mi ha detto che ieri era **c** _____ di mandarlo fuori.
Nella prova scritta di francese ha commesso **d** _____ . Nonostante mi
faccia **e** _____ di studiare di più, non riesce a migliorare.

---

promesse su promesse   errori su errori   sul punto   sul serio   su dieci

---

78 UNIT | The preposition *per*

il treno per Torino	*the train to Turin*
Lavori per niente?	*Do you work for nothing?*
entrare per la finestra	*to come/go through the window*

A **Per** translates:

- *by* (within a period of time/means)

per il 3 maggio	*by the 3rd of May*
mandare una lettera per posta	*to send a letter by post*

- *about* (a place)

andare in giro per la città	*to go about town*

- *on account of, out of, because of, due to, in order to*

fare qualcosa per ambizione	*to do something out of ambition*
per le condizioni del tempo	*due to the weather conditions*
per motivi di famiglia	*owing to family reasons*

- calculations, percentages

Cinque per tre fa quindici.	*Five times three is fifteen.*
dividere per cinque	*to divide by five*
il cinque per cento	*five per cent*
lo sconto del dieci per cento	*10% discount*

B Note also these expressions:

in fila per due	*two by two*
Per me …	*In my opinion …*
per l'appunto	*exactly/precisely*
per caso	*by chance*
per di più	*moreover*
per fortuna	*luckily*
per lo più	*generally/usually*
per tempo	*early*
gente per bene	*honest people*
giorno per giorno	*day by day*
per modo di dire	*so to speak*
chiamare per nome	*to call by name*

78 UNIT

The preposition *per* – Exercises

1 Join the two columns to make meaningful sentences.

a Scusi, a che ora arriva …
b Il ladro è fuggito …
c Devo finire questo libro …
d Ti mando il pacco …
e Va sempre in giro …
f Credevo che lavorasse soltanto …
g È assente …
h Quanto fa …
i Il tasso di interesse è
j L'ho pagato molto meno:
   mi hanno fatto lo sconto del …

1 … per motivi di famiglia.
2 … per posta.
3 … per la finestra.
4 … per settembre.
5 … per i boschi (*woods*).
6 … il treno per Rapallo?
7 … per ambizione.
8 … del cinque per cento.
9 … trenta per cento.
10 … sei per sei?

2 Add the appropriate expressions from the box to complete the dialogue below.

'Hai **a** _____ visto Margherita? **b** _____ arriva **c** _____ . Non riesco a capire perché sia tanto in ritardo.'

'Ah, sì, l'ho vista per le scale due ore fa. Stava andando a fare le pulizie dalla signora del piano di sopra.'

'Ho capito, si vede che non ha ancora finito.'

'**d** _____ la signora del piano di sopra la fa lavorare troppo. È una famiglia di persone per bene ma sono un po' tirchi (*stingy*).'

'**e** _____ Margherita non si è mai lamentata.'

'**f** _____ : Margherita non si lamenta mai e la gente se ne approfitta (*take advantage of her*).'

'**g** _____ c'è gente molto altruista come la famiglia Marchese che le fa tanti regali.'

'Altruista per modo di dire, perché qualche volta si dimenticano di pagarla. **h** _____ non le pagano nemmeno le marche (*stamps*) per la pensione.'

'Mamma mia, che gente meschina (*mean*)!'

'**i** _____ !'

---

	per fortuna	per di più	Per l'appunto!	
per lo più	per tempo		per me	per quanto io sappia
	per caso	per l'appunto		

> Tra and fra (between, among, within) are identical in meaning although one may be chosen instead of the other to avoid sounds like tra traumi or fra frati.
> Neither tra nor fra combines with the definite article.

Tra il dire e il fare c'è di mezzo il mare (*proverb*). *Easier said than done.*

A **Tra** and **fra** translate:

- *among/between*

Detto fra noi …	*Between you and me …*
Tra tutte queste auto preferisco quella rossa.	*Among all these cars I prefer the red one.*

⚠ Note the use of **quella** which in this context translates *one*: *I prefer the one (which is) red.*

Mi raccomando, che resti tra noi.	*Remember that it is between you and me.*

- *expressions of time*

Tra un mese arriva la macchina nuova.	*In a month's time the new car will arrive.*
Tra poco esco.	*I am going out in a while.*

- *place (in the middle of)*

tra la folla	*in the middle of the crowd*

- *distance (in)*

Tra un chilometro siamo arrivati.	*In one kilometre we will be there.*

- *movement towards a place (through)*

I raggi del sole filtravano tra le persiane socchiuse.	*The sun's rays passed through the half closed shutters.*

B Useful expressions to learn:

Ho detto fra me …	*I said to myself …*
tra l'altro	*besides, what is more*
Vive tra casa e ufficio.	*He lives only for work.*
Tra tutti saranno una dozzina.	*In all they must be a dozen.*
Tra i due preferisco il primo.	*Of the two I prefer the former/ the first one.*
Il sole filtrava tra i rami.	*The sun filtered through the branches.*
Il ladro è scomparso tra la folla.	*The thief disappeared in the crowd.*
Tra fare la spesa, cucinare e pulire non ho tempo per me.	*With the shopping, cooking and cleaning I have no time for myself.*

1 Join the two columns to make meaningful sentences, then read them aloud

a Detto fra noi mi sembra che …	**1** … preferisco scienze politiche.
b Tra una settimana arrivano …	**2** … ci sono dieci chilometri.
c Tra il tennis e in nuoto …	**3** … preferisco quest'ultimo (*the latter*).
d Tra tutte le materie (*subjects*) …	**4** … racconti fandonie (*tall stories*).
e Ho trovato questa vecchia lettera …	**5** … i miei amici francesi.
f Mi piace stare …	**6** … tra la gente.
g Tra il dire e il fare …	**7** … c'è di mezzo il mare.
h Tra casa mia e l'ufficio …	**8** … siamo arrivati.
i Tra dieci chilometri …	**9** … tra le pagine di un libro.
j Viale (*Avenue*) Roma è …	**10** … tra due filari di pioppi (*poplars*).

2 Yesterday the teacher took his class to the cinema, and this morning the children had to write about the film. This is Marietto's essay. Unfortunately he left out most of the prepositions, some of them with an article – add them for him.

IL FILM

Il ladro uscì **a** _____ casa **b** _____ un'anziana signora correndo verso (*toward*) il bosco. Il chiarore **c** _____ luna che filtrava **d** _____ i rami gli permetteva **e** _____ vedere appena (*just*) il sentiero che portava **f** _____ città. **g** _____ frattempo l'anziana signora, che durante la rapina si era nascosta tremante sotto (*under*) il letto corse **h** _____ telefono **i** _____ chiamare la polizia e scorse, **j** _____ le tende socchiuse, la figura **k** _____ 'uomo che, uscito dalla boscaglia, correva verso la città dove si svolgeva una grande festa religiosa **l** _____ la banda locale e i fuochi d'artificio. Il ladro fu trovato **m** _____ la folla ed arrestato. La vecchia signora venne a sapere che il ladro aveva rubato **n** _____ salvare la sua famiglia da una vita piena di tribolazioni e che si era pentito. La signora decise di perdonarlo e cominciò **o** _____ andarlo a trovare in prigione e, **p** _____ una visita e l'altra andava anche a trovare la sua povera famiglia **q** _____ tantissimi doni, cibo e giocattoli. Il giorno **r** _____ cui l'uomo uscì **s** _____ prigione andò **t** _____ attenderlo e lo portò **u** _____ sua grande casa **v** _____ tutta la sua povera famiglia. L'uomo diventò giardiniere ed autista **w** _____ signora e sua moglie cuoca.

The preposition *da*

The preposition **da** means **from** or **by**. It combines with the definite article.

da +	il	lo	la	l'	i	gli	le
	dal	dallo	dalla	dall'	dai	dagli	dalle

L'aereo parte da Genova.	*The plane leaves from Genoa.*
Era ammirato da tutti.	*He was admired by everyone.*
È stato assunto da loro.	*He has been employed by them.*

A Da is used:

- to translate *to someone's place (or shop)*

Vado da Giovanni.	*I am going to Giovanni's.*
Devo andare dal farmacista.	*I must go to the chemist.*

- to translate *since* or *for*

Sono qui da ieri.	*I've been here since yesterday.*
È assente da dieci anni.	*He has been away for 10 years.*

⚠ Italian uses the present tense with these expressions.

- indicate value and measurements:

un francobollo da ottocento lire	*an 800-lire stamp*
una moneta da mille lire	*a 1,000-lire coin*

- to indicate the purpose or use of an object

una tazza da tè	a tea cup
un orologio da uomo	a man's watch
una macchina da scrivere	a typewriter
una lampada da tavolo	a table lamp

- before an infinitive to mean *so as to, enough to*

Fa un caldo da impazzire.	*It's hot enough to drive one mad.*
Che cosa c'è da mangiare/ bere/vedere?	*What is there to eat/drink/see?*

- to indicate manner (*as a/like a/worthy of*)

Ho una fame da lupo.	*I am as hungry as a wolf.*
un pasto da re	*a meal worthy of a king*

B Other uses:

Fuggì/Entrò dalla porta.	*He escaped/came in through the door.*
dalle mie parti	*in my part of the country*
Ha studiato da avvocato.	*He studied to be a lawyer.*

80 The preposition *da* – Exercises

1 Match the pictures with the words in the box.

da sessanta watts	da tavolo	da ottocento lire	da mille lire
	da cucire	da scrivere	

2 Fill the blanks using *da, dal, dall', dallo* etc.

a Domani andrò _____ Andrea.

b A che ora parte il treno _____ Milano?

c Devo andare _____ fruttivendolo.

d Ho bisogno di un servizio _____ caffè.

e _____ quanto tempo abiti in Francia?

f Abito in Francia _____ '73

g Non vedo Mario _____ un mese.

h Non ho niente _____ dichiarare.

i Alle tre esco _____ università.

j Siamo qui _____ pochi giorni.

3 Supply the correct prepositions.

⚠ Note the use of the present tense throughout the passage to give 'immediacy' to the dialogue.

Leonardo Da Vinci nasce **a** _____ Vinci **b** _____ 1452. Anche sua madre, una contadina, e suo padre, un notaio, vengono **c** _____ Vinci. **d** _____ bambino mostra una grande passione **e** _____ il disegno e una grande incostanza **f** _____ studio **g** _____ lettere. Il padre lo manda **h** _____ Firenze **i** _____ bottega **j** _____ Verrocchio, come apprendista pittore, dove dimostra il suo genio che va **k** _____ arte **l** _____ tecnologia. In seguito viene chiamato **m** _____ corte **n** _____ molti re, duchi e mecenati. **o** _____ sua raccolta di annotazioni e disegni si può vedere la grande quantità **p** _____ progetti incompiuti o irrealizzabili che vanno **q** _____ bicicletta **r** _____ elicottero, **s** _____ idrometro (che serve **t** _____ misurare l'umidità **u** _____ aria) **v** _____ paracadute. Vive **w** _____ Milano, invitato **x** _____ Ludovico il Moro, poi **y** _____ Mantova, **z** _____ Venezia e **aa** _____ Roma. Trascorre gli ultimi anni **bb** _____ sua vita **cc** _____ Francia dove muore, **dd** _____ 1519, assistito **ee** _____ fedele amico Francesco Melzi.

161

Some adjectives, adverbs and present participles can also function as prepositions. They are often, but not always, followd by di or a.

accanto a (*near*)
al posto di (*instead of*)
assieme a (*together*)
a causa di (*because of*)
a dispetto di (*despite*)
ad eccezione di (*except for*)
a seconda di (*according to*)
attraverso (*through/across*)
circa (*about*)
contro* (*against*)
davanti a (*in front of*)
dentro* (*inside*)
dietro* (*behind*)
di fronte a (*opposite*)
dopo* (*after*)
durante (*during*)
eccetto (*except*)
fino a (*as far as/until*)
fuori di (*outside/out of*)
in cima (*at the top of*)
in fondo a (*at the bottom of*)
in mezzo a (*in the middle of*)
insieme con (*together with*)

intorno a (*around*)
invece di (*instead of*)
lontano da (*far from*)
lungo (*along*)
malgrado (*in spite of*)
nel mezzo di (*in the middle of*)
nonostante (*notwithstanding*)
per mezzo di (*by means of/through*)
prima di (*before*)
presso* (*near/not far from*)
riguardo a (*regarding*)
rispetto (*with respect to/as to*)
salvo (*except for*)
secondo (*according to*)
senza* (*without*)
sino a (*as far as/until*)
sopra* (*above*)
sotto* (*under/beneath*)
tramite (*by means of/through*)
tranne (*except for*)
verso* (*towards*)
vicino a (*near/next to*)

A The prepositions with an asterisk take **di** when followed by **me, te, lui, lei, noi, voi** or **loro**.

To understand if a word is an adverb or a preposition, you need to remember that an adverb modifies the meaning of a verb, while a preposition precedes a noun, a pronoun, an infinitive or another preposition.

➤ *See pronouns with a preposition in Unit 38.*

1 Complete the sentences using the prepositions in the box.

a L'automobile è _____ .

b Il gatto è _____ .

c Il cane è _____ .

d Gli alberi sono _____ .

e La collina è _____ .

f La bicicletta è _____ .

| davanti | sotto | dietro | in cima | in mezzo | vicino |

2 Choose a word or expression from the box to complete the sentences.

| tramite | nonostante | invece di | durante | circa |
| a dispetto del | senza | assieme a | secondo |

a _____ tutto è sempre molto contento.

b L'ho vista passare _____ suo marito.

c Ho mandato il pacco _____ il corriere.

d _____ guardare la TV, perché non esci?

e Non devi attraversare la strada _____ ben guardare prima a sinistra, poi a destra, poi ancora a sinistra.

f _____ l'estate arrivano i turisti.

g Avrà _____ cinquant'anni.

h _____ del maltempo uscì e camminò per molti chilometri.

i _____ loro Marianna non ha mai lavorato.

3 Translate the following into Italian.

a The car stopped in the middle of the road.

b They were all present except for two.

c I couldn't hear because of the noise (**rumore**).

d Is Lucca far from here?

e The fountain is next to the Basilica.

f Today the pound is up (**in rialzo**) with respect to the dollar (**dollaro**).

82 UNIT | Adverbs

A In English, most adverbs are formed by adding *-ly* to the adjective: *slow* (adjective) becomes *slowly* (adverb). In Italian, **-mente** is added to the feminine form of the adjective: **lenta** (adjective) becomes **lentamente** (adverb).

- Adjectives ending in **-e** just add **-ment**e: **veloce** → **velocemente**.
- Adverbs are usually placed next to the verb they modify.
  Lavora intensamente.   *He works constantly.*
- Most adjectives ending in **-le** and **-re** drop their final vowel before adding **-mente**: **facile** → **facilmente**, **regolare** → **regolarmente**.

B As well as a verb, adverbs can modify an adjective or another adverb.
  Siamo molto lieti di conoscerLa.   *We are pleased to make your acquaintance.*

In this example, **molto** is the adverb modifying the adjective **lieti**.

  Il professore ha spiegato la lezione *The teacher has explained the lesson very clearly.*
  molto chiaramente.

In the above example, the adverb **molto** illustrates the adverb **chiaramente**.

C Adverbs are invariable, so remember that when **molto**, **tanto** or **troppo** are used as adverbs, they remain as they are, whereas when used as adjectives they agree with the noun.
  molto bella *very beautiful*   molte telefonate *many telephone calls*

D Other adjectives which can be used as adverbs are: **vicino** (*nearby*); **lontano** (*far away*); **chiaro/chiaramente** (*clearly*); **forte** (*loudly*); **duro** (*hard*); **solo** or **soltanto/solamente** (*only*): Parla troppo forte. *He speaks too loudly.*

E In English, *better* and *worse* can be either adjectives or adverbs. In Italian, they have two different forms as follows:

adverbs	**bene** (*well*)	**meglio** (*better*)	**male** (*badly*)	**peggio** (*worse*)
adjectives	**buono** (*good*)	**migliore** (*better*)	**cattivo** (*bad*)	**peggiore** (*worse*)

  Parla italiano molto bene.   *S/he speaks Italian very well.*
  Va di bene in meglio.   *It's getting better and better.*

► See irregular adjectives in Unit 30.

82 UNIT Adverbs – Exercises

1 Form the adverb from the following adjectives.

a chiaro	i probabile	q cortese
b cattivo	j agile	r molle
c veloce	k gentile	s freddo
d difficile	l maggiore	t particolare
e grande	m forte	u sensibile
f rapido	n duro	v sincero
g magnifico	o elegante	w affettuoso
h inutile	p ovvio	x diretto

2 Choose a suitable adverb from the box to complete each sentence.

costantemente	impulsivamente	terribilmente	precipitosamente
attivamente	vigorosamente	allegramente	confusamente

a Marietto non riesce a tacere (*to be quiet*) un momento: parla _____ .

b Gli studenti uscirono dall'aula _____ .

c Partecipa _____ a molte opere di beneficenza.

d Negò tutto _____ .

e Agì _____ .

f Ha preso lo scherzo _____ .

g Il discorso è stato _____ noioso.

h A causa del buio vedeva _____ .

3 Change the expressions in bold to a suitable adverb.

E.g. **Ha cambiato il suo modo di vivere in maniera radicale.** → **Ha cambiato il suo modo di vivere radicalmente.**

a Si esprime **in modo chiaro**.

b Lavora **con un ritmo molto lento**.

c Parla italiano **in modo corretto**.

d Non parlare **a voce alta**!

e Questo è un lavoro **non ben fatt**o.

4 Translate the following into Italian.

a I speak Italian better (*adverb*) than you.

b You speak English better than me.

c This wine is good but that one is better.

d In my opinion (**Secondo me**) English tea is better than Italian tea.

e In my opinion, Italian coffee is better than English coffee.

83 UNIT | Other adverbs and expressions

As well as adverbs deriving from adjectives, there are adverbs with a form of their own.

A Adverbs of manner express the way in which something happens. These include most of those ending in **-mente** dealt with in the previous unit.

B Adverbs of time include:

ora/adesso (*now*); allora (*then/at that time*); ancora (*still/yet/again*); annualmente (*yearly*); appena (*just/scarcely/hardly*); domani (*tomorrow*); dopo (*afterwards*); dopodomani (*the day after tomorrow*); finora (*until now*); già (*already*); ieri (*yesterday*); mai (*never*); mensilmente (*monthly*); oggi (*today*); ormai (*by now/by then*); poi (*next/then*); presto (*soon/quickly*); raramente (*seldom*); sempre (*always*); settimanalmente (*weekly*); spesso (*often*); subito (*immediately/at once*); tardi (*late*).

Adverbial expressions of time:

per tempo (*early*), per ora (*for the time being*), di quando in quando (*every so often*).

C Adverbs of place include:

altrove (*somewhere else*); davanti (*in front*); dappertutto (*everywhere*); dentro (*inside*); dietro (*behind*); fuori (*outside*); laggiù (*over/down there*); lassù (*up there*); lì/là (*there*); lontano (*far away*); oltre (*farther/further*); qui/qua (*here*); quaggiù (*down here*); quassù (*up here*); sopra/su (*up*); sotto (*underneath*); vicino (*nearby*).

Adverbial expressions of place include:

di sopra (*upstairs*); di sotto (*downstairs*); in su (*upwards*); in giù (*downwards*); per di qua (*this way*); per di là (*that way*).

D Adverbs of quantity include:

abbastanza (*sufficiently/enough*); parecchio/alquanto (*quite/rather*); altrettanto (*equally*); assai (*a lot/much*); meno (*less*); molto (*a lot/(very) much/a great deal*); niente/nulla (*not at all*); poco (*little*); quanto (*how much/how many/how far*).

Adverbial expressions of quantity include:

pressapoco/all'incirca (*approximately*); né più né meno (*no more no less*).

E Other adverbs or adverbial expressions:

certo/certamente/sicuro/sicuramente (*certainly/of course/sure*); appunto (*exactly*); nemmeno/neanche, eppure (*not even*); non (*not*); forse (*perhaps*); quasi (*almost*); eventualmente (*if needs be/if necessary*); probabilmente (*probably*); da lontano (*from a distance*); da vicino (*closely*); in generale (*in general*); in breve (*in short*); di solito (*usually*).

1 Match the two halves of the sentences.

a Pago il lattaio …   1 … in discoteca.
b Ricevo lo stipendio …   2 … ma oggi sto bene.
c Pago le tasse …   3 … è troppo tardi.
d Ieri stavo male …   4 … mensilmente.
e Ormai …   5 … annualmente.
f Vado spesso …   6 … settimanalmente.
g Vieni qui …   7 … immediatamente.

2 Translate into Italian the adverb or adverbial expressions in this dialogue between Marcella and her friend Elisa.

MARCELLA Non riesco a trovare il gatto, ho guardato (**a** *everywhere*): (**b** *under*) il sofà, (**c** *up there*), sull'armadio, (**d** *outside*), ma non lo trovo.

ELISA Sarà (**e** *somewhere else*). Non ti preoccupare, lo sai che (**f** *every so often*) scompare.

MARCELLA Sì lo so, ma (**g** *usually*) scompare dopo aver mangiato. Non va (**h** *never*) via a stomaco vuoto. Non può essere andato tanto (**i** *far*).

ELISA Quando lo hai visto, l'ultima volta?

MARCELLA Mah, saranno state le otto …

ELISA Sarà (**j** *upstairs*).

MARCELLA Non credo perché sono scesa proprio (**k** *now*) e non l'ho visto.

ELISA (**l** *Then*) potrebbe essere dalla vicina, lo sai che al suo bambino piace giocare con lui.

MARCELLA (**m** *Perhaps*). Vado a vedere e torno (**n** *immediately*) perché il pollo al forno è (**o** *nearly*) pronto.'
(*after a little while*)

MARCELLA Non è (**p** *not even there*). Pazienza, vado un momento (**q** *upstairs*) e poi pranziamo.
(*a few moments later*)

MARCELLA Avevi ragione. il gatto è (**r** *upstairs*) (**s** *under*) la poltrona che si mangia il pollo!

84 UNIT | The position of adverbs

A With many adverbs, of manner in particular, the position of the adverb is free, its position only slightly changing the emphasis of its meaning.

Generalmente esco la domenica.
Esco generalmente la domenica. } *I usually go out on Sundays.*
La domenica esco, generalmente.

B Generally the adverb goes before the adjective or another adverb, as in English.

Questa casa è troppo rumorosa.　　*This house is too noisy.*

C When an adverb qualifies a verb, it usually goes after it ...

Abitano lontano.　　　　　　　*They live far away.*
Io mi siedo davanti.　　　　　　*I sit in front.*

... but **ieri**, **oggi** and **domani** tend to be placed before the verb.

Domani scade l'abbonamento　　*The TV licence is due tomorrow.*
alla TV.
Ieri ha fatto bel tempo.　　　　*The weather was fine yesterday.*

D With compound tenses, the adverbs of time **ancora**, **appena**, **già**, **mai** and **sempre** are placed, as in English, between the auxiliary and the verb.

Sono sempre andata in vacanza　　*I have always been on holiday to*
al mare.　　　　　　　　　　*the seaside.*
Marco è già partito.　　　　　　*Marco has already left.*
Quel film l'ho già visto.　　　　*I have already seen that film.*
Non ho ancora finito.　　　　　*I have not finished yet.*

⚠ Note the use of the direct object pronoun (**l'**). When the object is a noun at the beginning of the sentence (rather than after the verb as in **Ho già visto quel film**), it is followed by the direct object pronoun.

In other words, the object of the sentence needs to be repeated twice:

Hai la chiave (*object*)?　　　　*Have you the key?*
La chiave (*object*) la (*direct object*　*The key, have you got it?*
pronoun) hai?

OR La chiave ce l'hai? (**ce** is added to make the sentence flow better)

1 **Choose a suitable adverb from the box for each sentence and add it in the correct place.**

a È una persona che si emoziona.

b D'estate piove.

c Parla italiano.

d Se vuoi farti comprendere devi parlare.

e Ha continuato a negare.

f Vedo che hai studiato.

g Non ho finito.

h Ha rifiutato i loro consigli.

i Credo che Mario sia uscito.

j Non sono stata in Canada.

> lentamente e chiaramente
> diligentemente   raramente
> correntemente   facilmente
> fermamente   sempre
> ancora   mai   già

2 **Put the words in the right order.**

a onestamente lavorato sempre Ha

b alla domanda mia debolmente Rispose

c letto già Ho libro quel

d ricco Non molto interiormente è

e velocemente uscito È ma so dove non andato sia

3 **Each number corresponds to the same letter each time it is used. With the help of the clues, find the adverbs.**

a 12 2 8 4 5 4 6 7 3 9 10 11 9
 quasi certamente

b 12 8 13 13 6 4 6 7 3 9 10 11 9
 per quanto possibile

c 7 8 10 11 5 10 8
 non vicino

d 16 8 12 8 16 8 3 5 10 6
 tra due giorni

e 11 2 8 12 12 8
 più del necessario

f 3 9 14 7 6 8
 va di bene in ...

g 12 9 14 14 6 8
 il contrario di **meglio**

h 15 9 7 8 17 9 3 9 10 11 9
 rapidamente

85 UNIT | Conjunctions

Conjunctions are invariable. They join two words to make a single phrase, or two phrases to make a longer and more articulate sentence.

A Some conjunctions join two words or two separate phrases which otherwise could stand by themselves: *This book is expensive + this book is interesting = This book is expensive but/and interesting.*

B Among the most common conjunctions are:

- **anche** (*also/too*) È venuta anche Mariangela. *Mariangela came too.*

- **e** (*and*); to sound better **e** acquires a **-d** before a vowel – particularly before another **e** Ho visto Carla ed Enrica. *I saw Carla and Enrica.*

- **eppure/tuttavia** (*yet/nevertheless*)
  Tu non mi credi, eppure è vero.　　*You don't believe me, and yet it is true.*

- **anzi** (*on the contrary*)
  Oggi non fa freddo, anzi, fa　　*Today isn't cold, on the contrary it's*
  piuttosto caldo.　　*rather warm.*

- **quindi/dunque/perciò** (*so/therefore*) È tardi perciò vado. *It's late so I'll go.*

- **ma** (*but*) È superficiale ma onesto. *He is superficial but honest.*

- **però** (*however/but*)
  Questo cappotto costa caro però è　　*This coat is expensive however it's*
  di buona qualità.　　*of good quality.*

- **cioè** (*that is (to say)/namely*)
  Sarò lì alle cinque cioè tra due ore.　　*I'll be there at five, that is in two hours' time.*

- **infatti** (*in fact*)
  Mi sembrava troppo caro, infatti　　*I thought it was too expensive, in*
  c'era un errore nel conto.　　*fact there was a mistake on the bill.*

- **o ... o/oppure** (*either ... or*)
  o questo o quello　　*either this one or that one*

- **sia ... sia/sia ... che** (*both ... and*)
  Ho comprato sia la cassetta che il CD.　　*I bought both the cassette and the CD.*

- **né ... né** (*neither ... nor*) né carne né pesce *neither fish nor fowl*

- **non solo/soltanto ... ma** (*not only ... but*)
  È un libro non soltanto divertente　　*It's not only an amusing book but*
  ma anche istruttivo.　　*also educational.*

1 Combine the sentences using the conjunctions in bold.

a Questa mattina ho deciso di prendere il battello per Vernazza.

Fa bel tempo.

perché

Il mare è calmo.

e

b Ho indossato il costume da bagno.
Desidero prendere il sole sul battello durante il viaggio.

siccome

c Generalmente arrivo presto alla stazione marittima.
Mi pace sedere a prora.

poiché

ma

Non sempre ci riesco.

siccome

La gente, anche se arriva dopo di me, riesce sempre a salire prima. Durante il viaggio immagino di essere sola sul mio panfilo.

mentre

d La gente chiacchiera, riceve.

o

Fa telefonate, io mi rilasso osservando la bellissima costa, i gabbiani.

e

I riflessi del sole sulle piccole onde d'acqua fresca e trasparente.

e All'arrivo mi fermo sulla piccola spiaggia.
Vado al bar a prendere un succo di frutta.

oppure

f Verso l'una pranzo nel mio ristorante preferito.
Il ristorante 'Gambero Rosso'.

cioè

g Dopo il caffè faccio il giro delle viuzze (*lanes*).
Faccio qualche piccola spesa.

poi

Scrivo qualche cartolina agli amici.

e

h Verso le quattro e mezzo è ora di tornare.
Salgo sul battello.

quindi

i Una giornata tranquilla.

ma

Non noiosa.

anzi

Molto benefica.

sia

Fisicamente.

Per la mente.

che

86 UNIT | Conjunctions followed by the subjunctive

Below is a list of conjunctions joining two phrases together, one of which is subordinate to the other.

A In the phrase *I study Italian because I want to speak and understand it*, the first part (*I study Italian*) can stand by itself, this is the main clause; the second (*because I want ...*) is the dependent clause. Below is a list of conjunctions introducing a dependent clause which requires a subjunctive.

- **a condizione che/a patto che** (*on condition (that)*)
  Vengo a condizione che venga anche lui. | *I'll go on condition that he goes too.*

- **purché** (*as long as*)
  Ti aiuto purché tu non lo dica a Maria. | *I'll help you as long as you do not tell Maria.*

- **anche se** (*even if*)
  Uscirebbe anche se grandinasse. | *She would go out even if it was hailing.*

- **qualora** (*in case/if*)
  Qualora me ne dimenticassi, ti prego di ricordarmelo. | *In case I forget, please remind me.*

- **che** (*that*)
  Penso che sia uscito. | *I think he has gone out.*

- **benché/nonostante/sebbene** (*although/notwithstanding/even though*)
  Benché fosse in ritardo, se la prese con comodo. | *Even though she was late, she took it easy.*
  Sebbene abbia perso tutto, è sempre molto allegro. | *Although he lost everything, he is always cheerful.*

- **a meno che (non)** (*unless*)
  Non supererai l'esame a meno che non studi di più. | *You will not pass the exam unless you study more.*

- **prima che** (*before*)
  Pensaci prima che sia troppo tardi. | *Think about it before it is too late.*

- **affinché/in modo che** (*so that/in order that*)
  Protesto affinché sia fatta giustizia. | *I protest in order that justice be done.*

➤ *See subjunctive in Units 60–63.*

86 UNIT Conjunctions followed by the subjunctive – *Exercises*

1 Match the two halves of the sentences.

a Ti do la macchina a patto che…	**1** … prima che perda la pazienza.
b Ti permetto di andare in discoteca …	**2** … a meno che non piova.
c Rimarrebbe calmo anche se …	**3** … non ho ricevuto la lettera.
d Nel caso che io non ritornassi in tempo …	**4** … sono stato bocciato.
e So che lui …	**5** … è una persona onesta.
f Nonostante abbia studiato …	**6** … fai tu la spesa.
g Sebbene lui mi abbia scritto …	**7** … cascasse il mondo.
h Domani pianterò i fiori in giardino …	**8** … tu compri la benzina.
i Vai via …	**9** … purché ritorni per mezzanotte.
j Affinché sentissero …	**10** … dovette parlare più forte.

2 Join the two clauses in each line using the conjunction in brackets. You will need to modify the sentence, e.g. change the verb into the subjunctive tense, omit other conjunctions where necessary, or even delete a verb.

E.g. Siamo ancora in inverno ma fa abbastanza caldo. (Benché) →
Benché faccia abbastanza caldo siamo ancora in inverno.

a È un attore di mezza età. Recita la parte di un giovanotto. (Benché)
b Ti presto i soldi, se me li rendi domani. (a patto che)
c Vive solo ma ha sempre moltissima gente in casa. (Sebbene)
d Domani vado in gita, spero che non piova. (a meno che)
e Gli ho scritto per fargli sapere che sono arrivata. (affinché)
f È meglio tornare a casa, sta per piovere. (prima che)
g Parto giovedì se ci sono posti sull'aereo. (purché)
h Se tu hai bisogno di aiuto telefonami. (qualora)
i Andò a Roma ma nessuno lo sapeva. (senza che)

3 Translate the following into Italian.

a Although she doesn't say it, she would like to go to the mountains.
b Despite the fact that he has won the lottery, he lives as before.
c She is always very cheerful, as long as one does not mention Bruno.
d You must book (**prenotare**) the hotel before it's too late.
e If you need something, you must let me know.
f Unless you work, you cannot buy that boat (**barca**).
g I think she has arrived.
h He bought this flat (**appartamento**) without my knowlege.

87 UNIT | Interjections and exclamations

An interjection is an invariable part of speech and is used to express a mood or to call someone's attention.

A Among the most common interjections are: **ah! oh! eh! uh! ih!**, the meaning of which depends mainly on the tone of one's voice.

B Others, not depending on the tone of the voice, are:
- auff! uff! uffa! (*to show impatience*) Uffa, che noia! *How boring!*
- ehi!/ehilà! (*hey! hullo! you there! ahoy!*)
- ohi! ohé! (*to call someone*) ho! hey! he!
- mah! (*who knows!*) (to show uncertainty, doubt or resignation; the latter often accompanied by a very slight shake of one's head)
- ahimè!/ohimé (*alas!*)
- puh! puah! phew! pshaw! (*to show repulsion*)

C Interjections are usually followed by an exclamation mark which can appear at the end of the sentence in which case the interjection is followed by a comma: Ehi, sto parlando a te! *Hey I am talking to you!*

D Some other expressions used as exclamations are:

Alla buon'ora! (*At last! Finally!*)
Mamma mia! (*Dear me!*)
Santo cielo! (*Goodness gracious!*)
Bravo! Brava! (*Well done!*)
Evviva! Viva! (*Hurray! hurrah!*)
Salve! (*Hello!*)
Bene! (*Well! All right! Ok!*)
Sicuro! (*Of course! Sure!*)
Su!/Dai! (*Come on! Come (now)!*)
Che fregatura! (*What a rip-off*)!
Povero me! (*Poor me!*)
Coraggio! (*Take heart!*)
Per carità! (*For pity sake!/please!*)
Che barba! (*How boring!*)
Per amor del cielo! (*For heaven's sake!*)
Via! (*Go away!/(to start a race or similar) Go!/ (to incite) Come on!*)

Vallo a raccontare ad un altro! (*Tell that to the marines!*)
Meno male! (*Thank goodness!*)
Che bugiardo! (*What a fibber!*)
Che stupido! (*How stupid!*)
Che coraggio! (*How brave!*)
Accidenti! (*My goodness!/Damn it!*)

1 Match the two halves of the sentences.

a Quando eravamo in Italia siamo andati a trovarli …

b Me lo hanno fatto pagare il doppio.

c Per amor del cielo,…

d Mamma mia, …

e Povero me, …

f Evviva, …

g Coraggio, …

h Su, …

i Uffa, …

j Ehi, …

1 … dico a te! Sei sordo?

2 … che barba!

3 … fai presto!

4 … che presto arriva l'ambulanza!

5 … la nostra squadra ha vinto!

6 … ho perso il passaporto!

7 … che carattere che hai!

8 … non dirle nulla!

9 … Che fregatura!

10 … ma, ahimè, loro erano in Francia!

2 Choose one of the expressions in the box in response to each sentence of your friend's account of his holiday in Kenya.

> Dai, vallo a raccontare ad un altro! Che coraggio! Che stupido!
> Accidenti che sfortuna! Che bugiardo che sei! Meno male!

a Quando ero in Kenia ho noleggiato una jeep e sono andato a fare un safari da solo …

b Ad un certo punto ho visto un leone, allora ho fermato la macchina e sono sceso.

c Avevo lasciato la portiera aperta nel caso che il leone mi attaccasse …

d Soltanto che una folata di vento ha chiuso la portiera.

e Pensa che io ero completamente solo e disarmato ma mi è bastato schioccare le dita per farlo fuggire!

f Non mi credi? Eppure ti assicuro che è vero.

88 UNIT The negative

A A pronoun cannot be separated from the verb, so **non** in this case precedes the pronoun.

Ti è piaciuto il film?	*Did you like the film?*
No, non mi è piaciuto.	*No, I didn't like it.*

! Remember that **no** (*no*) isn't a substitute for **non** (*not*).

B Negative words or expressions such as **niente/nulla** (*nothing*), **nessuno** (*none/nobody*), **in nessun luogo/da nessuna parte** (*nowhere*), **mai** (*never*), **per niente** (*at all*), are used together with **non**.

Non c'è nessuno.	*There is nobody.*
Non lo trovo da nessuna parte.	*I cannot see it anywhere.*
Non viene mai nessuno.	*Nobody ever comes.*

! When a negative word is used as a subject, **non** is omitted.

Nessuno sa chi sia.	*Nobody knows who he is.*
Niente può fermarlo.	*He stops at nothing.*

C Negative expressions

- **non ... mai** (*never, not ever*)
  Non lo vedo mai.   *I never see him.*
- **non ... nessuno** (*not anybody, nobody*)
  Non vedo nessuno.   *I don't see anybody.*
- **non ... mai nessuno** (*never anybody*)
  Non vedo mai nessuno.   *I never see anybody.*
- **non ... niente/nulla** (*nothing/not anything*)
  Non vedo nulla.   *I can't see anything.*
- **non ... mai niente** (*never anything*)
  Non dice mai niente.   *He never says anything.*
- **non ... per niente/affatto** (*not ... at all*)
  Non mi piace per niente.   *I don't like it at all.*
- **non ... neanche/neppure/nemmeno** (*not ... even*)
  Non l'ha neppure ringraziato.   *She didn't even thank him.*
- **non ... più** (*no more/no longer/not any more*)
  Non dipingo più.   *I no longer paint.*
- **non ... da nessuna parte** (*not anywhere, nowhere*)
  Carla non va da nessuna parte.   *Carla doesn't go anywhere.*
- **non ... né ... né** (*neither ... nor*)
  Non voglio né l'uno né l'altro.   *I want neither the one nor the other.*

1 Change these sentences to mean the opposite

E.g. Compro sempre il giornale. → Non compro mai il giornale.
Mi piacciono tutti e due. → Non mi piace né l'uno né l'altro.
Vai ancora in vacanza a Lucca? → No, non ci vado più.

a C'era molta gente.
b C'è sempre molta gente.
c Ha molto da fare.
d Ha sempre molto da fare.
e Sa tutto.
f Sa sempre tutto.
g Mi piace moltissimo.
h Mi ha ringraziato.
i Scrivi ancora romanzi?
j Li compro tutti e due.

2 Answer the questions in the negative.

E.g. Vi è piaciuta la commedia? → No, non ci è piaciuta.
Scrivi spesso a Marianna? → No, non le scrivo mai.

a Ti sono piaciuti i film?
b Vi è piaciuto lo spettacolo?
c Lo vedi spesso?
d C'era qualcuno nel parco?
e Hai qualcosa per me?
f Giochi ancora (*still*) a tennis?
g Hai trovato le chiavi?
h Vuoi questo o quello?

3 Match the questions and answers.

a Dove andrete in vacanza per il ferragosto?
b Hai fatto il compito?
c Quanto hai pagato questo vestito?
d Io non ci credo, e tu?
e Che cosa ti ha detto Teresa?
f Chi di voi ha preso la mia auto?
g Faresti il paracadutista?
h Hai visto Mario o Goffredo?

1 Neanch'io.
2 Niente, l'ho fatto io.
3 No.
4 Nessuno.
5 Mai!
6 Né l'uno né l'altro.
7 Da nessuna parte.
8 Niente.

89 UNIT | False negatives and prefixes

There are some expressions using **non** *which are not negative. There are also some prefixes which give words a negative value.*

A Positive expressions containing **non**:

- **a meno che non** (*unless*) (requires the subjunctive)

  Arriverò alle tre a meno che non ci sia troppo traffico.
  I will arrive by three o'clock unless there is too much traffic.

- **finché non** (*until/till*)

  Non potrò uscire finché non avrò finito questo.
  I will not be able to go out until I have finished this.

- **non** + verb + **che** (*only/nothing but*)

  Non possiamo che attendere i risultati degli esami.
  We can only wait for the exam results./We can do nothing but wait for the exam results.

B As in English, some letters added at the beginning of a word (a prefix) may change the meaning of it.

- The prefix **ri-**, similar to the English **re-**, is often used in the sense of *again*: elaborare (*to elaborate*), rielaborare (*to elaborate/work out again*); vedere (*to see*), rivedere (*to see/meet again*); formare (*to form*), riformare (*to re-form/shape again*); provare (*to try*), riprovare (*to try again*).

- The prefix **s-** often (but not always) gives adjectives, verbs and nouns an opposite meaning:
  fiorire (*to bloom*), sfiorire (*to wither*); fiducia (*trust*), sfiducia (*mistrust/distrust*); legare (*to tie/fasten*), slegare (*to untie*); proporzionato (*proportional/proportionate*), sproporzionato (*disproportional*).

- The prefix **in-** gives a 'not' value and is used mainly before adjectives and nouns:
  abile (*able/capable*), inabile (*unable/incapable*); fedeltà (*fidelity/faithfulness*), infedeltà (*infidelity/unfaithfulness*).

- The prefixes **de-**, **di-** and **dis-**, also have a negative value:
  centralizzare (*to centralize*), decentrare (*to decentralize*); sperare (*to hope*), disperare (*to despair*); armare (*to arm*), disarmare (*to disarm*).

- **contro**, **contra** express opposition:
  indicato (*suitable/apt/advisable*), controindicato (*inadvisable*); dire (*to say*), contraddire (*to contradict*).

89 UNIT False negatives and prefixes – *Exercises*

1 Add *a meno che non* + subjunctive to the sentences below.

E.g. Concluderò l'affare _____ (esserci) problemi finanziari. →
Concluderò l'affare a meno che non ci siano problemi finanziari.

a Uscirò _____ (piovere).

b Arriveranno in ritardo _____ (partire) presto.

c Verrà questa sera _____ (essere) chiamato d'urgenza all'ospedale.

d Andrò col treno delle nove _____ ce ne (essere) uno prima.

e Ti aspetterò _____ tu (arrivare) in ritardo.

f Comprerò quell'auto _____ (essere) troppo cara.

2 Choose between *finché non ...* or *a meno che non ...* and complete the sentences below.

a Ti aspetterò _____ arriverai.

b Ti scriverò _____ sia troppo occupata.

c Non lo sapevo _____ me lo hai detto tu.

d Lo seguì con lo sguardo _____ lo vide scomparire dietro l'angolo.

e Lo comprerò _____ sia troppo caro.

f Verrò sicuramente _____ succeda qualcosa di inaspettato.

3 Translate the following into Italian.

E.g. She does nothing but talk about him. → Non fa che parlare di lui.

a They believe in no one but him.

b She only thinks about work.

c He does nothing but talk about sport.

d They do nothing but criticise.

e She does nothing but complain (**lamentarsi**).

f You think only of yourself.

4 Give the opposite meaning to the following sentences by adding or deleting the prefixes *s-, in-, de-, contro,* etc. as necessary.

a Questa medicina è indicata per i sofferenti di cuore.

b Quel macchinario è in uso dall'anno scorso.

c Dispero di riuscire.

d Il governo ha deciso di centralizzare i servizi pubblici.

e È una persona capace.

f Le piante sono presto fiorite.

90 UNIT | Relative pronouns

che = who, whom, which, that
di, **a**, **da**, etc. + **cui** = of, to, from, etc. whom/which
il, **la**, **i**, **le** + **cui** = whose

A **Che** is invariable and is used both as a subject and a direct object pronoun.

l'attore che ha recitato Amleto	*the actor who played Hamlet*
l'attore che ti ho presentato	*the actor (whom) I introduced to you*
il fax che ti ho spedito	*the fax (that) I sent you*

Il/la quale, i/le quali can be used instead of **che** to avoid ambiguity:

È il figlio della mia vicina che ha scritto da Cambridge. (Who wrote?)
He is the son of my neighbour who wrote from Cambridge.
È il figlio della mia vicina la quale ha scritto da Cambridge. (la vicina)
È il figlio della mia vicina il quale ha scritto da Cambridge. (il figlio)

⚠ Unlike English, the relative pronoun MUST NOT be omitted.

B **Cui** is invariable and is used instead of **che** before a preposition.

la città da cui vengo	*the town from which I come*
il ragazzo con cui esco	*the boy I go out with (with whom I go out)*
la nave in cui ho viaggiato	*the ship in which I travelled*

C **Il/la/i/le cui** + noun translate *whose* + noun:

La cliente il cui fax è arrivato ieri è al telefono.	*The client whose fax arrived yesterday is on the phone.*
Il libro, il cui autore è mio amico, è arrivato questa mattina.	*The book, whose author is a friend of mine, has arrived this morning.*

Whose can also be translated by **il/lo/la/l'/i/gli/le** + noun + **del/della quale**, **dei/delle quali**.

La cliente il fax della quale è arrivato questa mattina è al telefono.
Il libro, l'autore del quale è mio amico, è arrivato questa mattina.

Relative pronouns – Exercises

1 Match the two halves of the sentences, then read them aloud.

a la lettera che …	**1** … ti ho prestato
b l'autobus …	**2** … recitato 'Fedora'
c gli studenti che…	**3** … ho visto alla TV
d il programma che …	**4** … che ho preso
e il pittore che ti ha …	**5** … ti ho scritto
f l'attrice che ha …	**6** … fatto il ritratto
g i soldi che …	**7** … che ti ho presentato
h l'amico …	**8** … hanno superato l'esame

2 Add *di, a, da,* etc. + *cui* to the sentences below.

a La cittadina _____ viene si chiama Viareggio.

b La poltrona _____ siedo è molto comoda.

c La ragione _____ non ti scrivo è che non ho molto tempo.

d L'autobus _____ vado in ufficio è il numero 39.

e La persona _____ ho chiesto un'informazione era straniera.

f Gli amici _____ ti ho parlato arriveranno domani.

g L'uomo _____ ho viaggiato viene da Barletta.

3 Modify the sentences below using *il/la* etc. *cui* + noun.

> *E.g.* Lo scrittore, i libri del quale sono tanto apprezzati, ha cambiato lavoro.
> → Lo scrittore, i cui libri sono tanto apprezzati, ha cambiato lavoro.

a La casa, il proprietario della quale è stato arrestato, è in vendita.

b Il cane, il proprietario del quale è all'ospedale, è rimasto solo.

c Maria, il marito della quale ha vinto al lotto, vuole divorziare.

d Il cantante, i dischi del quale vanno a ruba (*sell like hot cakes*), terrà un concerto al Teatro Regio.

e Il giornalista, l'articolo del quale è tanto discusso, è stato denunciato.

f Gli studenti, il professore dei quali ha l'influenza, sono felicissimi.

4 Translate the following into Italian.

a The book I bought is not as good as I thought.

b The table I reserved is not this one.

c The lady whose daughter is in Rome asked me to go and see her.

d The window from which I see the park needs new curtains (**tende**).

e Our friend whose house was sold has rented (**ha affittato**) a flat.

f The people you are talking about have moved (**traslocato**).

91 UNIT | Other relative pronouns

English uses *what* as an interrogative pronoun (*What is this?*) as well as a relative pronoun (*what you say is right*). Italian uses two different words.

ciò che/quello che = *what*
tutto ciò che/tutto quello che = *all that*
chi = *he/she/those who*
colui che = *he who*
colei che = *she who*
coloro che = *those who*

A **Ciò che** and **quello che** have the same meaning.

Ciò che dici è molto interessante.	*What you say is very interesting.*
Quello che fai è affar tuo.	*What you do is your business.*

B **Tutto ciò che** and **tutto quello che** have the same meaning.

Questo è tutto quello che so.	*This is all I know.*
Di tutto quello che ha scritto gli hanno pubblicato soltanto un libro.	*Of all he wrote only one book was published.*

C **Chi** is invariable and can only refer to people. It is used in the singular even when referring to more than one person. It can be substituted by **colui che** (masculine), **colei che** (feminine) or **coloro che** (masculine and feminine plural).

Chi è interessato scriva al seguente indirizzo.
Coloro che sono interessati scrivano al seguente indrizzo. } *Whoever is interested must write to the following address.*

Chi is also used in proverbs.

Chi vuole vada chi non vuole mandi.	*If you want a thing done go, if not send someone.*
Chi s'aiuta, Dio l'aiuta.	*God helps those who help themselves.*
Chi più ha più vuole.	*Appetite comes with eating.*

➤ See interrogative pronouns in Unit 93.

Proverbio: 'Chi sa fa e chi non sa insegna'.

1 Match the two halves of the sentences.

a Ciò che fai …   1 … è falso.

b Quello che dici mi …   2 … sembra giusto.

c Ciò che conta …   3 … non m'interessa.

d Tutto quello che so è …   4 … è essere sereni.

e Tutto quello che dice …   5 … che c'è qualcosa che non va.

f Tutto quello che fa è …   6 … mangiare e dormire.

g Con tutto quello che guadagna …   7 … non ha mai una lira.

h Per tutto quello che ha fatto …   8 … ha ricevuto un premio.

2 Replace *chi* with *colui che, colei che, coloro che*, as required. Note that you will have to change some verbs into their plural forms.

a Chi ha scritto questa lettera di scuse è la zia di mio marito.

b Chi ha telefonato era la cugina di mio cognato.

c Chi desidera fare domanda (**to apply**) scriva alla segretaria.

d Chi hai visto erano le mie sorelle.

e Chi dorme non piglia pesci.

f Chi semina vento raccoglie tempesta.

3 Translate the following into Italian.

a He who is without sin cast (**scagli**) the first stone.

b What she does is not my concern.

c What counts is to be healthy.

d What they say is false.

e They gave her all (that) they had.

f Is this all you can do?

g This is all I know.

h They took all there was.

i We bought all (that) we could.

92 UNIT | Indefinite pronouns

These words stand instead of a noun. They are called indefinite because the exact number of person(s) or object(s) they represent is not specified.

A Common indefinite pronouns
- **chiunque** (*anybody/anyone/whoever*)
  Chiunque venga digli di attendere.   *Whoever comes tell him to wait.*
- **qualunque/qualsiasi cosa** (*anything*)
- **niente/nulla** (*nothing, anything*)
  Non si accorge mai di nulla.   *She never notices anything.*
- **ognuno** (*everybody/everyone/each one*)
  Ognuno ha donato dieci sterline.   *Each one gave ten pounds.*
- **qualcosa/qualche cosa** (*something/anything*)
  Vuoi qualcosa da bere?   *Would you like something to drink?*
- **qualcuno** (*someone/somebody, anybody/anyone, some*)
  C'è qualcuno che ti vuole.   *There is someone asking for you.*
  Ne prendo qualcuna.   *I'll take some.*

⚠ **Qualcuno** becomes **qualcun** before **altro** and **qualcun'** before **altra**.
Verrà qualcun altro.   *Someone else will come.*

- **uno** (*one/someone/somebody/each*)
  uno di noi   *one of us*
  Costano mille lire l'una.   *They cost a thousand lire each.*

⚠ **Ognuno**, **qualcuno** and **uno** have feminine forms, all the others are invariable.

B These indefinite words can function both as pronouns and adjectives.
- **alcun, alcuno** (-a,-i,-e) (*some* (usually plural))
- **ciascun, ciascuno, ciascuna** (*everybody/each (one)*)
- **nessun, nessuno, nessuna** (*nobody/no one/none/no*)
- **altro** (-a,-i,-e) (*another (one)/other*)
- **parecchio** (-a,-i,-e) (*quite a lot/several*)
- **molto/tanto** (-a,-i,-e) (*much/a lot*)
- **troppo** (-a,-i,-e) (*too much/too many*)
- **poco** (**poca, pochi, poche**) (*a little/a few*)
- **tutto** (-a,-i,-e) (*all/everything/everybody*)

➤ See indefinite adjectives in Unit 20.

1 Choose the correct word from the box to complete the sentences.

a Non vedo _____ .

b Non voglio _____ .

c _____ aveva qualcosa da dire.

d Vorrei _____ di più elegante.

e C'è _____ che vuole una fetta di torta?

f Chiedilo a _____ altro.

g È _____ del nostro gruppo.

h _____ sia digli di attendere.

chiunque
niente
nessuno
ciascuno
qualcun
uno
qualcuno
qualcosa

2 You are buying some delicious cakes. Take part in the dialogue using the English prompts.

YOU	**a** *'How much do they cost each?'*
COMMESSA	Duemila lire, signora.
YOU	**b** *They cost quite a lot!*
COMMESSA	Certo signora, ma sono ehm … eccellenti! Quanti ne vuole?
YOU	**c** *I would like quite a few (of them). Have you got a bigger box?* *(The shop assistant shows an extremely large box)*
COMMESSA	Sì signora, ho questa scatola.
YOU	**d** *Oh … you can put all of them in that box!*
COMMESSA	Li vuole tutti, signora?
YOU	**e** *No, I … all of them would be too many.*
COMMESSA	Allora tre? ... sei?
YOU	**f** *Six is not enough … give me eight (of them).*
COMMESSA	Allora, uno, due … e otto. Va bene, signora?
YOU	**g** *Yes … no … perhaps I'd better not buy any, since none of them appeal to me* (**mi attira**). *I was only practising my indefinite pronouns* (**volevo soltanto fare un po' di pratica sull'uso dei pronomi indefiniti**).

3 Translate into Italian.

a Would you like another one? (*feminine*)

b Each one of them had their share (**la sua parte**).

c Many believe in this medicine.

d Quite a lot of them were annoyed (**seccati**).

e Is there anyone who wants a slice (**fetta**) of cake?

f No one said anything.

g A few think that it is (*subjunctive*) possible

h She is capable of anything.

93 UNIT | Asking questions (1): interrogative pronouns

Interrogative words are usually placed at the beginning of a sentence. This and the next two units will show examples of their use.

Chi?	Who?
Che (cosa)?	What?
Quale?	Which (one)? What?
Quanto?	How much?

A Chi? is invariable and is used only for people.

| Chi è venuto alla festa? | Who came to the party? |
| Chi è? | Who is it? |

B Che (cosa)? is invariable and is used for things. You may ask either **Che ... ?** or **Che cosa ... ?** (lit: *What thing?*). Nowadays many people just say **Cosa ... ?**.

Che vuoi?
Che cosa vuoi? } *What do you want?*
Cosa vuoi?

C Quale? has a plural form (**quali?**).

| Quale preferisci? | Which one do you want? |
| Quali vuoi? | Which ones do you want? |

⚠ Quale becomes **qual** before **essere**.

| Qual è la tua opinione? | What is your opinion? |

The difference between **quale** and **che** is that the former implies a choice between two or more alternatives.

| Qual è la tua auto? | Which (one) is your car? |
| Che auto hai? | What car do you have? |

D Quanto (-a, -i, -e)? has masculine, feminine and plural forms.

Quante ne hai comprate?	How many did you buy?
Quant'è?	How much is it?
Quanto le devo?	How much do I owe you?
In quanti siete?	How many of you are there?

 ➤ See relative pronouns in Unit 90, asking questions in Units 94 and 95.

1 Complete the sentences with *chi?*, *che (cosa)?*, *quale(-i)?* or *quanto (-a -i- e)?*

a _____ c'era alla festa?

b _____ viene con me al cinema?

c _____ sigarette fumi al giorno?

d _____ soldi hai?

e _____ c'è in questa scatola?

f _____ vuoi per cena?

g _____ è la tua decisione?

h _____ hai deciso?

i _____ figli ha, Lei?

j _____ tavolo vuole?

k _____ ha mangiato la mia torta?

l _____ sceglieresti?

2 Form questions by joining phrases from the two columns as appropriate and then read them aloud.

a Chi hai visto ...   1 ... quell'uomo?

b Che cosa c'è ...   2 ... parlato?

c Che ...   3 ... di fare?

d Che cosa pensi ...   4 ... alla festa?

e Per quanti giorni ...   5 ... per cena?

f Quante sono ...   6 ... vuoi?

g Quanto ...   7 ... vai?

h Che cosa vai ...   8 ... queste paste?

i Chi ha ...   9 ... costano?

j Chi è ...   10 ... a fare?

3 Translate into Italian.

a Which is your husband?

b What is your job?

c Who went to the party?

d How much does the ticket cost?

e Which is your coat?

f What do they want?

g How long does it take?

h How many tickets have you sold?

94 UNIT | Asking questions (2)

Other common Italian interrogative pronouns are: **Come?** *(How?)*, **Quando?** *(When?)*, **Quanto** (-a, -i, -e) *(How much/many?)* and **Perché?** *(Why?)*.

A Come? *(How?)*

Come stai?	*How are you?*
Come mai …?/Com'è che …?	*How come …?*
Come ti chiami?	*What's your name?*
Come?/Come hai detto?	*Pardon?/Sorry?/What did you say?*
Com'è il tuo ragazzo?	*What is your boyfriend like?*

B Quando? *(When?)*

Quando parte?	*When does it leave?*
Da quando?	*Since when?*
Da quando sei qui?	*How long have you been here?*
Di quando è questo giornale?	*Which day's paper is this?*
Fino a quando continuerai così?	*How long will you go on like this?*
Per quando lo vuole, signora?	*When do you want it for, madam?*

C Quanto? *(How much/many?)*

Quanti soldi hai?	*How much money do you have?*
Quanti anni hai?	*How old are you?*
Quanto tempo?	*How long?/How much time?*
Quanto tempo ci vuole?	*How long does it take?*
Quanto (tempo) ci mette il battello?	*How long does the boat take?*
Quante volte? Ogni quanto?	*How many times?/How often?*
Quanti ne abbiamo oggi?	*What is the date today?*
Quant'è?	*How much is it?*
Da quanto lo vuole?	*Which one?* (price wise)
Da quanto tempo?	*Since when?*
Quanto è grande?	*How large is it?*
Quanto è alto (lungo/largo/spesso)?	*How tall/high (long/wide/thick) is it?*
Quanto dista?	*How far is it?*

D Perché? *(Why?)*

Perché non glielo chiedi?	*Why don't you ask him?*
Perché no?	*Why not?*
Perché mai …?	*Why on earth …?*

94 UNIT
Asking questions (2) – Exercises

1 **Match the two halves to form questions.**

a Come …	**1** … ore ci vogliono per andare a Fiesole?
b Quante …	**2** … è questo pane?
c Perché mai …	**3** … dovrò attendere?
d Quanti …	**4** … è entrata in vigore la legge (*the law was enforced*)?
e Per quando …	**5** … ne ha bisogno?
f Fino a quando …	**6** … sei così in ritardo?
g Di quando …	**7** … chilometri ci sono da qui a Sori?
h Da quando…	**8** … dice?

2 **Write the questions for these answers.**

a Il battello ci mette tre ore.
b Lo voglio da mille lire.
c Abito a Parigi da sette anni.
d Vado in Italia due volte all'anno.
e Non ho molti soldi.
f Ho venticinque anni.
g Per andare a New York ci vogliono sei ore.
h Oggi ne abbiamo venti.
i Perché non glielo chiedi tu?
j In tutto è trentamilacinquecentosettanta.
k Mia figlia è un tipo molto estroverso.
l Sono qui dal 1980.
m Questo tavolo è largo 80 centimetri.
n Io sono alto un metro e settanta (centimetri).

3 **Translate into Italian.**

a Excuse me, madam, what did you say?
b What is your name (sir)?
c How long have you been living in Brighton?
d What is your cousin Giacomo like?
e How long will they go on like that?
f How long does it take you to get dressed?
g How often do you go to the theatre?
h How come you never tell the truth (**verità**)?
i Why on earth do you want to wear such a (**un tale**) dress?

95 UNIT | Asking questions (3)

> More interrogative pronouns: Dove? (Where?), A che ora?
> (At what time?), Di chi è? (Whose is it?), Che tipo? (What kind?).

A **Dove?** *(Where?)*

Dove sono i miei occhiali?	*Where are my glasses?*
Dov'è il museo?	*Where is the museum?*
Da dove viene, signora?	*Where do you come from, madam?*
Di dov'è Lei, Signora?	*Where are you from, madam?*
Il treno per dove?	*The train going where?*

B **A che ora?** *(At what time?)*

A che ora è la colazione?	*What time is breakfast?*
A che ora comincia la festa?	*At what time does the party start?*

Che ora è?/Che ore sono? *(What time is it?)*

Scusi, sa che ore sono?	*Excuse me, do you know the time?*

C **Di chi?** *(Whose?)*

Di chi sono queste carte?	*Whose papers are these?*
Di chi è quel quadro?	*Whose painting is that?*

D **Che tipo?** *(What kind?)*

Che tipo di sciampo desidera?	*What kind of shampoo do you want?*
Che tipi ha?	*What kinds do you have?*
Che tipo è il tuo principale?	*What kind of person is your boss?*

E Other interrogative expressions

• **Che cosa succede?**	*What's going on?*
• **Che cosa ti/le/vi etc. succede?**	*What is the matter with you?*
• **Che cos'hai?**	*What is the matter with you?* or, in other contexts, *What have you got there?*
• **Che cosa danno al cinema?**	*What's on at the cinema?*
• **A chi tocca?**	*Whose turn is it?*
• **A che scopo?/ E perché?**	*What for?*
• **E con ciò?**	*So what?*

➤ See interrogative pronouns in Unit 93 and interrogative adjectives in Unit 22.

1 Match the questions and the answers.

a E perché?	1 Ho funghi, formaggio e ciliege.
b E con ciò?	2 Un'utilitaria che costi poco.
c A chi tocca?	3 Mie.
d Che cosa danno al cinema?	4 Perché non rispondi educatamente?
e Che cos'hai?	5 Perché sì!
f Che cosa succede?	6 Una commedia brillante.
g Che tipo di auto ha in mente?	7 Non mi sento bene.
h Di chi sono queste valigie?	8 Niente. Perché?
i L'autobus per dove?	9 A me.
j Che cos'ha di buono, oggi?	10 Lucca.

2 Write the questions for these answers.

a A me.

b Un film di cowboys.

c Mi sento male.

d Mario con Tonino si stanno picchiando (*are fighting*).

e Ne ho di molti tipi.

f Ho un cesto (*basket*) di ciliege.

g Perché te lo dico io!

h Vengo da Padova.

i Il gatto è sotto il tavolo.

j Mi dispiace ma non ho l'orologio.

k La partita comincia alle tre.

l L'ombrello è mio.

3 Translate the following into Italian.

a What kind of coffee do you want?

b What kinds do you have?

c What is the matter with you, madam?

d What's on at the Ritz?

e Whose turn is it?

f Whose shoes are these?

g What time is the train to Milan?

h What's the time?

i Where do they come from?

j What do you want it for?

There are many Italian words that, despite being very similar to English words, have a different meaning. Below is a list of the most common ones.

A

ITALIAN – ENGLISH	ENGLISH – ITALIAN
annoiare (*to bore*)	*to annoy* (infastidire)
anticipare (*to be early*)	*to anticipate* (prevedere)
argomento (*topic*)	*argument* (disputa)
atteggiamento (*attitude*)	*aptitude* (attitudine)
attendere (*to wait for*)	*to attend* (frequentare)
attuale (*current*)	*actual* (reale/vero/concreto)
attualmente (*at present*)	*actually* (veramente/in verità)
avvisare (*to warn*)	*to advise* (consigliare)
camera (*room*)	*camera* (macchina fotografica)
cantina (*cellar*)	*canteen* (mensa)
coincidenza (*(transport) connection*)	*coincidence* (coincidenza)
confetti (*sugared almonds*)	*confetti* (coriandoli)
confezione (*wrapping of a product/ ready-to-wear clothes*)	*confectionery* (dolciumi)
conveniente (*advantageous/cheap*)	*convenient* (comodo)
costipazione (*a bad cold*)	*constipation* (stitichezza)
educato (*well-mannered*)	*educated* (istruito)
facilità (*easiness/ease*)	*facilities* (attrezzature)
fattoria (*farm*)	*factory* (fabbrica)
firma (*signature*)	*firm* (ditta/società/compagnia)
grave (*serious/severe*)	*grave* (tomba)
incidente (*accident*)	*incident* (avvenimento/episodio)
intossicazione (*food poisoning*)	*intoxication* (ubriachezza)
libreria (*bookshop*)	*library* (biblioteca)
magazzino (*warehouse/department store*)	*magazine* (rivista)
marmellata (*jam*)	*marmalade* (marmellata d'arancia)
morbido (*soft*)	*morbid* (morboso)
parenti (*relatives*)	*parents* (genitori)
patente (*driving licence*)	*patent* (brevetto)
pavimento (*floor*)	*pavement* (marciapiede)
petrolio (*crude oil*)	*petrol* (benzina)
preventivo (*estimate*)	*prevention* (prevenzione)
sensibile (*sensitive*)	*sensible* (saggio/sensato/ ragionevole)

96 UNIT False friends – Exercises

1 Match the two halves of the sentences.

a Ti aspetto sul marciapiede…   1 … è di cachemire.

b Il malato è grave, …   2 … per la riparazione del tetto.

c Io prendo pane tostato con …   3 … vivo a Brighton.

d È un golfino molto morbido: …   4 … accanto al Duomo.

e Vorrei un preventivo …   5 … non bisogna disturbarlo.

f Attualmente …   6 … marmellata d'arancia.

g Devo andare in biblioteca …   7 … non occuparmi della faccenda.

h Devo andare in libreria …   8 … da superuomo.

i Veramente avrei preferito …   9 … a comprare un libro.

j Ha sempre un atteggiamento …   10 … a consultare un libro.

2 Fill the blanks to complete each sentence.

a Abbiamo una _____ da cento grammi e una da duecento grammi. Quale vuole?

b A Milano deve cambiare e prendere la _____ delle tre per Caronno.

c Vai a prendere il vino in _____

d A mezzogiorno mangio alla _____ .

e A Carnevale si usa gettare _____ alla gente che passa.

f _____ un attimo (*moment*) prego, vado a chiamarlo.

g Io vi ho _____ ; poi fate come volete.

h Cambiamo _____ di conversazione, se non vi dispiace.

i _____ un corso d'italiano all'università di Brighton.

j Ecco la _____ _____ . Fammi una foto.

k Cerca di non offenderlo, è un ragazzo molto _____ .

l I miei _____ si sono sposati 25 anni fa.

3 Translate the following into Italian.

a I had anticipated all this.

b She brought me some confectionery.

c Sign here, please.

d There is a connection at 2.30.

e I forgot the camera.

f I am going to the station to meet my relatives.

g The goods are (**La merce è**) in the storehouse.

h What do you advise?

i I work for an English firm.

j I need (some) petrol.

k The house has a (**il**) marble floor.

l I work in a factory.

193

KEY TO EXERCISES

UNIT 1

1 **a** La mamma prepara il pasto per il bambino. **b** I libri che ho ordinato arriveranno la settimana prossima. **c** Il treno delle 6.45 (sei e quarantacinque) arriverà in ritardo. **d** Mariella scrive una lettera.

2

Articoli	Sostantivi	Aggettivi	Verbi	Preposizioni	Congiunzioni
La	mamma	prossima	prepara	per	
il	pasto		ho ordinato	delle	
il	bambino		arriveranno	in	
I	libri		arriverà		
la	settimana		scrive		
Il	treno				
una	ritardo				
	Mariella				
	lettera				

UNIT 2

1 **a** Gino arriva da Roma dopodomani./Arriva da Roma dopodomani Gino./Da Roma arriva domani Gino./Dopodomani arriva Gino da Roma./Dopodomani Gino arriva da Roma. **2** **a** io parlo, parlo io! **b** io pago, pago io! **c** io vengo, vengo io! **3** **a** Posso andare? Non posso andare. Non posso andare? **b** Posso parlare? Non posso parlare. Non posso parlare? **c** Devo pagare il conto? Non devo pagare il conto. Non devo pagare il conto? **d** Devo scrivere la lettera? Non devo scrivere la lettera. Non devo scrivere la lettera? **e** Devo leggere questo libro? Non devo leggere questo libro. Non devo leggere questo libro? **4** Suggested answers: Francesco è un cantante famoso./Elisa legge un libro interessante./Filippo ha un'automobile enorme./Mario indossa un vestito blu. **5** **a** Non vado mai al cinema. **b** Gino va molto a teatro. **c** Ho sempre pagato i conti.

UNIT 3

1 **a** né **b** è **c** benché **d** sé **e** cioè **f** perché **g** poiché **h** tè **2** **a** lo **b** d' **c** dall' **d** d' **e** un **f** un' **g** un' **h** un **i** un' **3** **a** 4 **b** 3 **c** 2 **d** 1 **e** 5 **f** 6

UNIT 4

1 **a** il mal di denti **b** — **c** il mal di testa **d** il mal di cuore **e** il Mar Adriatico **f** un cuor d'oro **g** qual è? **h** sta' attento **i** un po' di vino **j** il professor Rossi **k** — **l** l'ingegner Bianchi **3** **a** un amico **b** un buon amico **c** quell'uomo **d** Qual è …? **e** buoni amici **f** poter andare **g** nessun amico **h** lavorar sodo **i** quel libro **j** to' **k** Il signor Cervi **l** Il dottor Green

UNIT 5

1 **a** aereo (*m.*) **b** cane (*m.*) **c** auto(mobile) (*f.*) **d** moto(cicletta) (*f.*) **e** mano (*f.*)

f radio (*f.*) **2** **a** problema, colore, orario, cane, dottore **b** foto, bambina, commedia, banca, oro **3** **a** programma **b** radio **c** problema **d** foto **e** clima **f** zia **g** poeta **h** tema **i** moto(cicletta) **j** pigiama **k** mano **l** cinema **m** dramma **n** crisi

UNIT 6

1 **a** fiore **b** bambino **c** problema **d** uomo **e** mamma **f** gonna **g** banca **h** luce **i** strada **j** borsa **k** fungo **l** scatola **2** Nouns with an **-h** in the plural: buchi, banche **3** **a** virtù **b** caffè **c** tè **d** qualità **e** quantità **f** giovedì **4** **a** viaggi **b** figli **c** zii **d** leggii **e** specchi **f** brusii

UNIT 7

1 **a** lo **b** la **c** l' **d** lo **e** lo **f** lo **g** l' **h** lo **i** l' **j** lo **k** il **l** l' **m** la **n** il **2** **a** gli gnocchi **b** le case **c** gli aerei **d** gli scioperi **e** gli psicologi **f** gli xenofobi **g** le auto **h** gli sci **i** le arance **j** gli specchi **k** i problemi **l** le ore **m** le zie **n** i fiori **3** **a** gli scioperi **b** gli dei **c** le auto **d** gli elicotteri **e** gli gnocchi **f** le unghie **g** gli pseudonimi **h** le borse **i** le ore **j** gli studenti **k** le isole **l** gli aerei **4** Individual responses

UNIT 8

1 **a** la **b** la **c** la **d** la **e** Londra **f** il **g** Milano **h** Roma **i** Cassino **j** la **k** la **2** **a** Abito in. Vado in. **b** Abito in. Vado in. **c** Abito in. Vado in. **d** Abito in. Vado in. **f** Abito in. Vado in. **j** Abito in. Vado in. **k** Abito in. Vado in. **3** **a** La Loren è un'attrice molto ammirata. **b** Sono le cinque. **c** Lavoro dalle dieci alle sei. **d** È mezzogiorno. **e** Il 1995 è stato un anno molto bello. **f** Vado a prendere l'ombrello. **g** Mi lavo la faccia. **h** Amo lo sport. **i** È mezzanotte. **j** Il pesce è caro. **k** Tutti e due/Ambedue/Entrambi i gatti sono neri. **l** I cani sono fedeli. **4** **a** Parla francese? Studia il francese? **b** Parla inglese? Studia l'inglese? **c** Parla tedesco? Studia il tedesco? **d** Parla spagnolo? Studia lo spagnolo? **e** Parla greco? Studia il greco? **f** Parla portoghese? Studia il portoghese? **g** Parla turco? Studia il turco? **h** Parla arabo? Studia l'arabo? **i** Parla russo? Studia il russo? **j** Parla olandese? Studia l'olandese? **k** Parla polacco? Studia il polacco? **l** Parla danese? Studia il danese? **m** Parla svedese? Studia lo svedese? **n** Parla norvegese? Studia il norvegese? **o** Parla finlandese? Studia il finlandese?

UNIT 9

1 **a** Costa tremila lire al litro. **b** Costa venticinque sterline all'ora. **c** È aumentato del dieci per cento. **d** Vado in montagna ogni anno. **e** Mi piace vedere/guardare la televisione. **f** Abito in campagna. **g** Vado in ufficio alle otto. **2** **a** Il vino Soave costa tremila lire al litro. **b** Mi piace vedere/guardare il calcio alla TV. **c** Il novanta per cento della popolazione ha un'automobile. **d** Una lezione costa venticinque sterline all'ora. **e** la Roma Imperiale **f** La cena è pronta. **g** A che ora è la colazione? **3** **a** in montagna **b** in campagna **c** in ufficio **d** in ufficio **e** in campagna **f** in montagna **g** in piscina **h** in piscina **i** in auto/in macchina

UNIT 10

1 **a** un **b** un **c** un **d** un **e** uno **f** uno **g** uno **h** uno **i** uno **j** una **k** una **l** una **m** un' **n** un' **o** una **p** una **q** un' **r** uno **s** un' **2** Individual responses **3** **a** un'arancia **b** uno sci **c** un uomo **d** un'ape **4** **a** uno zoo **b** un'elica **c** un attore **d** un'attrice **e** uno zero **f** un problema **g** una psicologa **h** uno psicologo **i** un album

UNIT 11

1 a – b – c una d un e un f – g un h – i un **2** a Che peccato!
b mezzo chilo di mele c mezz'ora d cento volte e mille volte f sei ore al giorno
g due volte all'anno h due volte al giorno i mezza pinta j Che bel ragazzo!
3 a Ho mal di gola. b Ho mal di testa. c Andrea ha mal di denti. d Goffredo ha il
raffreddore. e Angela ha un raffreddore terribile. f Ho una fretta! g Ho appetito.
h Ho un appetito! i Mario ha l'automobile. j Da bambina ero un maschiaccio.
4 a mezza mela b mille lire c mezzo chilo di spaghetti

UNIT 12

1 a la fonte b il fonte c il boa d la boa e la pianta f il pianto g la foglia
h il tappo i il mostro **2** a l'arco b una radio c il tasso d il manico e un foglio
f la posta g tappo h la capitale i le tappe j una foglia

UNIT 13

1 a la ciclista, i ciclisti, le cicliste b la turista, i turisti, le turiste c la violinista, i
violinisti, le violiniste d l'arpista, gli arpisti, le arpiste e la pianista, i pianisti, le pianiste
f l'artista, gli artisti, le artiste g la borsista, i borsisti, le borsiste h la ritrattista, i ritrattisti,
le ritrattiste i la giornalista, i giornalisti, le giornaliste j la parente, i parenti, le parenti
k la collega, i colleghi, le colleghe l l'atleta, gli atleti, le atlete m la pediatra, i pediatri, le
pediatre n la psichiatra, gli psichiatri, le psichiatre o la stratega, gli strateghi, le strateghe
p l'ipocrita, gl'ipocriti, le ipocrite q l'insegnante, gli insegnanti, le insegnanti r l'agente,
gli agenti, le agenti s l'amante, gli amanti, le amanti **2** a Il marito è una persona
intelligente. b Quell'uomo è una guida turistica. c La polizia è sulle sue tracce.
3 a il cervo b la femmina del leopardo c il bufalo d la volpe femmina
e la femmina della zebra f il maschio del puma g il rinoceronte femmina
4 Masculine nouns: e, g, h, m, p, q, r, v; Feminine nouns: b, c, i, k, n, o, t, u; Common
gender nouns: a, d, f, j, l, s.

UNIT 14

1 a il dio b il re c l'eroe d il cane **2** a la donna b il fratello c il marito
d la nubile e il genero f la femmina **3** a le qualità b le quantità c le virtù d le
città e i caffè f i tè **4** a metropoli b brindisi c ipotesi d tè e analisti f tesi
g oasi **5** a le b i c le d le e le f le g le h i i le j le k le l le
m le n i o le p i q le r i s gli t i u i v i w gli x i **6** a Un branco di
lupi. b Una folla di cinquecento persone. c La gente di Milano. d La polizia è efficiente.

UNIT 15

1 a un miglio b due miglia c un centinaio di persone d dieci dita e un migliaio di
lire f alcune migliaia di miglia g un dito **2** ACROSS 3 mura
4 braccia 5 membra 6 ossi DOWN 1 membri 2 bracci 5 muri 7 ossa

UNIT 16

1 a 11 b 5 c 8 d 4 e 9 f 1 g 10 h 7 i 6 j 3 k 2
2 a table b treasure c parcel d meadow e team f paper g man h stick
i tooth j elephant k book 1 waste paper 2 large book 3 little elephant 4 small
meadow 5 dear little treasure 6 big tooth 7 little stick 8 little parcel 9 small team
10 little man 11 little table **3** a un donnone e un ometto b un tavolino c un
omaccio **4** The altered nouns are: e paesino j pancione l uccellaccio m stradina
r ideuccia t finestrella x uccellino z gattone

UNIT 17

1 ACROSS **1** saliscendi **2** terrecotte **3** francobolli **4** cavalcavia DOWN
1 fabbriferrai **2** banconote **3** passaporti **4** benestare **2** **a** capolavori **b** capoversi
c capogiri **d** capigruppo **e** capisquadra **f** capitecnici **g** capistazione **h** capifila

UNIT 18

1 **a** 25 **b** 4 **c** 26 **d** 12 **e** 6 **f** 7 **g** 10 **h** 2 **i** 9 **j** 13 **k** 11 **l** 5 **m** 8
n 19 **o** 24 **p** 20 **q** 23 **r** 22 **s** 21 **t** 18 **u** 15 **v** 16 **w** 17 **x** 14 **y** 3 **z** 1
2 **a** e **b** a **c** a **d** a **e** i **f** a **g** o/o **h** i **3** **a** L'economia italiana
b L'economia inglese **c** Paul è ricco. **d** La retta annuale **e** Il presidente degli Stati
Uniti **f** La stanza è spaziosa **g** Milano è una città industriale **h** Un monumento artistico
i Un uomo intelligente **j** Filippo è bello **k** Clara è bella **l** Gino e Clara sono buoni (or
bravi = good *at* something) **m** Ennio è un vecchio amico **n** Un vestito vecchio

UNIT 19

1 **a** Questa. **b** Queste **c** Quest' **d** Questi **e** Questa **f** Questi **2** **a** Quella
b Quelle **c** Quell' **d** Quei **e** Quegli **3** **a** queste scarpe **b** quella casa **c** quegli
d questa; questo **e** questo tavolo **4** **a** Voglio questo. **b** Prendo questi. **c** Non voglio
quello. **d** Non prendo quelle.

UNIT 20

1 Suggested answers. **a** Devo pagare il lattaio ogni setttimana. **b** Devo pagare la
bolletta del telefono ogni tre mesi. **c** Devo pagare la tassa di circolazione ogni anno.
d Devo pagare la segretaria ogni mese. **2** **a** alcune riviste **b** alcune ore **c** alcuni giorni
d alcuni mesi **e** alcuni regali **3** **a** a qualsiasi costo **b** Qualsiasi cosa faccia è sempre
contento. **c** Ciascun libro costa tremila lire. **d** Ciascuna caramella è incartata. **e** Non
vedo nessun libro. **f** Il ragazzo non ha nessun amico. **g** La ragazza ha molti amici.
h Roberto ha molti soldi. **i** Lauretta mangia troppe caramelle. **j** Ho poco tempo. **k** Tutte
le ragazze erano assenti.

UNIT 21

1 **a** Questo è il mio giornale. **b** Questa è la mia macchina. **c** Questi sono i nostri
passaporti. **d** Questa è la mia mamma. **e** Questo è il mio papà. **2** **a** il **b** i **c** le **d** la
e le **f** Il **g** Le **h** – **3** **a** i nostri **b** la loro **c** Il mio **d** i suoi; i miei **e** la mia
f il suo **g** Il tuo **h** I suoi **4** **a** il suo libro **b** la loro casa **c** i nostri amici **d**
Questo non è il giornale di oggi, è quello di ieri. **e** le mie sorelle **f** la mia sorellina **g** il
mio fratello maggiore

UNIT 22

1 **a** Che **b** Quanti **c** Quante **d** Quanto **e** Quale **f** Quali **g** Che
h Quale **i** Quanti **j** Quanta **2** **a** 1 **b** 9 **c** 2 **d** 3 **e** 10 **f** 5 **g** 7 **h** 6 **i** 8
j 4 **3** **a** Che bell'uomo! **b** Che vita! **c** Che sorpresa!

UNIT 23

1 **a** Anselmo è più simpatico/bello/etc. di Giulio. **2** Giulio è meno simpatico/bello/etc.
di Anselmo. **3** **a** Giulio è più puntuale che attivo. **b** Giulio è più simpatico che bello.
c Giulio è più mascalzone che stupido. **d** Giulio è più studioso che intelligente. **e** Giulio
è più prudente che noioso. **f** Giulio è più ostinato che convincente. **4** **a** Carla è tanto bella/intelligente/etc. quanto Cristina. **5** **a** Cristina ha tante libri
quante Carla. **b** Cristina ha tanti vestiti quante Carla. **c** Cristina ha tante paia di scarpe

quante Carla. **d** Cristina ha tante borse quante Carla. **e** Cristina ha tante cassette quante Carla. **f** Cristina ha tanti dischi quanti Carla. **6** **a** 1 **b** 4 **c** 6 **d** 3 **e** 2 **f** 5

UNIT 24

1 **a** il; più **b** il più **c** le; meno **d** la più **e** il; più **f** la; meno
2 **a** bellissimo **b** piacevolissima **c** orgogliosissimo **d** intensissimi **e** interessantissimo **f** velocissima **g** intelligentissima **h** studiosissimo **i** noiosissimo **j** ostinatissima **3** Adjectives that cannot be modified by **-issimo** or **-errimo** are: **a**, **b**, **d**, **g** **4** **a** migliore; il migliore; ottimo **b** peggiori; i peggiori; pessimi **c** migliori; i migliori; ottimi

UNIT 25

2 **a** 3,800 **b** 2,500 **c** 6,300 **d** 1,600 **e** 3,200 **f** 4,600 **3** **a** venti **b** trenta **c** quaranta **d** cinquanta **e** cinquantuno **f** sessantotto **g** centotremilacinquecento-ventinove **h** millenovecentonovantanove **i** duemila **j** millenovecentosessanta **k** duemilacinquecentocinquantacinque

UNIT 26

1 primo, terzo, quinto, sesto, nono, undicesimo, quattordicesimo, quindicesimo, sedicesimo, diciasettesimo, ventitreesimo, centocinquantaquattresimo, trentatreesimo, settantesimo, centesimo, centocinquantacinquesimo, millesimo, millecinquecentesimo, duemillesimo, tremillesimo
2 **a** Papa Paolo Sesto **b** Pio Nono **c** Leone Decimo **d** Giovanni Ventitreesimo **e** Giovanni Paolo Secondo **f** Re Vittorio Emanuele Terzo **g** Gustavo Sedicesimo **h** Giorgio Sesto **i** Enrico Quarto **j** Regina Elisabetta Seconda **3** **a** l'undicesimo capitolo **b** la nona sinfonia di Beethoven **c** il terzo uomo **d** il diciassettesimo secolo **e** la seconda strada a destra **f** la quarta figlia **g** il secondo figlio **h** la terza tappa **i** la prima marcia **j** la Quinta Strada **k** la terza strada a sinistra **l** il decimo Comandamento **4** **a** Via 12 Ottobre **f** Via 25 Aprile **g** Via 24 Maggio **h** Via 22 Marzo

UNIT 27

1

	avanti Cristo	dopo Cristo	secolo (letters)	secolo (Roman)
100 a.C.	100	–	–	–
30 a.C	30	–	–	–
90 d.C.	–	90	–	–
1350	–	1350	il Trecento	XIV
1499	–	1500	il Quattrocento	XV
1875	–	1875	l'Ottocento	XIX
1492	–	1492	il Quattrocento	XV
1768	–	1768	il Settecento	XVIII
1650	–	1650	il Seicento	XVII
1899	–	1900	l'Ottocento	XIX
1999	–	1999	il Novecento	XX
2000	–	2000	il Novecento	XX

2 **a** Il terzo millennio va dal primo gennaio duemilauno al trentun dicembre tremila. **b** Dante è il grande poeta del Duecento. **c** L'attuale secolo si chiama il ventesimo secolo. **3** **a** true **b** true **c** true **d** true **e** false **f** true **g** false

UNIT 28

1 a un mezzo b due terzi c tre quarti d cinque ottavi e sette ottavi
f quattro quinti g cinque sedicesimi h diciannove trentaduesimi i cinque sesti j nove
decimi **2** a mezzo b mezza c mezza d mezza e mezzo f mezzo g mezz'
h mezzo i mezza j mezzo **4** a una coppia di sposi b un doppio whisky c Un
paio di bottiglie d un paio di camice e una decina di persone f tre alla volta g una
ventina di chili h un migliaio di chilometri i ad uno ad uno j Ambedue/Tutti e
due/Entrambi sono inglesi. k il primo semestre l Sono gemelli.

UNIT 29

1 a Ci vediamo lunedì. b Ci vediamo la settimana prossima. c Il martedì vado al
cinema. d Il mercoledì vado alla lezione d'italiano. e Vado in discoteca la domenica.
f Il lunedì pomeriggio vado in palestra. g Il sabato mattina vado a cavalcare. h Il venerdì
sera vado a teatro. i Che giorno è? È giovedì. j Che data è oggi? È il primo giugno.
k Che giorno è? È il cinque luglio. **2** Individual responses. **3** a il primo maggio
b il venticinque dicembre c ventisei dicembre d il ventidue novembre
millenovecentosessantatré e il venti luglio millenovecentosessantanove f il dodici aprile
millenovecentosessantuno g il quattro aprile millenovecentosessantotto h il dodici ottobre
millequattrocentonovantadue i il primo aprile

UNIT 30

1 a Quell' b Quella c Quell' d Quegli e quel f quello g Quelle h Quel
2 a Che bell'uomo! b Che begli occhi! c Che bel braccialetto! **3** a gran
b grande c grandi d grande e grandi f gran **4** a San b San c Santa
d Santi e Sant' f Santi g San

UNIT 31

2 a dormo b cammino c parto d parlo e guardo f vedo g compro h ascolto
i volo j rido k prendo l metto m vivo n piango o ballo p canto q suono
r respiro s prenoto t cresco

UNIT 32

1 a Vedete? b Non parlo tedesco. c Parlano sempre di Lei. d Parla sempre.
e Parli/Parla/Parlate/Parlano inglese? f Lo vedo ogni giorno/tutti i giorni. g Vedi i miei
occhiali? h Abito qui da un anno. i Parti oggi? j Partono domani. **2** a falso
b falso c falso d falso e falso f vero g falso h vero i falso j vero

UNIT 33

1 a finiamo b capiscono c preferite d agiscono e costruiscono
f puliscono g spariscono h ti restituiamo i guariscono j spedite **2** a sale b saliamo
c tengono d spengono e spengo f tieni g tengono h teniamo
i scegliete j rimango k scelgono l rimani **3** a sale b studia c segue d Vede
e ferma f Spegne g scende h parlano i capiscono j offre k ringraziano
l chiedono m hanno n studia o decide p uniscono q salgono

UNIT 34

1 a Oggi parto per Napoli. b Lui va a ballare, io vado a teatro. c Esco, ti serve
qualcosa? d Vanno in vacanza al mare. e Io esco e tu? f La domenica ceniamo alle otto.
g Noi ceniamo alle otto, loro cenano alle sette. h Sono inglese. i Io sono inglese e Lei?
j Mario ama la musica classica, io amo la musica pop. **2** a Rispondo io! b Rispondi tu?
c Risponde lui? d Compri tu le cartoline? e Comprate voi le cartoline? f Sì,

compriamo noi le cartoline. **3** **a** (Loro) parlano francese, signore? **b** (Loro) vedono spesso i loro amici? **c** (Voi) mangiate molto? **d** (Noi) vediamo Mario ogni giorno. **e** (Loro) partono domani, signori Rossi?

UNIT 35

1 **a** La vedo. **b** Li vediamo. **c** La domenica li vedo. **d** Vi vediamo. **e** Lo prendo. **f** La prendo. **g** Li prendo. **h** Sì, mi aiuta. **i** Li vediamo alla TV. **j** Sì, ci aiutano. **2** **a** preso **b** prese **c** comprata **d** venduta **e** invitati **3** **a** La vedo ogni giorno/tutti i giorni. **b** Lo vedo ogni giorno. **c** Ci vedono il sabato. **d** Marco ci aiuta. **e** Federico l'aiuta. **f** Li compriamo. **g** Le compriamo. **h** Li amiamo. **i** La studia. **j** Ci conoscono. **k** Mi capisce, signore? **l** Non la capisco. **m** Non mi capisce. **n** Vi aiutano?

UNIT 36

1 Maria ha fatto un regalo ... **a** me **b** a te **c** a lui **d** a lei **e** a noi **f** a voi **g** a loro **2** **a** Maria mi ha fatto un regalo. **b** Maria ti ha fatto un regalo. **c** Maria gli ha fatto un regalo. **d** Maria le ha fatto un regalo. **e** Maria ci ha fatto un regalo. **f** Maria vi ha fatto un regalo. **g** Maria gli ha fatto un regalo./Maria ha fatto loro un regalo. **3** **a** Voglio telefonarle. **b** Voglio telefonargli. **c** Voglio telefonarLe. **d** Voglio telefonarvi. **e** Voglio telefonar loro. **f** Voglio telefonar Loro. **g** Voglio parlarti. **h** Voglio parlarle. **i** Voglio parlargli. **j** Voglio parlarLe. **k** Voglio parlarvi. **l** Voglio parlargli./Voglio parlar loro. **m** Voglio parlar Loro. **4** **a** Le do un libro. **b** Gli do un libro. **c** Gli ho fatto/Ho fatto loro una foto. **d** Gli ho comprato/Ho comprato loro un lampadario. **e** Mi hanno comprato una valigia. **f** Le ho detto la verità.

UNIT 37

1 **a** Te lo darò. **b** Gliela darò. **c** Glielo darò. **d** Ve le darò. **e** Te le darò. **f** Gliela darò. **g** Ve le darò. **h** Te li darò. **2** **a** ne **b** Ne **c** ne **d** non ne ho **e** non ne ho **f** Ne **3** **a** Ne compro tre. **b** Ne compro due. **c** Ne ha venticinque. **d** Ne voglio un chilo. **e** Ne voglio mezzo chilo. **f** Ne voglio sei. **g** Sì, ne parla spesso. **h** Sì, ne sono sicuro. **4** **a** Voglio vederlo. **b** Voglio parlargli. **c** Voglio telefonarle. **d** Devo scrivervi. **e** Deve vederci. **f** Devo leggerlo. **g** Posso vederlo? **h** Posso telefonargli? **i** Puoi scriverci?

UNIT 38

1 **a** Chi viene con voi, bambini? **b** C'è un messaggio per me? **c** C'è una lettera per loro. **d** Mi ricordo di lui. **e** Viene con te? **f** Viene con Lei? **g** Viene con voi? **h** Viene con Loro? **2** **a** Mi ricordo di lui. **b** Vado da lui. **c** Chi viene con lei? **d** Marianna viene con noi. **e** C'è una lettera per voi. **f** Non mi ricordo di lui. **g** Non mi ricordo di lei. **h** Gisella viene con noi? **i** C'è un messaggio per te. **j** Mi ricordo di lei. **k** Questo pacco è per te. **l** Questi giornali sono per lui. **3** **a** C'è un supermercato qui vicino? **b** Ci vado ogni mese/tutti i mesi. **c** Vengo qui una volta all'anno. **d** Ci pensiamo sempre. **e** Ci sono sette giorni in una settimana. **4** Correct order: c, b, a, f, e, d, g.

UNIT 39

1 **a** Sì, è in discoteca. **b** Sì, sono in classe. **c** Sì, è in banca. **d** Sì, sono italiani. **2** **a** No, non sei alla partita. **b** No, non siamo a Capri. **c** No, non sono a casa. **d** No, non sono alla mensa. **3** **a** Dov'è Simone? **b** Dove siete? **c** Dove siamo? **d** Dove sono? **e** C'è **f** Ci sono **g** Ci sono; in questa via? **4** **a** è **b** è **c** È **d** pagare **e** sono **f** sono **g** Ci sono **h** ci sono **i** c'è

UNIT 40

1 Il signor Simoni scrive un libro.   La signora Simoni ha molti soldi e molti vestiti. Hanno un figlio e una figlia. Marianna, la loro figlia, ha i capelli biondi e gli occhi azzurri, e una barca. Ha ventitré anni. Ha molti amici. Paolo, il loro figlio, ha vent'anni. Ha una macchina nuova veloce. Loro hanno una grande casa con un giardino enorme. Hanno anche una casa in campagna. Purtroppo hanno sempre dei problemi.   **2** a 1 b 3 c 5 d 7 e 6 f 8 g 2 h 4 i 9 **3** a I Simoni hanno dei problemi? b Hanno figli?/Quanti figli hanno? c Quanti anni ha Paolo? d E Marianna (quanti anni ha)? e Hanno molti soldi?

UNIT 41

1 Oral exercise. **2** a 4 b 6 c 7 d 8 e 2 f 1 g 3 h 5 **3** a Chi va dal farmacista? b Da dove viene, signora? c Da dove vieni, Robert? d Ti dispiace se vengo con te? e Esco. f Io vengo da Roma, e Lei? g Di solito non vado con loro. h Esci, Antonio? i Esce ogni sera. j Escono i Rossi?

UNIT 42

1 a beviamo b dicono c Diciamo d fa e facciamo f Faccio **2** a 7 b 5 c 6 d 8 e 9 f 1 g 4 h 3 i 2 **3** a Fa molto caldo. b Roberta fa le valigie. c (Loro) fanno i biglietti. **4** a fanno b rifanno c riordinano d fanno e va f fare g va h va i fa j ritorna k fa l fa

UNIT 43

1 a danno b danno c diamo d dai e danno f dà g dai h date **2** a sai; so b sapete; sappiamo c sa; sanno d sapete e sai f sa g sai h so **3** a So b Conosco c Conosco d So e So f sa **4** a Quanti anni gli dai? b Che film danno alla TV? c I Simoni danno una festa. d Sai giocare a tennis? e Non sa giocare a carte. f Sanno che non posso andare. g Mi dai il tuo video? h Non sappiamo la verità. i Conosce bene il Sud'Italia/l'Italia del Sud. j Non sanno molto.

UNIT 44

1 a 3 b 5 c 1 d 2 e 4 **2** a Come sta, signora? b Dove sta? c per avere un bambino. d non sta mai fermo. e Come stai/sta? **3** a stai b sta c stiamo d Sta e stanno f sta g state h stiamo **4** a Stai a casa oggi? b Stanno per mangiare. c Il bambino sta dormendo? d Sta al Claridges. e Non stanno attenti. f Marianna non sta mai zitta. g Non ascolta mai nessuno.

UNIT 45

1 a 5 b 8 c 9 d 10 e 4 f 7 g 2 h 3 i 6 j 1 **2** a No, non può/posso. b No, non posso. c No, non puoi. d No, non possiamo. e No, non potete. f No, non possono. g No, non vogliamo. h No, non voglio. i No, non posso. j No, non può. k No, non lo deve a lui. l No, non possiamo. m No, non lo vogliamo. n No, non voglio. **3** a possiamo b può c vogliono d vogliono e possiamo f deve g dobbiamo h devo i devi

UNIT 46

1 All are transitive except **dormire**, **essere** and **piovere**. **2** Intransitive verbs: a, c, d, f, g, h; **Transitive verbs:** b, e, i, j **3** Active forms: a, d; Passive forms: b, c, e, f **4** a Il vino si tiene in cantina. b Il traffico aereo si controlla dalla torre. c Si richiedono ottime referenze. d Si vendono libri usati.

UNIT 47

1 **a** Mi sveglio **b** mi alzo **c** mi lavo **d** mi lavo i denti **e** mi trucco **f** mi vesto **g** mi pettino **h** si sveglia **i** si alza **j** si alza **k** si lava **l** si rade **m** si lava i denti **n** si spazzola i capelli **o** si veste **p** mantenersi in forma **g** abbronzarsi **r** si arrabbia **s** si annoia **t** si preoccupa **u** si chiama.

UNIT 48

1 **a** Vuoi cambiarti la giacca? **b** Mi metto il vestito. **c** Voglio farmi tagliare i capelli. **d** Ti sei lavato le mani? **e** Luigi si è tagliato un dito. **f** Ho dimenticato la patente. **g** Ieri ho visto tuo figlio. **2** **a** Si telefonano. **b** S'incontrano. **c** Si baciano. **d** Si vedono. **e** Si parlano. **f** (Si) bisticciano. **3** **a** Ci telefoniamo. **b** C'incontriamo. **c** Ci baciamo. **d** Ci vediamo. **e** Ci parliamo. **f** (Ci) bisticciamo. **4** **a** Il treno si è fermato a Lucca. **b** La finestra si è aperta. **c** Giulia ha aperto la finestra. **d** Quell'uomo è pieno di sé. **e** L'auto si è fermata e la portiera si è aperta. **f** L'allarme ha fermato il treno. **g** Giulia non crede in se stessa. **h** È andata lei stessa. **5** **a** si ferma **b** prepararsi **c** si ferma **d** si vedono **e** divertirsi

UNIT 49

1 **a** parlato **b** venduto **c** camminato **d** capito **e** studiato **f** riposato **g** ascoltato **h** ritornato **i** mangiato **j** continuato **k** salito **l** imparato **m** costruito **n** guarito **o** pagato **p** cercato **q** pulito **r** andato **s** saputo **t** stato **u** voluto **v** potuto **w** dovuto **x** avuto **2** **a** venuto **b** rotto **c** offerto **d** corso **e** fatto **f** messo **g** bevuto **h** preso **i** visto **j** rimasto **k** aperto **l** stato **m** chiuso **n** scritto **o** nato **p** mosso **q** letto **r** detto **s** sceso **t** vissuto **3** **a** N **b** V **c** A **d** N **e** V **f** A **4** **a** Il negozio è chiuso. **b** La farmacia è aperta. **c** Ho visto il film due volte. **d** Ho scritto una lettera. **e** Mi sono preso la libertà di venire. **f** Ho fatto una torta. **g** Ha vissuto bene. **h** Ho permesso a Marina di uscire. **i** Ho letto il libro. **j** Ho camminato per tre chilometri.

UNIT 50

1 **a** Sono andata **b** sono andati **c** siamo andati **d** abbiamo impiegato **e** Siamo arrivati **f** abbiamo fatto **g** ci siamo seduti **h** abbiamo preso **i** Abbiamo osservato **j** abbiamo deciso **k** siamo arrivati **l** Siamo andati **m** abbiamo mangiato **n** abbiamo bevuto **o** abbiamo preso **p** abbiamo pagato **q** siamo andati **r** Abbiamo parlato **s** è nato **t** è morto **u** si è sposato **v** ha divorziato **w** siamo andati **x** abbiamo raccolto **y** abbiamo fatto **z** abbiamo preso **aa** abbiamo trovato **bb** Abbiamo cenato **cc** siamo andati **dd** abbiamo ballato **2** **a** Sono stato in vacanza con Claire. **b** Abbiamo preso il battello per San Fruttuoso. **c** Abbiamo camminato tutto il giorno. **d** Abbiamo fatto un po' di spesa. **e** Siamo andati in discoteca. **f** Abbiamo bevuto un caffè e siamo usciti. **g** Hanno preso il treno. **h** Sono tornato a casa la settimana scorsa. **i** È arrivata a Portofino. **j** Il ladro è scappato. **k** Sono corso a casa. **l** Alessandro è nato nel 1978. **m** Sono stati una settimana. **n** Ho corso un miglio. **3** Individual responses.

UNIT 51

1 **a** è **b** è **c** ha **d** è **e** hanno **f** siamo/siete/sono **g** abbiamo **2** **a** Ho dovuto camminare per due miglia. **b** Sono dovuti partire/andare via presto. **c** Hai parlato al dottore? **d** Sei uscito/a/Siete usciti/e ieri sera? **e** Abbiamo guardato la partita di calcio alla TV. **f** L'ho visto ieri. **g** Glielo hanno detto subito. **h** Gli ha telefonato da Napoli. **i** Hanno parlato al presidente. **j** Abbiamo vissuto in India per tre anni. **3** **a** Sono arrivata

b ho passato   **c** ho avuto   **d** ho visto   **e** ho potuto   **f** ho avuto   **g** ho avuto   **h** ho visitao   **i** è nato   **j** ho potuto

UNIT 52

1 **a** ero;   volevo   **b** Suonavo;   ero   **c** andavo   **d** Nuotavo   **e** Mangiavo   **f** studiavo; ascoltavo; mangiavo   **g** uscivo   **h** Parlavamo   **i** ritornavo   **2** **a** abitavano   **b** iniziavano   **c** andavo   **d** era   **e** c'era   **f** si poteva   **g** c'erano   **h** Bastava   **i** si vedeva   **j** era   **k** c'era   **l** vendeva   **m** si vedeva   **n** conduceva   **o** potevano   **p** c'era   **q** andavano   **r** si sentivano   **s** giocavo   **t** osservavo   **u** si scaldavano.   **3** Individual responses.   **4** **a** Avevo avuto il raffreddore.   **b** Il treno era partito alle otto.   **c** Avevo mangiato poco.   **d** Avevo scritto una lettera.   **e** Avevo detto tutto a mia madre.   **f** Avevo studiato molto.   **g** Avevo imparato molto.   **h** Avevamo parlato di letteratura.

UNIT 53

1 **a** Bisogna   **b** ho bisogno di   **c** Bisogna   **d** ha bisogno   **e** Bisogna   **f** abbiamo bisogno di   **g** Bisogna   **h** Bisogna   **2** **a** ci vuole   **b** ci vogliono   **c** ci vuole   **d** ci vuole   **e** ci vogliono   **f** ci vuole   **g** ci vogliono   **h** ci vuole   **i** ci vogliono   **3** **a** Ne bastano due cucchiaini.   **b** Ne basta mezzo bicchiere.   **c** Ne bastano cento grammi   **d** No, basta studiare.   **e** No, basta avere la carta stradale.

UNIT 54

1 **a** piace   **b** piace   **c** piace   **d** piacciono   **e** piacciono   **f** piace   **g** piacciono; piacciono   **h** piace   **2** **a** 1   **b** 4   **c** 6   **d** 7   **e** 5   **f** 8   **g** 2   **h** 3   **3** **a** A Mario piacciono le fragole.   **b** Ad Anna e Paolo piacciono le automobili italiane.   **c** Mi piace leggere le riviste italiane.   **d** Le piace nuotare.   **e** Vorrei due panini.   **f** Ti piace camminare?   **g** Le piacciono gli spaghetti?   **h** Ti è piaciuto il libro?   **i** A Paolo e Lucia è piaciuto il film?   **j** Che cosa prende?   **4** **A Cristina** **a** non piace il calcio.   **b** piace suonare il pianoforte.   **c** non piacciono i cioccolatini.   **d** piace la musica.   **A Marco** **a** piace guardare la televisione.   **b** piace la/andare in motocicletta.   **c** non piacciono i dolci.   **d** non piace la frutta.

UNIT 55

1 **a** Leggerò il libro domani.   **b** Il treno partirà tra poco.   **c** L'autobus arriverà tra poco.   **d** Studierò la lezione domani.   **e** Andrò a piedi domani.   **f** Domani rimarrò a casa.   **g** Le telefonerò domani.   **h** La vedrò domani.   **2** **a** Sarà in giardino.   **b** Costerà almeno novecento sterline.   **c** Ne avrà ventitré.   **d** Avrà perso il treno.   **e** No, saranno in macchina/in auto.   **3** **a** nuoterò   **b** mi abbronzerò   **c** leggerò   **d** farò   **e** prenderò   **f** scriverò   **g** non guarderò   **h** non leggerò   **4** **a** avrò finito   **b** sarà partita   **c** avrà cucinato   **d** saranno arrivati

UNIT 56

1 **a** Studierei ma sono stanca.   **b** Scriveremmo ma non abbiamo tempo.   **c** Finiremmo ma è troppo tardi.   **d** Partirebbero ma non hanno i soldi.   **e** Guarderebbero la TV ma hanno altro da fare.   **f** Verrebbe ma non ha tempo.   **g** Partirebbero ma non vogliono lasciarmi sola.   **h** Lavorerebbe ma non trova un posto.   **i** Uscirebbero ma piove.   **j** Scriverebbe ma è malato.   **k** Telefonerebbero ma non hanno abbastanza soldi.   **2** **a** Sì, ci vorrebbe molta pazienza.   **b** Sì, bisognerebbe riposare.   **3** **a** L'avrei comprato ma non avevo i soldi.   **b** Gli avrei parlato ma non l'ho visto.   **4** **a** Vorrei una birra e un panino.   **b** Mi piacerebbe andare in vacanza.   **c** Dovresti dirglielo.   **d** Non potrei farlo!   **e** Non lo farebbe.

UNIT 57

1 a 4 b 7 c 6 d 3 e 5 f 2 g 1 **2** a Avrei finito se non fosse stato troppo tardi. b Sarebbe venuto se ne avesse avuto il tempo. c Avremmo scritto se non fossimo stati malati. d Avremmo guardato la TV se non avessimo avuta altro da fare. e Avrebbero telefonato se avessero avuto abbastanza soldi. **3** a L'avrei mangiato ma era finito. b Gli avrei telefonato ma non avevo monete. c L'avrei voluto ma costava troppo. **4** a Avrei voluto un tè ma c'era soltanto caffè. b Avrebbero venduto la casa ma non hanno avuto offerte. c Saremmo partiti ma l'aereo era al completo. d Sarebbe dovuta arrivare ieri e Faresti meglio a venire. f Preferirei non vederla.

UNIT 58

1 a Scrivigli la lettera. b Raccontagli tutto. c Le venda la macchina. d Gli compri un nuovo computer. e Gli consigli di stare a casa. f Parlategli del fatto. g Mandategli i documenti. h Regalale la collana. **2** a Scrivigliela. b Raccontaglielo. c Gliela venda. d Glielo compri. e Glielo consigli. f Parlategliene. g Mandateglieli. h Regalagliela. **3** a Non scrivere la lettera a Marcello. b Non raccontare tutto a Goffredo. c Non venda la macchina a Susanna. d Non compri un nuovo computer a Sandro. e Non consigli a Renzo di stare a casa. f Non parlate del fatto al presidente. g Non mandate i documenti al sindaco. h Non regalare la collana ad Anna. **4** a Non scrivergliela. b Non raccontarglielo. c Non gliela venda. d Non glielo compri. e Non glielo consigli. f Non parlategliene. g Non mandateglieli. h Non regalarglela. **5** a Sii gentile! b Compra! c Dormi! d Cammina! e Abbi fede! f Vendi! g Abbi pazienza! h Mangia! **6** a Sia gentile! b Compri! c Dorma! d Cammini! e Abbia fede! f Venda! g Abbia pazienza! h Mangi! **7** a Siamo gentili! b Compriamo! c Dormiamo! d Camminiamo e Abbiamo   fede! f Vendiamo! g Abbiamo pazienza! h Mangiamo! **8** a Siate gentili! b Comprate! c Dormite! d Camminate! e Abbiate   fede! f Vendete! g Abbiate   pazienza! h Mangiate! **9** a Siano   gentili! b Comprino! c Dormano! d Camminino! e Abbiano   fede! f Vendano! g Abbiano pazienza! h Mangino!

UNIT 59

1 a Dalle il libro! b Vai/Va' via! c Di' la verità! d Fa' attenzione! e Fa' presto! **2** a Le dia il libro! b Vada via! c Dica la verità! d Faccia attenzione! e Faccia presto! **3** a 3 b 2 c 1 d 4 **4** a 3 b 9 c 2 d 8 e 4 f 1 g 10 h 5 i 6 j 7 **5** a Mi faccia vedere i documenti. b Mi dia un bicchiere pulito, per favore. c Non fate rumore! d Mi facciano un favore!/Fatemi un favore!

UNIT 60

1 a venda b abbia c partano d meriti e vendano f piova g mangi h abbia **2** a abbiano comprato b abbia meritato c abbia mangiato d abbia avuto e abbia venduto **3** a Credo di avere l'influenza. b Immagino che lui abbia vinto al lotto. c Malgrado io provi non riesco a crederci. d Erica crede di essere intelligentissima. e Patrizio immagina di essere bellissimo. f Lo aiuto a condizione che smetta di fumare. **4** a Credo che sia onesto. b Suppongo di avere il raffreddore. c Benché le abbia parlato non mi ha voluto ascoltare. d Penso che abbia già cenato. e Esigo che tu finisca adesso. f Nel caso che tu parta per Londra portati un ombrello.

UNIT 61

1 a vendesse b avesse c partissero d meritasse e vendessero f piovesse g mangiassi h avesse **2** a avessi mangiato b avessero venduto c avesse avuto

d avesse meritato **e** fosse partito **3** **a** 6 **b** 5 **c** 3 **d** 7 **e** 4 **f** 8 **g** 2 **h** 1
4 **a** Se tu fossi in me, che cosa faresti? **b** Se fossi in te comprerei un pianoforte.
c Pensavo che i vicini fossero a casa. **d** Gli studenti pensavano che il professore li aiutasse.

UNIT 62

1 **a** Insistevano che noi andassimo via/partissimo subito. **b** Ho paura che il bambino
abbia preso il raffreddore. **c** Avevo paura che il bambino avesse preso il raffreddore. **d** Ci
tiene molto che lui finisca il lavoro. **e** È necessario che tu prenda il prossimo treno. **f** È
giusto che tu parta/vada via. **g** È strano che si comportino così. **h** Benché avessero ragione
non si sono lamentati/si lamentavano/si lamentarono. **2** **a** 3 **b** 5 **c** 2 **d** 1 **e** 6
f 4 **3** **Only** *che avesse ragione*: f, g, j; **Both:** a, b, c, d, e, h, i

UNIT 63

1 **Present:** a, c, f, h, j, i; **Imperfect:** b, d, e, g, i, k, m **2** **a** stessero
b togliessi **c** esca **d** uscisse **e** dicessi **f** fosse tenuto **3** **a** Voglio che tu esca di
più. **b** Credo che vogliano cambiare casa. **c** Pensavo che venisse. **d** Penso che lo tenga
nella scrivania. **e** Se dovessero scegliere andrebbero in Francia. **f** Voleva che (lui) le desse
una mano. **g** Spero che tu vada domani. **h** Spero che vada.

UNIT 64

1 **a** Garibaldi nacque a Nizza nel 1807. **b** Dopo che ebbe partecipato ad un attentato per
conquistare Genova, dovette fuggire in Sud America. **c** Quando ritornò partecipò alla lotta
per l'Unità d'Italia. **d** Dopo l'Unità d'Italia non volle nessun riconoscimento. **e** Si ritirò a
Caprera dove visse fino alla morte. **f** Morì nel 1882. **2** **a** nacque **b** fu **c** ritornò
d ritornò **e** ritirò **f** visse **3** **a** uscì **b** iniziò **c** Pensò **d** Si fermò **e** diventò
f cominciò **g** ritornò **h** Cominciò **i** volle **j** arrivò **k** poté **l** salì **m** fermò **n** arrivò
o poté **p** Fu

UNIT 65

1 **a** ha suonato **b** era **c** ho deciso **d** ho premuto **e** ha cominciato **f** era
g aveva telefonato **h** parlavamo **i** ha suonato **j** era **k** aveva rotto **l** voleva **m** ho
fatto **n** tornavo **o** è arrivato **p** ha/hanno cominciato **q** è stato **r** ha telefonato **s** ha
visitato **2** Individual response. **3** **a** era **b** Viveva **c** maltrattavano **d** Faceva
e ordinavano **f** offrì **g** raccomandò **h** accettò **i** vide **j** s'innamorò **k** lasciò
l perse **m** ritrovò **n** sposò **o** vissero

UNIT 66

1 **a** parlando **b** Sbagliando **c** lavorando **d** Continuando **e** Avendo **f** Essendo
g Dicendo **h** Facendo **2** **a** Non essendo stanco è andato a piedi. **b** Essendo chiusi i
negozi è andato al ristorante. **c** Avendo comprato i biglietti sono tornato a casa. **d** Avendo
commesso tale gaffe preferì tacere per il resto della serata. **e** Attraversando la strada inciampò
e cadde. **f** Uscendo di casa decise di prendere l'ombrello. **3** **a** Sto scrivendo una lettera
a Ronaldo. **b** Sto leggendo un articolo su Sting. **c** Sta mangiando una bistecca alla
fiorentina. **d** Sto ascoltando il Requiem di Verdi. **e** Sta riparando la lavatrice. **f** Sta
bevendo un doppio whisky con ghiaccio. **g** Stanno raccontando una barzelletta. **h** Stiamo
giocando a scacchi. **4** **a** 3 **b** 4 **c** 5 **d** 2 **e** 1

UNIT 67

1 **a** amante **b** proveniente **c** brillante **d** sorridente **e** divertente **f** inconcludente
g nascente **h** calante. **2** **a** sorridente **b** calante **c** nascente **d** inconcludente

e divertente **f** brillante **g** amante **h** proveniente **3** **a** Paolo è sempre sorridente. **b** Francesco è un uomo abbiente. **c** Questo treno è proveniente da Roma? **d** Era un film divertente. **e** Conosci l'amante di Maria? **f** Giovanni è uno studente brillante. **g** il sole nascente **h** la luna calante **4** **a** Francesco è un dirigente importante. **b** Durante il secolo scorso molti emigranti italiani andarono in America. **c** Ambedue i contendenti sono molto bravi. **d** I nostri concorrenti stanno perdendo i loro clienti. **e** È un mio conoscente. **f** La mia lavatrice non funziona. **g** Voglio una nuova canna da pesca per Natale.

UNIT 68

1 **a** vivere **b** parlare **c** spendere **d** lavorare **e** fumare **f** Leggere **g** bere **h** Divertirsi **2** **a** venire **b** continuare **c** pensare **d** dire **e** vedere **f** giocare **g** uscire **h** tornare **i** avere studiato **j** essere arrivato **3** **a** Studia per diventare avvocato. **b** Risparmiano per comprare un'automobile. **c** Vanno a nuotare ogni giorno. **d** Marianna **e** Paolo vanno a pescare quando possono. **e** Sono stanco/a di ripetere le stesse cose. **f** Non sono riusciti a convincerlo.

UNIT 69

1 **a** produce; prodotta **b** posto; poste **c** trae; traggono; esposto; espongono **2** **a** compongo, componi, compone, componiamo, componete, compongono **b** attrassi attraesti, attrasse, attraemmo, attraeste, attrassero **c** traduci!, traduca!, traduciamo!, traducete!, traducano! **d** traduco, traduci, traduce, traduciamo, traducete, traducono **e** riprodotto; introdotto; ridotto; posposto; disposto; proposto; contratto; attratto

UNIT 70

2 **a** 7 **b** 8 **c** 6 **d** 1 **e** 2 **f** 3 **g** 4 **h** 5 **2** **a** Se lo fa. **b** Se la fa. **c** Se la prepara. **d** Se li stira. **3** **a** Ci siamo abbronzati. **b** Quando vieni a trovarci/ci vieni a trovare? **c** Ci siamo presentati. **d** Sei mai stato/a a Roma? Sì, ci sono stato/a tre volte. **e** Eccovi! **f** Ci siamo conosciuti/incontrati in vacanza. **g** Non ci credo! **h** Vi ho mandato un fax ieri. **i** C'è una banca qui? **j** Ce n'è una in via Roma. **k** Ci sono gabinetti pubblici qui vicino? **l** Ce n'è uno in quel bar. **m** Ci aiutiamo molto. **n** Vi vedete spesso? **o** No, c'incontriamo soltanto una volta all'anno. **4** **a** In estate ci si abbronza di più se si mangiano molti pomodori. **b** Per avere i capelli lucidi ci si sciacqua i capelli con acqua e aceto. **c** Se ci si preoccupa troppo a causa degli esami si rischia di imparare di meno.

UNIT 71

1 Individual responses. **2** **a** 8 **b** 7 **c** 6 **d** 5 **e** 4 **f** 3 **g** 2 **h** 1 **3** **1** volere **2** (orizzontale) odiare **2** (verticale) occorrere **3** dovere **4** osare **5** bastare **4** **a** dovere **b** Occorre **c** odia **d** osato **e** voluto **f** basta

UNIT 72

1 **a** di **b** a **c** a **d** a **e** a **f** a **g** a **h** al **i** ad **j** di **k** di **l** a **m** a **n** di **o** a **p** di **2** **a** Teresa impara/sta imparando a suonare il piano. **b** Paolo ci tiene molto a giocare a tennis. **c** Non vedo l'ora di vederti. **d** Siamo stufi di tradurre questi esercizi. **e** Erano sicuri di aver ragione. **f** Ricordati di scrivere una cartolina allo zio. **g** Faresti meglio ad accettare il loro invito. **h** Ho intenzione di comprare una macchina sportiva. **i** Avete ragione a volervi divertire. **j** Ho paura di prendere il raffreddore. **k** Si sono rifiutati di dargli alcun consiglio. **l** Ho voglia di andare a una festa.

UNIT 73

1 **a** Con questo rumore è difficile lavorare. **b** Prendo il caffè con due cucchiaini di zucchero. **c** Paolo è arrivato con l'automobile di sua madre. **d** Marianna è stata gentile con loro. **e** Eleonora ha deciso di andare al cinema con la sua amica. **f** Con mia grande sorpresa ha accettato l'invito. **g** Dovrebbero imparare a prendersela con calma. **h** Ieri sono andata al cinema con lui. **2** **a** ad **b** di **c** con **d** a **e** con **f** con **g** con **h** Con **i** con **j** con **3** **a** Grazie per essere venuta con questo tempo. **b** carne con peperoncino **c** Nel 1915 l'Italia era in guerra con la Germania. **d** Ha fatto questo tavolo con legno usato. **e** Con tutti i loro problemi sono riusciti a stare insieme. **f** Era stato così gentile con loro che non poterono rifiutargli il favore. **g** Sono gentili con lei. **h** Con loro grande sorpresa ha lasciato il lavoro. **i** Dovrebbe imparare a prenderla con calma. **j** In Italia gli impiegati pubblici se la prendono con calma con pratiche di questo genere.

UNIT 74

1 **a** della **b** del **c** della **d** dei; degli; delle **e** della **f** dello **g** del **h** della **i** dei **j** del **2** **a** un vestito di seta **b** un bicchiere rotto **c** un bicchiere di vino **d** Il mio giardino è più piccolo del tuo. **e** Hai visto niente di interessante? **f** Sono inglese. **g** Soffre di gotta. **h** la città romana **i** la città di Firenze **j** Ti consiglio di scrivergli. **k** un tavolo di legno **l** la scrivania di Giorgio **m** Ho deciso di venire. **n** Sono di Londra. **o** una scatola di pomodori **3** **a** di ora in ora **b** C'è niente d'interessante alla TV? **c** Vorrei qualcosa di meglio. **d** Ho comprato l'intera opera di Shakespeare. **e** l'itinerario dell'autobus **f** una statua di marmo **g** Gli attori lavorano di notte e dormono di giorno. **4** **a** 4 **b** 5 **c** 2 **d** 1 **e** 3

UNIT 75

1 **a** scuola **b** all'aeroporto **c** alla spiaggia **2** **a** Abito a Londra e passo le vacanze a Capri. **b** L'altro ieri sono andata all'aeroporto alle undici. **c** Sono partita alle quattro e cinquanta e sono arrivata a Napoli alle diciotto e cinquanta ora locale. **d** A Napoli ho preso un tassì per andare al porto a prendere il battello. **e** I miei amici mi avevano dato le chiavi del loro appartamento così sono andata a casa loro. **f** Dopo una doccia sono andata a cena al ristorante. **g** Ho ordinato spaghetti con le vongole e pesce alla griglia. **h** Ieri mi sono alzata all'alba per andare a fare un'escursione. **i** Ho passato la mattinata salendo sulle colline al sole. **j** A mezzogiorno sono tornata a Marina Grande e mi sono seduta in un bar con una birra fresca. **k** Ero contenta di avere trovato un posto all'ombra e di starmene seduta ad osservare la gente passare/i passanti. **3** **a** a **b** a **c** a **d** all' **e** a **f** a **g** di **h** con **i** A **j** di **k** della **l** A **m** al **n** All' **o** a **p** con **q** al

UNIT 76

1 **a** 7 **b** 8 **c** 5 **d** 4 **e** 3 **f** 2 **g** 1 **h** 6 **i** 9 **2** **a** Quando sono in Italia vado spesso in Toscana. **b** Quando vivevo in Cornovaglia andavo in Francia ogni anno. **c** Non ho deciso se andare in Sicilia o all'isola d'Elba. **d** Vivo/Abito in città. **e** Questo pomeriggio vado in città. **f** Mia sorella è andata a vivere in campagna. **g** La famiglia Simoni è/I Simoni sono in montagna. **h** Francesco sta facendo il jogging nel parco. **i** Il mio corso d'italiano comincia in/d'inverno. **j** Nel 1999 andrò in Australia. **k** Il mio treno è arrivato in orario. **l** Vado in vacanza in/d'estate.

UNIT 77

1 **a** 3 **b** 4 **c** 2 **d** 1 **e** 6 **f** 5 **g** 7 **h** 9 **i** 8 **j** 10 **2** **a** Il telefono è sul tavolo. **b** La penna è sulla rivista. **c** Sul televisore c'è un gatto. **d** Sulla rivista c'è scritto *gente*. **e** Ho visto le notizie/il telegiornale alla televisione. **3** **a** Il faro è sulla roccia. **b** Roma è sul fiume Tevere. **c** Il mio/La mia insegnante è sulla cinquantina. **d** Il mio/La mia collega scrive saggi sulla psicologia. **e** Le mie scarpe sono fatte su misura. **4** **a** sul serio **b** su dieci **c** sul punto **d** errori su errori **e** promesse su promesse

UNIT 78

1 a 6 b 3 c 4 d 2 e 5 f 7 g 1 h 10 i 8 j 9 **2** a per caso b per lo più c per tempo d Per me e Per quanto io sappia f Per l'appunto g Per fortuna h Per di più i Per l'appunto!

UNIT 79

1 a 4 b 5 c 3 d 1 e 9 f 6 g 7 h 2 i 8 j 10 **2** a dalla b dell' c della d tra e di f in g Nel h al i per j tra k dell' l con m tra n per o ad p tra q con r in s di t ad u nella v con w della

UNIT 80

1 a una macchina da cucire b una lampada da tavolo c una macchina da scrivere d una lampadina da sessanta watts e un francobollo da ottocento lire f un gelato da mille lire **2** a da b da c dal d da e Da f dal g da h da i dall' j da **3** a a b nel c da d Da e per f per lo/nello g delle h a i nella j del k dall' l alla m a n da o Nella p di q dalla r all' s dall' t per u dell' v al w a x da y a z a aa a bb della cc in dd nel ee dal

UNIT 81

1 a davanti alla casa b sotto la macchina c in mezzo alla stradina/al vialetto/alla strada d in cima alla collina e dietro la casa f vicino alla macchina **2** a Nonostante b assieme a c tramite d Invece di e senza f Durante g circa h A dispetto i Secondo **3** a La macchina/L'auto si è fermata in mezzo alla strada. b Erano tutti presenti ad eccezione di due. c Non potevo sentire a causa del rumore. d Lucca è lontano da qui? e La fontana è vicino alla Basilica. f Oggi la sterlina è in rialzo rispetto al dollaro.

UNIT 82

1 a chiaramente b male c velocemente d difficilmente e grandemente f rapidamente g magnificamente h inutilmente i probabilmente j agilmente k gentilmente l maggiormente m fortemente n duramente o elegantemente p ovviamente q cortesemente r mollemente s freddamente t particolarmente u sensibilmente v sinceramente w affettuosamente x direttamente **2** a costantemente b precipitosamente c attivamente d vigorosamente e impulsivamente f allegramente g terribilmente h confusamente **3** a chiaramente b lentamente c correttamente d forte e fatto malamente/male **4** a Io parlo italiano meglio di te. b Tu parli inglese meglio di me. c Questo vino è buono ma quello è migliore. d Secondo me il tè inglese è migliore di quello italiano. e Secondo me il caffè italiano è migliore di quello inglese.

UNIT 83

1 a 6 b 4 c 5 d 2 e 3 f 1 g 7 **2** a dappertutto b sotto c lassù d fuori e altrove f ogni tanto g di solito h mai i lontano j di sopra k adesso (ora) l Allora m Forse n immediatamente o quasi p neppure là q di sopra r di sopra s sotto

UNIT 84

1 a È una persona che su emoziona facilmente. b D'estate piove raramente. c Parla italiano correntemente. d Se vuoi farti comprendere devi parlare lentamente e chiaramente.

e Ha continuato a negare fermamente. **f** Vedo che hai studiato diligentemente. **g** Non ho ancora finito. **h** Ha sempre rifiutato i loro consigli. **i** Credo che Mario sia già uscito. **j** Non sono mai stata in Canada. **2** **a** Ha sempre lavorato onestamente. **b** Rispose debolmente alla mia domanda. **c** Ho già letto quel libro. **d** Non è molto ricco interiormente. **e** È uscito velocemente ma non so dove sia andato. **3** **a** probabilmente **b** possibilmente **c** lontano **d** dopodomani **e** troppo **f** meglio **g** peggio **h** velocemente.

UNIT 85

1 **a** Questa mattina ho deciso di prendere il battello per Vernazza perché fa bel tempo e il mare è calmo. **b** Ho indossato il costume da bagno siccome desidero prendere il sole sul battello durante il viaggio. **c** Generalmente arrivo presto alla stazione marittima poiché mi piace sedere a prora ma non sempre ci riesco siccome la gente, anche se arriva dopo di me, riesce sempre a salire prima. Durante il viaggio immagino di essere sola sul mio panfilo. **d** Mentre la gente chiacchiera, riceve o fa telefonate, io mi rilasso osservando la bellissima costa, i gabbiani e i riflessi del sole sulle piccole onde d'acqua fresca e trasparente. **e** All'arrivo mi fermo sulla piccola spiaggia oppure vado al bar a prendere un succo di frutta. **f** Verso l'una pranzo nel mio ristorante preferito, cioè il ristorante 'Gambero Rosso'. **g** Dopo il caffè faccio il giro delle viuzze, poi faccio qualche piccola spesa e scrivo qualche cartolina agli amici. **h** Verso le quattro e mezzo è ora di tornare, quindi salgo sul battello. **i** Una giornata tranquilla ma non noiosa, anzi, molto benefica sia fisicamente che per la mente.

UNIT 86

1 **a** 8 **b** 9 **c** 7 **d** 6 **e** 5 **f** 4 **g** 3 **h** 2 **i** 1 **j** 10 **2** **a** Benché sia un attore di mezza età, recita la parte di un giovanotto. **b** Ti presto i soldi a patto che tu me li renda domani. **c** Sebbene abbia sempre moltissima gente in casa, vive solo. **d** Domani vado in gita a meno che non piova. **e** Gli ho scritto affinché sapesse che sono arrivata. **f** È meglio tornare a casa prima che piova. **g** Parto giovedì purché ci siano posti sull'aereo. **h** Qualora tu avessi bisogno di aiuto, telefonami. **i** Andò a Roma senza che nessuno lo sapesse. **3** **a** Benché non lo dica, vorrebbe andare in montagna. **b** Nonostante (il fatto che) abbia vinto alla lotteria, vive come prima. **c** È sempre molto contenta a patto che non si parli di Bruno. **d** Devi prenotare l'albergo prima che sia troppo tardi. **e** Nel caso che tu avessi bisogno di qualcosa, devi farmelo sapere. **f** A meno che tu non lavori, non puoi comprare quella barca. **g** Penso che sia arrivata. **h** Ha comprato questo appartamento senza che io lo sapessi.

UNIT 87

1 **a** 10 **b** 9 **c** 8 **d** 7 **e** 6 **f** 5 **g** 4 **h** 3 **i** 2 **j** 1 **2** **a** Che coraggio! **b** Che stupido! **c** Meno male! **d** Accidenti che sfortuna! **e** Che bugiardo che sei! **f** Dai, vallo a raccontare ad un altro!

UNIT 88

1 **a** Non c'era molta gente. **b** Non c'è mai molta gente. **c** Non ha niente da fare. **d** Non ha mai niente da fare. **e** Non sa niente. **f** Non sa mai niente. **g** Non mi piace per niente. **h** Non mi ha ringraziato. **i** Non scrivi più romanzi? **j** Non ne compro nessuno. **2** **a** No, non mi sono piaciuti. **b** No, non ci è piaciuto. **c** No, non lo vedo mai. **d** No, non c'era nessuno. **e** No, non ho niente. **f** No, non gioco più. **g** No, non le ho trovate. **h** Non voglio né l'uno né l'altro. **3** **a** 7 **b** 3 **c** 2 **d** 1 **e** 8 **f** 4 **g** 5 **h** 6

UNIT 89

1 **a** a meno che non piova **b** a meno che non partano **c** a meno che non sia **d** a meno che non ce ne sia **e** a meno che tu non arrivi **f** a meno che non sia **2** **a** finché non

b a meno che non **c** finché non **d** finché non **e** a meno che non **f** a meno che non
3 **a** Non credono che in lui. **b** Non pensa che al lavoro. **c** Non parla che di sport.
d Non fanno che criticare. **e** Non fa che lamentarsi. **f** Non pensi che a te stesso/a.
4 **a** Questa medicina è controindicata per i sofferenti di cuore. **b** Quel macchinario è in
disuso dall'anno scorso. **c** Spero di riuscire. **d** Il governo ha deciso di decentralizzare i
servizi pubblici. **e** È una persona incapace. **f** Le piante sono presto sfiorite.

UNIT 90

1 **a** 5 **b** 4 **c** 8 **d** 3 **e** 6 **f** 2 **g** 1 **h** 7 **2** **a** da cui **b** in cui **c** per cui
d con/in cui **e** a cui **f** di cui **g** con cui **3** **a** La casa, il cui proprietario è stato
arrestato, è in vendita. **b** Il cane, il cui proprietario è all'ospedale, è rimasto solo.
c Maria, il cui marito ha vinto al lotto, vuole divorziare. **d** Il cantante i cui dischi vanno a
ruba, terrà un concerto al Teatro Regio. **e** Il giornalista, il cui articolo è tanto discusso, è stato
denunciato. **f** Gli studenti, il cui professore ha l'influenza, sono felicissimi. **4** **a** Il libro
che ho comprato non è (tanto) bello quanto credevo. **b** Il tavolo che ho riservato non è
questo. **c** La signora la cui figlia è a Roma mi ha chiesto di andarla a trovare.
d La finestra dalla quale vedo il parco ha bisogno di nuove tende. **e** Il nostro amico, la cui
casa è stata venduta, ha affittato un appartamento. **f** Le persone di cui parli hanno traslocato.

UNIT 91

1 **a** 3 **b** 2 **c** 4 **d** 5 **e** 1 **f** 6 **g** 7 **h** 8 **2** **a** Colei che ha scritto questa
lettera di scuse è la zia di mio marito. **b** Colei che ha telefonato era la cugina di mio cognato.
c Coloro che desiderano fare domanda scrivano alla segretaria. **d** Coloro che hai visto erano
le mie sorelle. **e** Coloro che dormono non pigliano pesci. **f** Coloro che seminano vento
raccolgono tempesta. **3** **a** Chi è senza peccato scagli la prima pietra. **b** Ciò/Quello che
fa non mi riguarda. **c** Ciò/Quello che conta è la salute. **b** Ciò/Quello che dicono è falso.
e Le hanno dato tutto quello che/tutto ciò che avevano. **f** Questo è tutto quello che/tutto ciò
che puoi fare? **g** Questo è tutto quello che/tutto ciò che so. **h** Hanno preso tutto ciò
che/tutto quello che c'era. **i** Abbiamo comprato tutto ciò/tutto quello che abbiamo potuto.

UNIT 92

1 **a** nessuno **b** niente **c** Ciascuno **d** qualcosa **e** qualcuno **f** qualcun **g** uno
h Chiunque **2** **a** Quanto costano l'uno? **b** Costano proprio molto! **c** Ne vorrei
parecchi. Ha una scatola più grande? **d** Può metterli tutti in quella scatola! **e** No, io ...
tutti sarebbero troppi. **f** Sei non bastano ... me ne dia otto. **g** Sì ... no ... forse è meglio
che non ne compri nessuno siccome nessuno mi attira. Volevo soltanto fare un po' di pratica
sull'uso dei pronomi indefiniti. **3** **a** Ne vorresti/vorrebbe un'altra? **b** Ciascuno di loro
ha avuto la sua parte. **c** Molti credono in questa medicina. **d** Non pochi di loro erano
seccati. **e** C'è qualcuno che vuole una fetta di torta? **f** Nessuno ha detto niente. **g** Pochi
pensano che sia possibile. **h** È capace di tutto/qualunque cosa.

UNIT 93

1 **a** Chi **b** Chi **c** Quante **d** Quanti **e** Che cosa **f** Che cosa **g** Qual **h** Che
cosa **i** Quanti **j** Che **k** Chi **l** Quale/Che cosa/Chi **2** **a** 4 **b** 5 **c** 6 **d** 3 **e** 7
f 8 **g** 9 **h** 10 **i** 2 **j** 1 **3** **a** Qual è tuo marito? **b** Che lavoro fai? **c** Chi è
andato alla festa? **d** Quanto costa il biglietto? **e** Qual è il tuo cappotto? **f** Che cosa
vogliono? **g** Quanto ci vuole? **h** Quanti biglietti hai venduto?

UNIT 94

1 **a** 8 **b** 1 **c** 6 **d** 7 **e** 5 **f** 3 **g** 2 **h** 4 **2** **a** Quanto ci mette il battello?

b Da quanto lo vuoi/vuole? **c** Da quanto tempo abiti/abita a Parigi? **d** Quante volte/Ogni quanto vai/va in Italia? **e** Quanti soldi hai/ha? **f** Quanti anni hai/ha? **g** Quante ore ci vogliono per andare a New York? **h** Quanti ne abbiamo oggi? **i** Perché non glielo chiedi? **j** Quant'è in tutto? **k** Che tipo è tua/sua figlia? **l** Da quanto tempo sei/è qui? **m** Quanto è largo questo tavolo? **n** Quanto sei/è alto? **3** **a** Scusi signora, che cosa ha detto? **b** Come si chiama, signore? **c** Da quanto tempo abiti/abita a Brighton? **d** Com'è tuo/suo cugino Giacomo? **e** Fino a quando continueranno così? **f** Quanto tempo (ti) ci vuole per vestirti? **g** Ogni quanto/Quante volte vai/va a teatro? **h** Come mai non dici/dice mai la verità? **i** Perché mai vuoi mettere/indossare un tale vestito?

UNIT 95

1 **a** 5 **b** 4 **c** 9 **d** 6 **e** 7 **f** 8 **g** 2 **h** 3 **i** 10 **j** 1 **2** **a** A chi tocca? **b** Che cosa danno al cinema? **c** Che cos'hai?/Come ti senti? **d** Che cosa succede? **e** Che tipi ha?/Quanti tipi ne ha? **f** Che cos'ha? **g** E perché? **h** Da dove viene? **i** Dov'è il gatto? **j** Che ore sono? **k** A che ora comincia la partita? **l** Di chi è l'ombrello? **3** **a** Che tipo di caffè desidera? **b** Che tipi ha? **c** Che cosa le succede, signora? **d** Che cosa danno al Ritz? **e** A chi tocca? **f** Di chi sono queste scarpe? **g** A che ora è il treno per Milano? **h** Che ore sono? **i** Da dove vengono? **j** Perché/A che scopo lo vuole?

UNIT 96

1 **a** 4 **b** 5 **c** 6 **d** 1 **e** 2 **f** 3 **g** 10 **h** 9 **i** 7 **j** 8 **2** **a** confezione **b** coincidenza **c** cantina **d** mensa **e** coriandoli **f** Attenda **g** avvisato **h** argomento **i** Frequento **j** macchina fotografica **k** sensibile **l** genitori **3** **a** Avevo previsto tutto ciò. **b** Mi ha portato dei dolciumi. **c** Firmi qui, per favore. **d** C'è una coincidenza alle due e trenta. **e** Ho dimenticato la macchina fotografica. **f** Vado alla stazione a prendere i miei parenti. **g** La merce è in/nel magazzino. **h** Che cosa consiglia? **i** Lavoro per una ditta inglese. **j** Ho bisogno di benzina. **K** La casa ha il pavimento di marmo. **l** Lavoro in una fabbrica.

GLOSSARY

This section is intended for those students who may not be familiar with all the grammar terms occuring in this book.

ACCENTS In Italian, accents are placed on a few vowels which need to be pronounced with a stress when they occur at the end of a word. The vowel **e** is the only vowel which can carry either a grave accent (**è**) or an acute accent (**é**). In the former case it is pronounced as in *well* and in the latter as in *they*. The vowels
a, **i**, **o**, and **u** normally only have a grave accent: **à**, **ì**, **ò** and **ù**.

ACTIVE The most common form of a verb which occurs when the subject carries out the action of the verb: *Sting sings the song*. (See also **passive**.)

ADJECTIVES Words used to describe a noun. These can be:

> **descriptive** *beautiful, red, large, easy, sad, happy*, etc.
> **demonstrative** *this book, that car, these books, those cars*
> **indefinite** *every time, some books, each room*
> **possessive** *her desk, his umbrella, their car*
> **interrogative** *which car? how much sugar? how many cars?*
> **comparative** expressing a comparison: *more ... than, less ... than, as ... as*
> **superlative** *the most, the least*

ADVERBS Words which modify a verb: *Paul plays **well***. They can also modify an adjective: *Paul is **very** handsome*, or another adverb: *Paul plays **very** well.*

CONJUNCTIONS Words connecting other words, clauses or sentences: *bread **and** butter, slowly **but** surely, I'll go **if** they ask me.*

CONJUGATION A verb is conjugated when it is formed into its various forms of mood, tense and person. The present tense of **essere** (*to be*) is conjugated as follows:

sono	sei	è	siamo	siete	sono
I am	*you are*	*s/he it is*	*we are*	*you (pl.) are*	*they are*

GERUND A verb mood. English words ending in *-ing* are most often gerunds: *coming, living.*

IMPERSONAL VERBS Verbs without a specific subject. They are only used in the third-person singular: ***It is said*** *that he is very rich.*

INFINITIVE The mood of the verb which merely expresses its meaning without saying who is carrying out the action nor when the action is occurring: *to go*, *to say*, *to do*. In Italian, the infinitive is expressed by one word, usually ending in **-are**, **-ere** or **-ire**: **andare**, **vedere**, **dire**. A few verbs end in **-urre**, **-orre** or **-arre**.

INTRANSITIVE Verbs normally used without an object (i.e. the action of the subject doesn't transit to the object): *It's raining*. Sometimes a verb can be used both transitively and intransitively: *He eats* (what?) *a roll* is transitive. *He eats at seven* is intransitive. (See also **transitive**.)

MOODS The manner in which the action is carried out: whether it is really happening or has happened or is going to happen (indicative mood = *I speak/ I spoke/I was speaking/I will speak*, etc.), whether it is an order or suggestion (imperative mood = *go!*), whether it depends on a condition (conditional mood =
I would if I could), whether it is only probable or a wish (subjunctive mood = *I wish I were rich*, etc.).

NOUNS Words used for naming people (*Carla*), animals (*giraffe*), objects (*table*), places (*Italy*), and concepts (*beauty*), the latter being called an **abstract noun**. They can be **singular** or **plural** (usually referred to as **number**) and – in Italian – they have a **gender**, either **masculine** or **feminine**. The gender can be found in the dictionary (*m.* or *f.*) but most often it can be recognised by the noun's ending or by the article which precedes it.

OBJECT The person, animal, being or thing undergoing the action carried out by the subject.

PASSIVE The form of a verb where the action is carried out by the object rather than the subject: *The song is sung by Sting*. (See also **active**.)

PREPOSITIONS Used to mark the relation of a word with another, in space (*on, under, below, near, in front of* etc.) or time (*before, after,* etc.). In Italian they can be **simple** (e.g. **di** = *of*) or **combined** (when they are combined with the definite article, e.g. *of the* = **del/dello/della/dell'/dei/degli/delle**).

PRONOUNS Words used to replace the noun or the name of a person in order not to repeat it. There are several kinds of pronouns.
    subject pronouns *I, you, he/she/it, we, you (plural), they*; these denote the person or subject carrying out the action of the verb: *I am writing a book*.
    object pronouns Denote the object of the verb. They can be **direct**: *me, you, him/her/it, us, you (plural), them* (e.g. *I see **them***) or **indirect**:

to me, to him/to her/to it, to us, to them: *I gave the book **to them***.

NOTE Although in English you can say *I gave them a book*, *them* in this case is really *to them* and is therefore an indirect object pronoun.

pronouns preceded by a preposition (other than *to*). Also known as **disjunctive pronouns** *for me, by him*, etc.

reflexive pronouns *myself, yourself, him/herself*, etc. are so called because they are used as the object of reflexive verbs: *I wash **myself***.

possessive pronouns *mine, yours, theirs*, etc.

relative pronouns *who, whom, which, that, whose*.

interrogative pronouns *Who? Whom? What? Which (ones)?*, etc.

demonstrative pronouns *this (one), these (ones)*, etc.: *I'll take this one*.

REFLEXIVE VERBS Verbs that express an action which reflects back to the subject: *I wash myself*.

SUBJECT The being or thing carrying out the action of the verb: *I read the book* (the book 'receives' the action of my reading it). (See also **pronouns** and **passive**.)

SYLLABLE Each individual sound which makes up a word: *by-ci-cle*.

TENSE Indicates the time during which something is happening: *I speak/I am speaking* = **present**; *I spoke* = **past**; *I will speak* = **future**; *spoken* = **past participle**; *speaking* = **gerund**.

TRANSITIVE Verbs where the action passes from the subject to the object: *We sold the house*. (See also **intransitive**.)

INDEX

Numbers refer to the Units of the Grammar.